FUELLING INSECURITY

Energy Securitization in Azerbaijan

Aurora Ganz

BRISTOL UNIVERSITY PRESS

First published in Great Britain in 2022 by

Bristol University Press
University of Bristol
1-9 Old Park Hill
Bristol
BS2 8BB
UK
t: +44 (0)117 954 5940
e: bup-info@bristol.ac.uk

Details of international sales and distribution partners are available at bristoluniversitypress.co.uk

British Library Cataloguing in Publication Data
A catalogue record for this book is available from the British Library

ISBN 978-1-5292-1669-1 hardcover
ISBN 978-1-5292-1670-7 ePub
ISBN 978-1-5292-1671-4 ePdf

Cover design by Nicky Borowiec
Front cover image: Pixabay
Bristol University Press uses environmentally responsible print partners.
Printed and bound in Great Britain by TJ Books, Padstow

FSC www.fsc.org MIX Paper from responsible sources FSC® C013056

To my always-missed friend Stephen Tindale

Contents

1

Introduction

James Bond's convertible runs fast through a giant oilfield in remote Azerbaijan. Miles of drilling bits and pumps penetrate the arid and dusty ground to extract the oil. An English visionary magnate is building a pipeline to transport Azerbaijan's oil to Europe, but the Russians threaten to bomb the corridor and Bond needs to stop them. That is what the British spy is after: energy security. It was 1999 when the film *The World Is Not Enough* was released; the Baku–Tbilisi–Ceyhan (BTC) pipeline was only a project but a far-sighted one. Today, the BTC pipeline – together with the South Caucasus Pipeline – connects Azerbaijan's oil and gas reserves to Europe's energy-hungry market, making the 20th-century dream of connecting the west to the Caspian energy wealth a lucrative reality. Despite its questionable sensationalism and stereotyped geopolitics, the Bond film shows a common reality of the energy sector: the presence of security and military professionals in the oil and gas fields. This points to an overlap between energy and security and ties energy to practices of defence and enforcement. This book examines the large network of security professionals and the wide range of energy security practices that have spread in Azerbaijan's energy sector. I should stress that these practices share little with the extraordinary lustre of popular imaginaries: the military and security professionals called to secure energy in Azerbaijan are much more ordinary versions of James Bond. For instance, these agents are employed to patrol infrastructure, guard access to facilities and administrative buildings, work behind their desks to monitor security technology, conduct due diligence on workers, enforce land expropriation and participate in different forms of training and capacity building. While I recognize the ontological plasticity of security (Chapter 2), in this monograph I am primarily concerned with those security practices that imply the actual or potential use of force. Hence, this study does not primarily aim at exploring the infinite conceptual and policy possibilities behind energy security. Conversely, it is interested in exposing how the particular rendering of energy security as a conventional security threat expands military and enforcement, defence and policing, coercion and control, towards uncharted territories. By exploring the space where energy and security are conjoined, this book pays particular attention to security discourses and practices, as well as to the increasingly transnational governance that shapes energy security in Azerbaijan. To do so, it investigates the interaction of state, supra-state, and private security organizations in securing energy: who are the security and military professionals that perform energy security practices in Azerbaijan? What do they do? What shapes and delimits their work?

In Azerbaijan, as energy security increasingly intertwines with the national security agenda, corollary defence and enforcement practices have proliferated. In the country, several thousand security and military professionals – from both military and civil agencies – operate to protect the country's energy assets. Close to the country's large oil and gas facilities, it is common to see police cars, armed soldiers, or security guards on their horses, who patrol and defend the energy sites. Control and surveillance technologies, including CCTV cameras, real-time videos, sensors, radar and drones, are employed to secure these spaces along with more traditional military equipment. Off the coast, in the middle of the Caspian Sea, the navy's and the coastguard's large vessels and military ships – often equipped with advanced anti-ship cruise missiles and missile-defence radar – defend the offshore fields from potential armed attacks. Protecting the national oil and gas deposits has been used to justify Azerbaijan's military build-up and reinforce the militarized character that energy security has gained in the country in the past three decades. Sometimes the significant presence of security and military professionals deployed across the territory to secure energy is less obvious, less comprehensible, less visible: some pipelines, for example, are hidden and invisible to the eye; they run underground, and their exact position is unknown to the public and obscured to open-access satellites and GPS technologies. In those cases, any adventurous explorer that manages to approach the surrounding sites will be stopped, interrogated and, in the best case, asked to leave. When in the field, the invisibility of energy security made me wonder about the effects of energy materiality on security: what delimits, if anything, the space of energy security? Can the vastness, mobility and invisibility of energy enlarge the space of its security and justify the more visible and tangible aspects of security practices? This book shows that the spatial and temporal boundaries of energy security in Azerbaijan have gone through considerable expansion since the end of the 1990s: military and security professionals have enlarged their remits, spread their geographical scope, and become a permanent presence in all those sites that are considered to be critical for energy security not just at the local level but at the global level too.

The hunger for security that has grown in Azerbaijan's energy sector has multiplied the presence of foreign security professionals. They include personnel from international security organizations, such as the North Atlantic Treaty Organization (NATO), and third states' military forces, especially from the US, as well as contractors from private security companies and energy firms such as British energy company BP. The first question that came to mind when reflecting on their presence was whose energy is being secured. Whose interest guides NATO–Azerbaijan energy security cooperation? And what about BP: does the company work according to its corporate goals, or does the national interest prevail? Is the diversity of interests among actors reconcilable? While western states and companies seek access to the country's lucrative market for profit and geopolitical ambitions, Azerbaijan welcomes transnational engagement as an opportunity to enhance its role and reputation in the international arena, protect foreign investments, consolidate its military capabilities and conform to a westernized way of problematizing energy and security. Observing the interventions of NATO and BP in Azerbaijan's energy security, I noticed that when transnational actors intervene, the conceptual and physical boundaries of energy security become less clear. By exploring how state, supra-state, and private organizations interact in energy security, this research illustrates that different actors have different ways of thinking about and doing energy security. This has multiple ramifications: the growing engagement of non-state actors in securing energy creates complex configurations of global-local, national-international and public-private arrangements, which escape the traditional contours of international politics. In Azerbaijan international organizations, energy companies and security enterprises have increased their involvement in energy security practices, supplying services and conducting operations that were once considered to belong in the state's monopoly over force. Securing energy has offered them an opportunity to increase their capacities, resources and powers of action; this has inevitably affected the way the state secures energy.

These are not just theoretical questions of how to problematize energy security; they point to a more palpable matter: while diverse practitioners operate in the same space, they do not always coordinate; each of them responds to a different chain of command, which has its own regulatory mandate, modus operandi and specific, sectorial interests. When it comes to non-national actors such as NATO and BP, even the space of energy security is transformed, disaggregated: practices conducted *in* Azerbaijan are often designed and approved outside the country, in the offices of multinational companies and the headquarters of international organizations in western Europe. During my fieldwork, I was surprised to see how many inconsistencies, opposed interests and contradicting practices coexisted, often thanks to intentional silences, ambiguity and neglect. These aim at ignoring any areas of disagreement, even – or especially – when fundamental and irreconcilable, but also illustrate that the complexity of energy security has implications for governance, the definition of authority and the configuration of power. Energy security in Azerbaijan points to a space where institutions, practices, discourses and knowledge assemble and disassemble.

The consequences of this intricate web go beyond governance effects. The considerable expansion of security practices has facilitated the proactive, constant and diffuse involvement of security and military professionals into and beyond Azerbaijan's energy sector. This has fuelled a system of fear, violence, oppression and control. The widespread use of surveillance technology and the significant investments in the state's military capability to secure energy add to the government's dictatorial exercise of state power and its manifold ways of spying, censoring and suppressing citizens. Transnational security interventions are often blind to the multiple negative implications of these practices on the local communities: energy security interventions have facilitated the intimidation and harassment of local communities; enabled the suppression of energy workers' rights, including unionism and freedom of speech; affected land management and ownership through practices of land grabbing, land expropriation and degradation. Energy security practices in Azerbaijan have consolidated a system of patronage, corruption and everyday insecurity. The autocratic rule of President Ilham Aliyev has recorded an unsettling number of human rights violations, which are largely ignored by the country's complicit political elite. Azerbaijan is also one of the most militarized nations in the world: the country, in a state of war against Armenia since 1988, has invested massively in its military capabilities for over three decades. The prominence of defence and enforcement over alternative understandings of energy security has contributed to downgrading the efforts that try to reorient energy security policies towards the protection of energy users, energy workers, local communities and the natural environment. Interviewees indicated that security professionals impede residents' access to vital resources, including sources of potable water, when deemed to be too close to the protected site. Communities living near the pipelines noted a worrying surge of gendered violence and abuse, including human trafficking and prostitution, sharper economic inequalities and a decline in health records. Energy security in Azerbaijan contributes to an obscure and intricate web of energy, power and security, which generates multiple forms of insecurity. A central component of this research lies, therefore, in the identification of what energy security does (and does not do), including the recognition of its paradoxical relationship with insecurity.

This book's sensitivity, intent and conclusions aim to challenge not just how we understand energy security, but also what we study about it and why. This study is interested in understanding and questioning the fixation on this particular notion of energy security in Azerbaijan, explaining its processes and unpacking its implications. To undertake this task, this book answers the attendant questions: how is energy securitized in Azerbaijan?

By whom? Through what discourse and what practices? What contextual dynamics allow energy securitization to happen in the country? What are the implications? Answering this question means examining the discursive and non-discursive practices that constitute energy securitization and the dominant and marginal actors that enact them. It also requires exploring how energy security interacts with other fields of Azerbaijan's politics while acknowledging its wider reverberations beyond the security of the powerful actors.

Examining the overlap between energy and security in Azerbaijan is important for at least three main reasons. First, as the merging of energy and security is often taken for granted, our understanding of this entanglement remains superficial and misinterpreted. The attention on the military obfuscates the diversity of security practices; the focus on the state negates the agency and complicity of non-state actors; the emphasis on security shadows alternative logics, policies and structures; the putative centrality of security distracts from its unexpected production of insecurity. Moving beyond the abstractions and generalizations of the energy security ideal type, this book pays attention to the heterogeneity and idiosyncrasies of the social world. It explores how energy security is enacted in Azerbaijan; in particular, it analyses how discourses conceptualize and problematize energy security, how practitioners *do* energy security on the ground, how these actors work in the everyday, what practices and networks energy security has created. Interrogating energy security practices – hereby intended as inclusive of discourse – can tell us about the development of transnational security networks, the creation of new modes of governance, as well as the expansion and transformation of the conceptual and material space of energy security. This is particularly relevant as energy security practices are intimately linked with the exercise of power and the ways it manifests itself, including the forms of security and insecurity it (re)produces.

Building on this point, the second contribution of this book lies in the critical ethos of its approach. It acknowledges the political origins of energy security, it questions how energy security relates to political structures and power arrangements, and it devotes attention to what energy security *does*, politically, culturally, socially and materially, as well as what it does not. This book has a political spirit even if it does not take an explicit normative pathway. Its careful attention to power draws from the growing critical security scholarship and its efforts in exposing the Janus-faced nature of security. Energy security cannot simply be understood as an obvious and objective reaction to unquestionable threats; the relationship between politics and geography cannot be the result of predefined, linear and always valid causality. The fixation on conventional security and the passive acceptance of geopolitical principles and biases is a risky practice in itself: in the case of energy security, it has long hidden the ways in which dominant energy security discourses and practices have consolidated and developed forms of domination, inequality and oppression.

Third, this book offers an alternative to conventional understandings of energy security through the case of Azerbaijan, a barely accessible country that has been under-researched from postpositivist perspectives. Not only does this research divert the attention away from the geopolitics of so-called great powers, but, through its novel case study, it also opens up the critical field beyond its traditional focus on the west. Interrogating security in a non-democratic context, while still uncommon, is a much-needed political act: authoritarian practices have been proven to increase the risks of transforming security into unrestrained, punitive practices of social control. Research can contribute to overturning the dialectical paralysis that despotic governments obtain through citizens' fear of retaliation, and often thanks to the blind eye turned by international society. This does not neglect the indispensable, brave and honourable resistance and opposition that has developed in Azerbaijan but builds on their activism and scholarly inquiry; my research adds to these efforts by denouncing the ways in which energy security, especially as a global project, feeds the local illiberal practices of the Aliyev's regime.

The politics of energy securitization

Problematizing energy as a security problem implies a different preoccupation and a distinct set of solutions from problematizing it as, for example, an economic issue or an environmental question. As anticipated in the previous section, energy security in Azerbaijan has come to include defence, enforcement and policing. This can first be ascribed to the peculiar genealogy of security, which has historically been associated with the military realm and the use of force, to which it has remained semantically, culturally and politically attached. This does not mean that security *is* necessarily about force; it is widely accepted that security does not have a definitively settled meaning, its essence is contested, and its definitions are always relational and contextual. The rendering of energy as a security concern embodies distinct rationales (Huysmans 2006) or logics (Shepherd 2008) of security. Security can mean different things to different people, but each meaning is defined by a particular way of thinking – precisely, a rationale, a logic – about the problem. For instance, when describing the logics of security, Laura Shepherd (2008, p 294) explains that this refers to 'a distinct primary focus, referent object and perspective on the arrangement of the international system' and informs the consequent policy decisions. Similarly, Huysmans (2006, p 147) affirm that 'security rationalities define the meaning of security'. It is, therefore, this security rationality – which is essentially aggressive and force oriented – that defines energy security practices, identifies certain objects and subjects as threatening, and outlines specific forms of governance. Rather than questioning the malleability of energy security discourses, this book is interested in explaining the fixation on a specific interpretation of energy security: how and why has the merging of energy with security, defence and enforcement been normalized? Why has it been taken for granted? To respond to these questions, we need to shift the attention from the semantic variation of energy security discourses to the fixation of and on a specific way of problematizing energy security: despite their differences, discourses and practices share a common way of thinking and doing energy security that circulates among actors, across spaces and through materiality. Accepting energy security as a subset of national security and the product of power politics, for example, implies and justifies a set of defence-oriented measures, which range from aggressive military build-ups to the deployment of armed forces, the reinforcement of national and international bases, the presence of security agents in a foreign country and the interference in third states' politics to either support or dismantle local governments, all in the name of energy security. At the same time, understanding energy security as a national security priority downgrades alternative energy concerns – for example, access, availability and affordability of electricity, environmental and infrastructure degradation, or energy sustainability – and makes invisible the insecurity connected to its practices and the violence they create. It becomes, therefore, imperative to question and problematize the fixation on and success of energy securitization.

This book suggests understanding this particular rendering of energy security as the result of a process of securitization. Energy securitization refers to the construction of energy as a conventional security concern; it implies affirming energy security as a critical and vital issue, identifying energy insecurity as an existential threat, and calling for the widespread establishment of military and paramilitary measures. In this sense, energy securitization is a strategic, pragmatic and deeply political process that designates what and who constitutes a threat, what measures need to be applied and who retains the power to do so. In securitization, this logic institutionalizes and normalizes a way of doing security that is fundamentally aggressive, praises the use of force, and divides the world along the categories of 'enemy' and 'friend'.

This means that this research is less concerned with what energy security *is* – which can lead to abstraction, simplification, and essentialism – and does not aim at evaluating whether energy security threats are based on real or perceived dangers. In turn, it is attentive to what energy securitization *does* and *does not do*. The core of its inquiry questions the functioning and implications of the securitization process itself. Attention to energy securitization as a set of practices transcends the practices themselves and moves foremost from an interest in the effects they carry: rather than focusing on what security is, the focus on securitization moves from a concern with what security does. Securitization does not only point to the constructed ontology of security but also to an understanding of security as practice, a performance, an act, to the extent that security practices determine problems and solutions, often by dictating and controlling behaviours; as in Burke (2002), security 'imagines, directs and acts upon bodies, spaces and flows'. Security is a political act, which is nested in specific power relations and within a specific order and has the ability to facilitate particular policies, empower certain actors as security providers, and depict certain subjects and objects as dangerous and others as vitally critical.

Sharing the ethos of Critical Security Studies, this book is concerned with the power relations that security enables, supports and normalizes and sees security, especially securitization, as a negative practice, detrimental to democracy and emancipatory politics. Rightly, many critical scholars note that security has become an all-pervading and sticky policy principle, able to catalyse, drive and give salience to most political debates. As securitization embodies an aggressive logic of security, its way of ordering the social tends to impose hierarchies and forms of domination. This happens along undemocratic principles of inclusion/exclusion. Moving beyond security as a given object defined by necessity and naturalness creates the possibility for a critique of security. Security concerns are, in fact, never self-evident and should always be questioned and challenged; it is through a critical spirit that we can identify the forms of insecurity tied to securitization and find an escape from its oppressive and exclusionary practices and discourses.

This book adds to those critical voices that interrogate and challenge the monopolistic and sticky character of security, showing that its perceived determinism and omnipresence are not ontological characteristics but belong in a distinct culture and political project. I am interested in exposing the fact that security hides a particular mode of understanding and governing the world. Often, this embraces logics of division, exclusion, and categorization: it determines what (and who) matters and deserves protection against the definition of what (and who) represents a threat and needs to be annihilated. This is the case also in the case of energy.

While it has a strong political intent, this project is not openly prescriptive. Its critique holds a normative sensitivity but does not indicate one single path for political change. This book's priority is to unpack the loopholes and contradictions of security in a world that seems to pay attention to issues only when they are framed as security problems. Huysmans (2002, p 43) wrote that 'speaking and writing about security is never innocent'. Security has become a tool for control: it moulds all spaces of social life around the need to manage all forms of insecurities through a pervasive and divisive way of doing politics that is willing to put a halt to civil freedoms, human rights and democratic processes whenever considered necessary.

As Huysmans (2014, p 4) puts it: 'security practice always securitises; it necessarily inscribes insecurities in the world'. Through their work, critical security scholars have taken a clear stance against the undemocratic drift and the perils of authoritarian, fascist tendencies that find a home in the security realm. Neocleous (2008) explains that the critique of security belongs in a wider critique of power. Breakthrough research has been done on migration, health, borders, trafficking and surveillance, often with the aim of exposing how security discriminates, violates and harms certain bodies. It has become clear that security produces insecurities. In this context, energy security has been overlooked. Energy tends to be seen and dealt with as a technical sector, ruled by scientific and engineering jargon that leaves little room for social science research. In some cases, it is the vicious relationship between oil, money and politics that desanitizes the discussion and puts energy back into the political debate. While there is some truth in this, these narratives tend to assume conspiracy tones that reverberate with disturbing stereotypes of oil-as-blood and substitute the political nature of these policies with empty determinism, limiting our imagination and pushing the possibility for change further away.

While affirming the need for an analysis of energy security that is attentive to its social and political dimension – including the profound commingling of energy, security and money – this book does not fall into the trap of conspiracy thinking. The critical ethos that moves this research challenges and takes distance from the alleged determinism and objectivism of mainstream energy security normativities, their geopolitical eschatology and technical jargon. In turn, this book embraces a sensitivity towards historical contingencies, social dynamics, collective imaginaries, and representations. It analyses energy security practices to unpack their political and social stakes. It aims to show that increasing emphasis on security has pushed the energy sector further away from inclusive and democratic policy efforts and towards centralized, elitist and aggressive choices that produce or tolerate different forms of insecurity. Here energy is not treated as a purely passive object but emerges as a multiplier that exacerbates the effects of security, especially the predisposition of security towards the exercise of force.

Beyond the material/ideational dichotomy

A quick glance at energy securitization in Azerbaijan shows that its practices are heterogeneous and diffused. The multiplicity of actors involved in energy security points to a diversity of interests, perceptions and priorities, which can result in different policy objectives and outcomes. It has become widely accepted that energy security means different things to different audiences. The definitions of energy security depend, among other things, also on the agency and identity of the actor that defines it. This book shows that energy securitization in Azerbaijan builds on sedimented ideas and imaginaries of oil and gas and the politics around them, transforming energy into a site of security intervention. I refer one more time to the James Bond film that I cited earlier because its exaggerated and caricatured fiction uncovers mainstream representations of oil and gas politics, especially in the ex-Soviet region. Much of the film's plot borrows from a widespread understanding of energy and security in Azerbaijan and the Caspian region: persistent geopolitical codes and Cold War stereotypes depict a context of dangerous rivalries, where the competition over energy is tangled with clashing national interests, military strategies, and power politics. Traditionally, it has been called the new Great Game: a mix of diplomacy and conflict that powerful states – especially, Russia, European countries, the US, China, Iran, Turkey – *play* in the Caspian region to gain and maintain control over its oil and gas resources, pipelines and political influence. The rush for hydrocarbons is translated into a quest for power in and over the Caspian region. The most popular narratives on energy security in the Caspian region read like spy stories or chess manuals: they narrate historical anecdotes about KGB agents, Churchill's ambitions and Hitler's secret plans; make aseptic calculus and prophecies on the division of resources and power among rival states; and often employ sports terminology like 'players', 'pawns', 'chessboard' and 'derby' to describe states' competition over resources and power. Obsessed with geopolitical struggles among hungry powers, these conservative renderings of energy security tend to embrace a realist thinking whereby states' willingness to use force to protect their vital interests in oil and gas is an obvious necessity: their conclusions inevitably lead to the idea that energy security belongs in national security. Despite their alleged determinism, these considerations of energy security are neither neutral nor objective; they hinge on a specific ideological and politicized way of problematizing energy security, which mobilizes resources and defines intervention.

A focus on the ideational and constructed character of energy security should not, however, exclude or prescind materiality from the analysis. While this book recognizes energy security as a social construction, it does not neglect the importance of materiality, especially in the peculiar case of energy. Yet rather than approaching it through a purely materialistic lens, I am interested in understanding how energy materiality intertwines with socially situated and intersubjective dynamics. The extension of energy security as both a concept and a set of practices echoes energy materiality, including the vastness and complexity of the physical space where energy and security conjoin. Energy is the material spine of Azerbaijan and stretches over large parts of its territory; the country's infrastructure runs across the national steppes and cuts through its mountains; the national reserves of oil and gas lie below vast sections of Azerbaijan's lands and waters. Oil and gas permeate the country. Energy materiality has important implications for securitization, especially for determining its own materiality and spatiality. Energy materiality is a unique and controversial space with unstable sectorial, geographical and temporal boundaries. For instance, while oil and gas deposits and facilities are geographically situated, once resources are processed, they move across large territories. Similarly, electricity is diffuse and virtually everywhere and energy markets are increasingly interconnected and work on a global scale. Energy materiality is also defined by different forms of ownership. Oil and gas resources are nationally owned, but the infrastructure used to extract, process and transport them are mainly private and multinational. Energy emerges simultaneously as both a public good and a private commodity. Interconnections among facilities, from production to storage, transformation and distribution, integrate local elements into complex, interdependent regional and transregional systems. Because the energy industry is not self-sufficient, its functioning cannot be restricted to what happens in the energy fields but depends on the multiple and constant material interactions with other sectors, such as engineering and transport.

This complexity suggests that while ideas and imaginaries may affect which energy objects become security concerns and get prioritized, energy materiality enacts and constrains what can be said and done to secure them. Hence, what energy object becomes political depends on the significance that is attached to its materiality; however, energy materiality affects, informs and concurs in defining this perception. The relationship between the ideational and the material is, therefore, characterized by relationality. The political dimension of energy securitization emerges in the plurality of these relations between multiple elements, which are both material and non-material. According to Barry (2013, p 183) 'the political significance of materials is not a given; rather, it is a relational, a practical and a contingent achievement'. He claims that the task of politics is to 'channel actions into particular directions with a whole material apparatus, practices and atmospheres that need to be studied to see how politics is made and becomes possible in the first place' (p 425).

The diverse and (dis)entangled nature of the space of energy requires us to rethink how we understand energy security, including the ways in which the ideational and the material intertwine. Most energy security literature maintains a stark distinction between the material world and the ideational, discursive realm. While the positivist, geopolitical tradition has privileged the former, the constructivist scholarship has focused on the latter.

I use the 'positivist' label to point to those approaches that in International Relations (IR) and Security Studies are often called also 'rationalist', 'foundationalist', 'traditional' or 'mainstream' (see Lake 2013) and are characterized by a general commitment to social science as a scientific, objectivist method. Their explanatory and predictive models aim to establish social phenomena as products of causal relationships. Despite their differences, the positivist literature of IR tends to share a predominant focus on the state as the only analytical unit and favours geopolitical analysis that reads the influence of geographical factors on politics in deterministic, causal and one-directional ways. Positivist accounts of energy security hinge on a widespread but cosmetic definition of energy security as a balance between the demand and the offer of oil and gas supplies: there is energy security when access to oil and gas supplies is granted. This articulation of energy security, which favours consumers' needs over producers' interests and neglects any energy source but oil and gas, is the starting point of the rich geopolitical literature. These works are interested in the material – namely the geographical and geological – conditions that affect IR as the exclusive drivers of international politics: hard data are believed to determine one actor's position within a hostile international arena. For instance, the ownership of oil and gas offers political leverage and an advantage when balancing power. A significant portion of the literature adheres to realist principles and understands security as the result of materially defined power politics, which, due to its inner rivalry, often leads to conflict. Given that resources are allocated unequally across the world, economic, political and military competition emerges between those who own the resources and those who need them. As relations between and among states are understood as convoluted and conflicting, especially between suppliers and importers, access to oil and gas becomes functional to the survival of the state. These studies maintain the centrality of conflict and take for granted the military and defence dimension of energy security as a natural component of both the concept and the policies of energy security. Regional studies on the Caucasus and Central Eurasia contribute to the success of these positivist renderings of energy security, especially the acceptance and spread of the geopolitical paradigm. (Neo)realist paradigms drive most of the empirical studies conducted on energy politics and security in the Caspian and Caucasus regions. While it is still limited, also the IR literature on Azerbaijan follows these trends. The country's energy wealth is understood as a decisive source of bargaining power to gain western support, strengthen Azerbaijan's regional influence over its rival neighbours, and balance Russia's protection to Armenia. In the positivist and geopolitical literature, the security component of energy emerges out of the alleged causality between resource scarcity and interstate conflict: although this thesis is now highly contested, some scholars have long argued that the uneven geographic allocation of oil and gas and the ever rising energy demand against the finite nature of these resources inevitably lead to conflict between those who have and control fossil fuels and those who need them. Based on rationalist and materialistic models of economic resource scarcity, these accounts do not consider the complexity of the energy security challenge, including the social and cultural contingencies that affect political choices. Similar rationalist readings argue that energy causes conflict not only between countries, but also within a state: oil and gas abundance are commonly read as 'a curse' that engenders multiple forms of violence, from militarization to authoritarianism. This observation has brought many scholars to assume a cause-effect relationship between energy wealth and poor governance. In particular, the so-called law of petropolitics argues that 'the price of oil and the pace of freedom always move in opposite directions in oil-rich states' (Friedman 2009, p 31). While this thesis is still widespread, conspicuous literature has countered its arguments, even with reference to the case of Azerbaijan (Gould and Sickner 2008; Shaw 2013): these counter studies have proved that resource wealth does not necessarily bring war, underdevelopment or dictatorships; instead of deterministic causality, the relationship between energy wealth and government needs to be understood as the result of policy choices, affected by historical, social and cultural factors and defined by the contingencies of the specific context. In other words, there is no structural necessity, universal law or eschatological fate that determines the illiberal character of resource-rich regimes. A more convincing argument suggests that rather than causing authoritarianism, the presence of profitable resources might reinforce the undemocratic nature of the already illiberal regimes as democratization might be perceived as undesirable and potentially destabilizing: despotic rulers might be more prone to reinforce their grip on power as a political choice to guarantee and secure the access to and the growth of wealth that could be jeopardized in regimes where power is decentralized. In agreement with these studies, scholars have noticed that in Azerbaijan oil wealth has not generated authoritarianism but has reinforced the already illiberal character of Heydar and Ilham Aliyev's regimes and frozen power allocation around well-established poles. Collins (2004) notes that the consolidation of oil as a driver of the country's clan politics made less relevant the rule of law, the creation of an autonomous civil society, the separation of powers, and the establishment of a system of party representation. Decentralizing power – for example by instituting democracy – is often perceived as a driver of political instability, which could deter capital and investments. In this sense, wealth is not only a means to finance and sustain an autocratic regime and its elites, but also it emerges as a critical object for the state's stability and security to the extent that its special protection might even justify extraordinary force and an illiberal exercise of power. The relationship between energy, security and politics cannot be grasped only by looking at material capability. The emphasis on the material fails to take into account the social, cultural and political dynamics of the context and the relationality between the ideational and the material that affects the role that energy occupies in the political space.

This book distances itself from the positivist tradition. Couched in abstract generalization and driven by determinism and geopolitical eschatology, material power politics risks simplifying the complexity of the energy security challenge, while also making the possibility for political change and alternative accounts of energy security seem absurd and irrelevant. Thus, this research recalibrates the analytical sensitivity away from purely materialistic and rationalist accounts to recognize the value of historical, cultural and social contingencies and forms of knowledge, upon which energy security depends.

Anti-foundationalist approaches to energy security offer an alternative to the stasis of positivist materialism. As per the positivist security scholarship, this scholarship is a pluralistic field and uniting its different trends under the same label is a difficult and dangerous task. Thus, I use the term 'anti-foundationalist' to indicate those studies that tend to favour interpretative epistemologies and problematize those methods based on alleged scientism, empiricist objectivism, and meta-narratives. They emphasize that the social world is shaped by intersubjective beliefs, perceptions and ideational factors. Knowledge of our world cannot come from an observation of what is *out there* because how we understand and interact with the *out there* is constructed through social processes and interactions. Rather than the mere hard facts, they introduce identity, societies and culture as constitutive elements of the way we appreciate, problematize and tackle energy security. In other words, energy materiality acquires its socio-political relevance according to ideational factors, such as what we think, feel and know about it. This does not mean that energy security threats are not *real* but that what energy security (or insecurity) *is* depends also on intersubjective factors, including our beliefs and interests in certain aspects of energy materiality. For example, when a state mentions only oil and gas in its national security strategy and excludes any other form of energy, or when it deploys large military convoys around its oil plants, it is giving a sign of what ideas of energy and security it accepts and prioritizes. Energy security decisions are not only based on technical expertise or material calculations; rather, they intertwine with the definition of one's identity and imply envisaging social priorities, imaginaries and values.

In affirming the socially constructed nature of energy security, anti-foundationalists emphasize its hybrid, multifaceted and context-dependent nature and pay attention to how energy security acquires a specific meaning in a given context. Most of these works belong in the constructivist and poststructuralist tradition and reflect on the construction of energy security through language: the ideational is recognized to be ontologically and epistemologically discursive. Our knowledge of the social world does not exist independently of our interpretation of it; it is language that accords meaning to social phenomena. In other words, knowledge is mediated through discourse. On the relationship between security and discourse, Huysmans (2006, p 7) writes that (in)security 'is then not simply constructed through policy reactions to a threat but first of all by discourses of danger, speech acts of security, or language games that reframe an event into a condition of insecurity'. Within the anti-foundationalist scholarship, an important contribution to energy security comes from securitization theory, which explores the process of construction of energy as a subset of national security and emphasizes the performative and constitutive role of language in that process. When securitized, objects are 'framed as threatened in their existence and are subsequently lifted out of ordinary democratic politics and into the realm of emergency politics' (Floyd 2016, p 678). In other words, according to securitization theory, when a societal or economic issue is transformed into a security problem through discourse, that issue acquires a particular salience as it becomes an existential threat and calls for emergency interventions and countermeasures. A recent but growing literature (see Chapter 2) has explored energy securitization, particularly the ways in which certain states have moved energy away from the economic domain and pushed it into the security realm.

This book shares some important premises with securitization theory. In particular, it embraces the shift from thinking of energy security as a given object to appreciating it as a social construct. Drawing from securitization theory, I understand energy securitization as a strategic, pragmatic and deeply political process that designates what and who constitute a threat, what measures need to be applied and who retains the power to do so. In securitization, the security logic institutionalizes and normalizes a way of doing security that is fundamentally aggressive, praises the use of force, and divides the world along the categories of 'enemy' and 'friend'. Securitization fits this book's interest in and focus on the use of force. Analysing energy security through securitization allows zooming into the ways in which security becomes entangled with defence and enforcement, facilitates militarization, enables exclusionary practices and increases power in the hands of the securitizing actors.

However, the traditional formulation of securitization theory does not do justice to the complexity and variety of the social world. The literature of energy securitization explains the processes as a mere discursive construction, which favours state centrism, exceptional policies and realist thinking. This approach has significant limitations. Energy securitization is ontologically and epistemologically much deeper, broader and more diversified than the ideal type of securitization. In the first instance, energy security discourses assemble with practices and energy materiality. Second, exceptional narratives coexist with and may succeed to routinized everyday practices. Moreover, rather than a loose enlargement of national security, the constant intersections between and among local, national, global and private forms of authority thwart the strict focus on the national. Similarly, the existence of states' agencies and bureaucracies, which hold different mandates and priorities, refutes the wholeness of the state as a unitary securitizing actor.

This heterogeneity tells us that the security rationales that subtend energy security practices cannot be confined to nationalist thinking and geopolitical paradigms. Even if predominant, conventional geopolitics does not exhaust the security culture behind energy security; neither does it offer a satisfactory explanatory framework. This diversity of energy security practices makes it much harder to draw a line between local, national and international interventions, or to neatly separate the private and the public sectors. This encourages us to move beyond the ideal type of securitization as a state-driven approach and focus on *actually existing* securitizations (see Chapter 2) as processes that fully embrace the complexity and diversity of the social world. In this sense, energy securitization requires us to also rethink the state as a unitary analytical unit and to finally approach it through the social diversity it encompasses. While traditionally the space of security was defined by the space of the state and the impulse to protect the internal from the external, energy securitization shows that the military and the civil security fields overlap, and defence coexists and often fuses with policing and enforcement, the internal and the external space of security constantly interpenetrate each other, assemble and disassemble in a complex configuration that dismisses the neat distinction of geopolitical boundaries. Securitization theory fails to overcome the dichotomies that have long challenged the social sciences, especially IR: discourse and practice, ideational and material, exceptional and ordinary, state and non-state. Conversely, actually existing energy securitizations point to a complex interplay across boundaries that cannot, even analytically, be kept separate. Therefore, I approach energy securitization as a heterogeneous sociological process. This allows the constant ontological and epistemological tension between the material and the ideational to be reconciled, without falling into the trap of privileging one over the other. By recognizing their relationality, this book explores the ways in which material and ideational factors are embroiled in the formation of energy security.

A sociological approach to energy securitization

The recent critical turn of energy security studies, especially the energy securitization scholarship, has largely welcomed the linguistic focus of constructivism and poststructuralism to reflect upon and expose the liminality and contingency of energy security discourses. However, understanding the interaction between the ideational and the material requires moving beyond language. The starting point of this book is to see energy security not as a technical, neutral value, but as a political practice, subjected to socio-historical contingencies and intersubjective processes of reproduction.

While Chapter 2 delves into the theoretical framework, this section offers an overview of the epistemological and methodological elements of this research. As anticipated in the previous paragraphs, this book moves beyond the idea that energy securitization pertains exclusively to the speech act: the social world is made of 'bundles of ideas and matter that are linguistically, materially, and intersubjectively mediated in the form of practices' (Adler and Pouliot 2011, p 28). This book approaches energy securitization as constituted of practices. To cite a few, certain energy security practices aim at ensuring physical protection of energy objects through the deployment of armed personnel on the ground, patrolling operations; others focus on anticipating, deterring and managing potential threats through intelligence operations, due diligence, counterespionage activities or the use of surveillance technologies; additional practices include educational activities like training, drills, conferences and research activity.

The extensive work on border security practices has served as a guiding light and a source of inspiration for finding new pathways to studying energy security. Adler and Pouliot (2011, p 4) explain that 'practices are competent performances. More precisely, practices are socially meaningful patterns of action, which, in being performed more or less competently, simultaneously embody, act out and possibly reify background knowledge and discourse in and on the material world'. Thus, *practice* offers an exceptional tool to mediate between the ideational and the material. On one side, 'practice' identifies a wide set of meaning-making processes, which still include discourse but also open the inquiry to what practitioners *do* rather than say. The *doing* of 'practice' is still understood as a social, intersubjective and performative process. Intentions, interests, beliefs and rationales are still contained in those practices that embody specific forms of knowledge about security problems and solutions. These constellations of ideas construe the linkages between energy and security and suggest ways in which practices and technologies can intervene to mediate those relations. Thus, energy security practices rely upon a certain shared regime of truth, made of assumed meanings, rationalities and concepts, which belong in the ideational. On the other side, practices offer a way of including the material in the analysis as practices have a clear material dimension: practices are *also* deeds performed in the world. Practice-oriented studies identify tangible activities, operations, and security tools, from military equipment to surveillance technologies and capacity building tools. However, attention to materiality is not limited to the concreteness of practice and its tools, but also to the objects that make up the world and exist regardless of the ideas, perceptions and beliefs around them. 'Materiality' points to the corporeal, physical matter that composes the world. In the case of energy, its materiality is important as much as discourse and wider practices. As energy objects transcend national borders, no line can be easily drawn to define the territorial, temporal and even professional configurations of energy security. The difficulties in limiting the physical space of energy contribute to making its practices boundless and permanent.

Methodologically, this implies relying on an interpretative approach that has solid theoretical foundations but also engages seriously with the empirical, while avoiding transcendental abstractions of timeless structures. The importance of the empirical as the primary driver of any research project is part of the transformative approach of Critical Security Studies to understanding the world. Traditional, positivist approaches to International Relations and Security Studies favour metatheory, ideal types and universal laws over the possibilities of the empirical. Positivism believes that knowledge derives from fixed models and explanatory theories rather than empirical descriptions; positivists argue for subordinating the empirical level of research to the meta level. Critical scholars disagree with these assumptions. The positivist stance on research reduces 'the potential infinity of data to something manageable and, ideally, explicable' (Salter and Mutlu 2013, p 43). Critical theorists share Nietzsche's concern that positivism, with its explanatory, abstract and reductionist claims, would 'abolish the real world' (Nietzsche 1968, p 40). However, they also recognize that, as Foucault (1981, p 68) puts it, 'we must not imagine that the world turns towards us a legible face which we would have only to decipher'. Hence, critical research aims at questioning rather than explaining 'the doubt rather than the certainty that comes with an entrenchment in disciplinary practices' (Salter and Mutlu 2013, p 31). In this process, the emphasis lies in the 'continuous reflexive wandering' (p 31), where the researcher is aware and conscious of 'the way different kinds of linguistic, social, political and theoretical elements are woven together' (p 29) in the interpretative moment.

Notes on the methods

The emphasis given to interpretation requires the researcher to be particularly mindful of their role in defining how to approach a specific issue, understand its ontological grammar and narrate the findings of their research. A common voice is rising among IR scholars that calls for understanding IR theory as a practice in itself. As Alexandria Innes (2015, p 7) elegantly puts it, 'IR scholarship is not a separate world but is implicit in international politics (even if distantly); thus, it is an ethical obligation for IR theory to be reflexively self-aware in its own production of international political phenomena'. Embedding reflections on positionality in the research design is fundamental not just for methodological rigour and intellectual honesty, but also to place the research in its larger socio-political context and identify the gendered, racialized and wider intersectional structures that facilitate or obstruct the research process. Azerbaijan's socio-political context imposed certain limits on the extent of my immersion in the field.

One year before my fieldwork started, Giulio Regeni, an Italian citizen and PhD student at the University of Cambridge, was tortured to death while in the custody of Egyptian forces under false accusations of espionage. Other scholars have been arrested, incarcerated, accused of treason and espionage, or sentenced to life imprisonment because of their academic work. In an almost self-evident way, these stories are testimony to the insecurities that are viscerally tied to security practices. Several academics have addressed the problem of safety when conducting research on Central Asia (Gentile 2013; Koch 2013; Janenova 2019). Their concerns resonate with my experience. While practice-oriented approaches entail a deep immersion in the field, ethnography, especially long observation of critical energy sites, soon appeared not to be a viable option for my research project. I therefore opted for a multi-method approach based on semi-structured interviews, discourse analysis and mapping. This allowed overcoming most problems raised by the palpable socio-political challenges I would face in Azerbaijan, while respecting the epistemological fundamentals of my work. The three methods aimed at maintaining a dialectical relationship between materiality and discourse and recognizing the importance of local knowledge.

Discourse analysis is particularly useful to expose how language accords meaning to specific social phenomena and how the reiteration of those discourses constructs specific truths. Barnett and Duvall (2005, p 56) argue that 'discourses are sites of social relations of power, because they situate ordinary practices of life and define the social fields of action that are imaginable and possible. This approach is grounded in Foucault's understanding of discourse as a system of power-knowledge relations, embedded in a definite historical juncture.' A Foucauldian conceptualization of discourse implies that language is a productive technology of social practice, which sets up a constitutive relationship between meaning and power. Recognizing the performative ability of discourse, discourse analysis is concerned with the symbolic and meaning-making systems that sustain and legitimate certain policies and allows 'captur[ing] the dynamic relationships between discourse and society, between the micropolitics of everyday text and the macropolitical landscape of ideological forces and power relations, capital exchange, and material historical conditions' (Luke 2002, p 100). Discourse manifests and connects the heterogeneous multitude of representations, imaginaries and beliefs that sustain the energy security debate in Azerbaijan. To conduct my discourse analysis, I selected the texts that contained the core security strategy for the three case studies I wanted to focus on, namely Azerbaijan's government, NATO and BP. In terms of primary sources, I used Azerbaijan's 2007 National Security Concept, the 2010 Military Doctrine, the 2013 Maritime Security Strategy; the NATO–Azerbaijan Individual Partnership Action Plans Reviews of 2009, 2014 and 2019; and all the 14 Annual Sustainability Reports published by BP between 2003 and 2016.

Some scholars suggest that the focus on language can never be self-contained but needs to work in conjunction with methods that allow overcoming the false dichotomy between the material and the discursive. As Loughlan et al (2014, p 23) put it, research needs to navigate 'the empirical muddy waters where discourse, institutions, and materialities entangle'. Mapping has emerged as one of the most appropriate and suitable methods to complement discourse analysis. Drawing on a sociological tradition, mapping was introduced into security studies to analyse the social space in which security actors act, with an emphasis on the banal nature of their security practices. In simple terms, mapping provides a systematic analysis of actors, the relational dynamics among them, their mandates and the acts they perform. As a method, mapping allows simplification and ordering of their heterogeneity and complexity, charting of objectives, strategies and tactics, and examination of the patchwork of security and military professionals that share the field. Mapping is a process of ordering and categorization that allows the outcomes, the activities, and the tools that underpin different energy security practices to be located. Each practice bears a distinctive cognitive logic and a certain knowledge of how to do energy security; it embodies a form of expertise and institutional culture.

Mapping has been an innovative method to challenge the conventional conceptualizations of security space and temporality: through mapping, the research is not forced to define the space according to topographical principles and national borders but is able to reframe the space through its social character, situating security in the realm of the everyday and as an actually existing practice. Mapping as a method implies being attentive to institutional relations; a focus on the social space implies understanding how the tension between the local and the global is resolved – or not – in the social, looking at how discourses and practices circulate among actors, how they are absorbed, reformulated and exported across spaces. The data used for mapping were gathered through open sources, complemented by data gathered through the texts used for the discourse analysis and the semi-structured interviews. I used a broad range of institutional websites, such as NATO's, BP's and Azeri security agencies' portals to map actors and practices. A few legislative databases (like e-qanun.az and legalacts.az) were handy to get easy access to laws and decrees that are rich in information on institutions' mandates and modi operandi. Sources in the Azeri language were translated using online software and counterchecked by a native speaker. Interviews complemented some missing pieces of information. During my time in Azerbaijan, I engaged as much as I could with Azerbaijan's think tank Centre for Economic and Social Development (CESD), where I formally interviewed local energy and security experts, and with leading Azeri scholars working on the country's political context. As energy security in Azerbaijan combines a wide set of heterogeneous practices that are not confined by the country's geographical boundaries, I conducted interviews also in Europe, where NATO, the Organization for Security and Co-operation in Europe (OSCE) and BP have their headquarters. I interviewed BP's former Vice President for Strategy and Policy Development in London, BP's Vice President for the Caspian region, BP's Team Leader in Social Investment Strategy, the NATO Director of the Energy Security Section, the OSCE's Senior Programme Officer Energy Security, and the OSCE's Counter-Terrorism Officer. To approach interviewees, I relied on different strategies. With energy stakeholders, my previous experience in the sector and my wide network of contacts in the industry proved to be essential. Chance encounters in Baku led to serendipitous discoveries, giving me access to former policymakers in the high ranks of the Azerbaijan political entourage and former security guards. Contacts with local citizens happened on sites and thanks to the kindness and helpfulness of the communities themselves. Some sources were interviewed twice to review and discuss important pieces of information. Some challenges to accessing the field remained. In Azerbaijan, the regime's grip over information jeopardizes access to primary sources and transparency. There is palpable distrust and suspicion when it comes to discussing national security issues, and interviewees from the political and economic entourage dread the risk of (Armenian) espionage. Local citizens fear governmental reprisal when expressing discontent with official policy decisions and most agreed to participate in the research only on condition of anonymity. Being a white, European woman was a double-edged sword. My interest in the country raised curiosity and pride; my gender and my distance from the political context reassured most interviewees. Nonetheless, I was also perceived as an outsider who could be easily tricked with propaganda. Sometimes sharing the information I had collected before the interviews was effective to facilitate the discussion and establish myself as a reliable and credible voice in the field. When confronted with stonewalling, I decided to recognize reticence as a valid and revealing piece of information per se.

My selection of Azerbaijan as the main site of research often raises curiosity: Azerbaijan is a small, non-western country, which rarely features in books on International Relations and Security Studies, and when it does, it is mostly as a functional piece of the geopolitical chessboard. As mentioned earlier, only a few works take a constructivist approach to researching the South Caucasus region, assigning the study of energy security to the realm of geopolitics. As such, Azerbaijan is a novelty also for critical approaches, including securitization studies: despite the popularity of the framework, securitization theory is seldom applied to small, non-western contexts. In the case of energy securitization, research has favoured consumer states and great powers over suppliers and small countries. Yet, Azerbaijan offers the types of social, political and economic conditions that sparked my interest in energy securitization in the first place, especially the tension between energy, security and power; the economic and political centrality of the oil and gas industry; and the multitude of foreign actors that have entered the sector following the opening of the industry. I was interested in understanding how energy securitization functions in a context where energy is central to the economy and politics, and where security is subjected to multiple and constant vulnerabilities and attacks. Azerbaijan is not only an energy-rich state, but also an insecure place torn by the authoritarian ruling of the Aliyev family and the war against Armenia. Given the relatively recent nature of Azerbaijan's independence, the study of energy securitization in the country allows exploration of energy security practices in relation to nation building and ideas of nationhood. Azerbaijan's transition out of the Soviet economy and towards integration with the global, liberal market forces us to move beyond looking at securitization as a purely nationalistic and militaristic process and to recognize the umbilical connection between securitization and globalization, particularly processes of internationalization and privatization. These dimensions are reflected in my comparative case studies. In fact, while some criticism may still arise regarding my exclusive focus on Azerbaijan and the subsequent lack of comparison with other countries, this responds to a clear methodological rationale: I wanted to retain, in my research design, the ambition to shift away from a state-based conceptualization of the analytical space. Hence, this book still offers a comparison, but rather than across topographical borders, it compares three different selves that reflect the heterogeneous character of energy securitization. In particular, they embrace three social universes that characterize energy securitization: Azerbaijan's state security actors stand for the national dimension of energy securitization, NATO for the international, and BP for the private. The first case study focuses on state security institutions and explores how energy securitization intersects with the processes of state and nation building in Azerbaijan since its independence. I want to emphasize that this attention to state actors and dynamics still retains the analytical sensitivity towards social heterogeneity and diversity of this research project. Thus, instead of claiming an ideal unity, the first case study approaches the state as a politically, institutionally and even materially fragmented space. In the second case study, the analysis of NATO enables a reflection on the role of international actors in securitizing energy in Azerbaijan. Accounting for the global dimension of energy securitization allows reflection on its ontology, including the nature and scale of the threats, as well as of the reference objects, and the forms of governance that are established by international actors through western multilateralism. The study of NATO's discourse and practice shows how energy securitization is situated within the larger western, liberal project, whose ideational and material politics it embraces and reproduces. Finally, the third case study looks at the non-state and non-national dimension of energy securitization. My research uses the example of BP to examine the role and impact of a private and foreign actor in securitizing energy in Azerbaijan. This third case unpacks the interpenetration of the private with the public sectors and the skein of authority and expertise that their assembly forms. It recognizes that securitized discourses and practices cannot be understood outside neoliberalism.

Outline of the book

This introductory chapter has outlined the research area, explained the motives behind the book and its aims, and introduced the epistemological and methodological approach. Chapter 2 lays out and develops the theoretical framework and situates this study within its scholarship. Drawing on the work of International Political Sociology, this book rediscovers securitization theory beyond the early formulations of the School of Copenhagen, with the intent of fostering a more critical engagement with the politics of energy security. Willing to encompass the *actually existing* complexity of energy securitization, this book approaches it a multi-layered terrain where manifold processes intertwine and unfold, assemble and disassemble. In this context, energy securitization in Azerbaijan emerges as a sociotechnical assemblage, generated from the entanglement and disentanglement of ideational, material, social and technical elements. Chapter 2 sets forth five theses on the ontology of energy securitization.

The core of the book presents the empirical findings, which investigate the interaction of state, supra-state, and private organizations in securitizing energy in Azerbaijan. Chapter 3 focuses on Azerbaijan's national security discourse and argues that it securitizes energy by conflating it with the security of the state and by merging it with the country's process of nation building. It puts forward three main arguments: first, in the national security discourse, energy security is constructed as a function of state security and emphasizes the physical protection of energy infrastructure as a symbol of the country's history, territory and sovereignty; second, it signals that the construction of energy security and the fabrication of national identity are co-constituted in an ontological but also political way; third, energy securitization validates processes of militarization and power centralization that legitimize the Aliyev family's regime and instil a political culture of obedience.

In Chapter 4, the analysis shifts the attention towards the security professionals and the practices that produce energy securitization. Its central argument is that energy securitization interlaces with Azerbaijan's process of state building. The empirical analysis shows that the prioritization of energy security and the corollary enlargement of the military and paramilitary machine have provided the elites with abundant financial resources, larger mandates, increased responsibilities and, finally, greater political power.

Chapter 5 provides an account of the global dimension of energy securitization through the case study of NATO's energy security interventions in Azerbaijan. It analyses the global ontology of energy securitization, as well as the forms of global governance it creates; this allows an understanding of the particular vision of order, the forms of authority and the patterns of social organization around which this specific problematization of energy security as a global issue coheres. Through the empirical analysis, this chapter demonstrates that NATO energy security discourse and practices securitize energy by insisting on the exceptional, critical, global and novel character of its threats. This has enabled the creation and proliferation of energy security programmes and the enlargement of its institutional architecture through the formation of ad hoc energy security-oriented units. Energy securitization renovates NATO's security mandate, proves its continuing relevance, and enlarges its authority to the extent that it positions the Alliance as *the* global expert of energy security. Under the rubric of interoperability, cooperation, alignment and integration, NATO's energy securitization in Azerbaijan concurs in (re)producing and cementing liberal norms and values as the only possibility for and pathway towards global energy security.

By analysing the role of BP in providing security, Chapter 6 exposes the privatized dimension of energy securitization. It situates energy security in discourses and practices of security that are defined ontologically and politically by private property. Chapter 6 shows that energy securitization embodies and diffuses neoliberal principles, such as autonomy, efficiency and privatization, creating a legitimate space for energy companies and private security contractors to provide security services. In the case of BP, energy securitization and neoliberalism interlace in a particular way, whereby security enlarges private profits and the neoliberal propensity towards the maximization of profits reinforces security as securitization. This analysis demonstrates that BP has enlarged its corporate structure and created an ad hoc security department, expanded its business portfolio, increased its resources, expanded its remits, spread its network, deepened its ties with the state, boosted its role and power in the country, and established itself as a source of expertise and a legitimate administrator of force.

Chapter 7 reorients attention to the implications of energy securitization and exposes the Janus-faced relation between security and insecurity, showing the multiple vulnerabilities created by energy securitization in Azerbaijan. In these sections, the analysis reveals how security professionals have reoriented their rights to use force to protect energy sites against activists, workers, ordinary people and local communities. Energy securitization is tied to forms of abuse, violence and harassment. Moreover, despite the criticality attached to energy by the multiple processes of securitization, Azerbaijan's energy system is unreliable. The study discusses the country's lack of access to, and affordability and availability of, electricity, the low degree of sustainability of its energy system, the impact on the environment, and the inadequacy of public investment in the domestic energy industry.

Chapter 8 sets out the conclusions of the book, offering a summary of the main conceptual arguments and findings of the empirical work. It reaffirms the relevance of this work and its contribution to understanding energy securitization and its implications.

2

An Analysis of Actually Existing Energy Securitizations

This book explores energy securitization in Azerbaijan through an innovative approach to securitization theory, which combines discourse analysis to a practice-oriented approach. Overall, securitization studies champion a way of thinking that appreciates the possibility of change against the long metaphysical tradition of positivist theories of security and recognizes that security is inherently political. In this sense, securitization forces us to understand and question what is at stake in security – including the related forms of insecurity that security generates – and the conditions that make it possible. Securitization acknowledges security as an intersubjective process of construction, socially enacted and politically consequential, rather than as a universal and neutral value. This chapter locates the book's theoretical framework within the field of International Political Sociology (IPS) and its rediscovery of securitization beyond the early formulations of the School of Copenhagen and its speech act-centred theory. When developing the theoretical arguments underpinning the book, this chapter explains how a new, highly transdisciplinary, perspective of energy securitization can offer more latitude in understanding the complexity and heterogeneity of securitization. In particular, IPS moves away from the linguistic tradition of the speech act theory and grounds securitization in French and continental philosophy with the intent of fostering a more critical engagement with the politics of security. While still recognizing the importance of discourse, IPS positions language within a wider set of practices, the analysis of which can help identify and question the ways in which power and authority intersect. Against the rhetoric of the extraordinary highlighted by the School of Copenhagen, IPS demands attention to less spectacular forms of security: it brings into the analysis everyday practices and taken-for-granted forms of knowledge along with the attention to the discourses that fixate certain ideas of security and even disguise governmental practice.

This chapter starts with a reflection on the concept of energy security and its application; by doing so, it offers an exploration of the principal debates of energy security studies and sketches the conceptual trajectory of the phrase. It then introduces securitization as a theoretical framework to problematize the relationship between energy and security. Since its formulation at the end of the 1990s, securitization theory has experienced as much success as criticism and, to a certain extent, has followed the path of security studies, becoming something of a cottage industry – to steal Baldwin's metaphor. However, I believe that the proliferation of works on securitization has not deprived the concept of its persuasive power and revolutionary force: not only has the theory introduced an innovative way of analysing security, but also it has come to epitomize a specific modality of doing security, a recognizable political practice and, finally, a certain art of governing. Its popularity has even emancipated the concept; it has embedded its terminology in everyday vocabulary and, in doing so, has spread its inner critical spirit outside books and academic inquiry.

The last section outlines five theses on energy securitization and in so doing it delineates an alternative theoretical approach to securitization, which, unlike traditional applications of the theory, accounts for the heterogeneous, contingent and liminal character of energy securitization. The re-elaboration of securitization theory has happened under multiple labels – 'critical', 'post-structuralist', 'sociological' and 'emancipatory', among others. Drawing clear boundaries between so-called critical orientations is difficult and risks imposing artificial demarcations that miss the many overlapping zones that these approaches share. These include a shared recognition of the socially constructed nature of securitization, an understanding of securitization as a performed strategy of power, and an ontology and epistemology of (energy) security aimed at overcoming the dichotomy between the material and the ideational. By positioning my work within the field of IPS, I want to make more explicit the theoretical foundations of this book. At the most superficial level, compared to other so-called critical approaches to security, IPS evokes a rising determination of complement the focus on security discourses with a pressing interest in security practices and practitioners. This points to a commitment, pursued by this book too, to understand the social as formed by relational, assembled, contextual processes. This is done not only to keep broadening and deepening the inquiry into security, but also to bring it closer to the social reality where security develops; in this way, security is seen in its banality, rather than exceptionality, and embedded into the quotidian and micro space where international politics happens. Together with an attention to the sociological dimension of security as practice, IPS invites researchers to adopt an anthropological eye, which questions and problematizes the specific cultural beliefs behind the fixation on certain understandings of (energy) security, their claim to necessity and universality, as well as the transmission across spaces of peculiar forms of knowledge and *truths*. The truly interdisciplinary ethos of IPS bridges the empirical devotion of sociology and anthropology with the theoretical insights of critical social theory and international political theory. As this chapter explains, I have hooked securitization on French and continental philosophy, with the intent of deepening the critique of security. The seminal work of Foucault and Deleuze and the rich literature of Critical Security Studies inspired by 20th-century continental and French philosophy have helped me build my research architecture and have lent a useful and identifiable terminology that enables the empirical analysis to be located in a clear theoretical tradition. In particular, I borrow the concept of assemblage, an effective theoretical tool that social sciences have adopted to highlight the blurred, heterogeneous, complex and ever changing nature of security and securitization.

The original sin of energy security

As a concept, energy security was introduced to indicate the relationship between the demand and the offer of oil and gas supplies. Although often assumed to be a technical, neutral and self-evident term, what energy is a security concern and what security energy requires are not straightforward decisions and can be contested. As the introductory chapter has anticipated, the study of how energy and security intertwine is not an easy field of inquiry, especially given the conceptual complexity of security and the material fluidity of energy. Historically, the roots of the phrase 'energy security' are often situated in the first decades of the 20th century, when western European societies began a revolutionary industrial transition from coal-based to oil-based production. This process was initially pushed by the investments that European states made in their national defence industries: fomented by the two world conflicts, the defence sector – which was at the forefront of technological innovation – went through a phase of modernization based on the introduction of petrol-based machines to ameliorate armaments and make them more efficient. The launch of internal combustion engines favoured a process of military automation, which not only revolutionized war making, but also put oil at the centre of larger processes of industrial renovation. The use of petrol and internal combustion spread beyond the military and was soon introduced in numerous civilian sectors, such as transportation, electricity and heating, all over Europe, in the US and in many other countries worldwide. Western countries, however, had to confront a material challenge that complicated the extent and progress of the oil revolution: the continent lacked oil reserves. While coal had provided European and American industries with an abundant, cheap and local source of fuel, the shift towards petrol required western economies to rely on oil imports from foreign countries, especially the Middle Eastern states. The oil trade soon became politicized. In the 1970s, following western support to Israel in the Yom Kippur War, Arab oil providers responded with an embargo on sales of oil to Europe and the US: between 1973 and 1974, the price of oil quadrupled, paralysing European and US industries and affecting private households, where electricity outages and high energy bills became the norm. In 1979, following Iran's Revolution, a significant decrease in oil production and exports caused a second crisis. European and US cities experienced energy shortages, high inflation and higher production costs, which caused a decline in production in the local manufacturing sectors. Long queues at petrol stations and concerns about heating and electricity blackouts terrified western citizens. The idea of energy security, which became so popular in those years, developed around western anxiety and fear over import dependence. It was the overlap between energy trade and foreign policy interests that was perceived as potentially dangerous, a political weapon in the hands of oil-rich states. In the west, political attention arose, generating concerns about the need to stabilize oil prices and diversify supplies by finding alternatives to Middle Eastern suppliers. As the consumption of gas started growing in the west, making it one of the three main sources of energy (together with oil and coal) in most developed economies, European and US energy dependence deepened. In particular, European dependence on the gas imported from Russia generated new concerns. Mistrust between Brussels and Moscow, due to enduring animosity and historically difficult diplomatic relations, resulted in the gas crises of 2006 and 2009. In those years and within the context of the Russia–Ukraine conflict, clashes over the cost of and access to gas escalated to the point that Moscow decided to cut the supplies destined for Ukraine and Europe.

While it is not my intent to provide a detailed account of the history of energy security and energy politics, these brief remarks serve to contextualize the genealogical formation of energy security in its historical context in order to better understand its conceptual and policy trajectory. For decades, the definitions of energy security have prioritized the historical experience, the material geological conditions, and even the psychological and emotional charge of western, especially European, states. Western states' fear of supply disruptions and price distortion has been echoed in the multilateral efforts to define energy security in terms of supply security and the prominent use of international regulation to govern access to foreign oil and gas markets. The meaning of energy security has long remained centred on the 'uninterrupted availability of energy sources at an affordable price' (IEA 2017). Over the decades, some light rewording has led to rhetorical and conceptual nuances, including 'access to cheap oil and gas', 'positive patterns of availability and prices of oil and gas', 'the good functioning of energy markets' (Isbell et al 2007; Müller-Kraenner et al 2008; Kalicki and Goldwyn 2013). According to these definitions, the degree of energy security should be measured using the so-called four As, namely the availability, accessibility, affordability and acceptability of oil and gas supplies. In line with these approaches and as a response to the oil crises, international governance and institutions – such as the International Energy Agency (IEA) and the International Monetary Fund (IMF) – started intervening through a set of market regulations that pushed oil-rich countries to open their markets. The privatization and liberalization of the national energy markets has been promoted as a tool to depoliticize energy, reinsert it into the efficient and functioning realm of technocracy, and, thus, make it *secure*. Embedding energy security in (neo)liberal economic principles, defined by an ideology of market liberalization and profits, has long aimed at stripping energy out of politics and political dynamics – perceived as inherently conflictive – to let it be managed by the allegedly *unbiased* invisible hand of the market. Two main considerations can be drawn from the liberal economic rationality that constitutes energy security. First, albeit apparently neutral and technocratic, the market-oriented definitions of energy security are *political* to the extent they embrace liberalism, which is in itself a political project. Building on Neocleous (2008, p 31), who argues that 'the new form of economic reason to which liberalism gave birth also gave new content to the idea of reason of state', I contend that liberal principles have also shaped the whole space of the political, redesigning an idea of order and transforming international and transnational relations. This is something that emerges clearly in the empirical analysis of energy securitization in Azerbaijan: energy security practices are increasingly driven by neoliberal principles that push towards the maximization of profits over the allocation of public resources, the standardization and replicability of security practices, automation and efficiency, and the creation of new forms of authority and legitimate power based on private property. This has implications: security becomes about the stability of the neoliberal market and defined by quantification and comparison of goods and services that secure continuous economic transactions. Access, availability, affordability and acceptability tend to be approached as quantitative values, measured through quantitative methodologies, rather than quality-based criteria.

To reinforce this statement, my second point is that, despite efforts to couch energy security in technical jargon, the political and geopolitical dimensions of the 'four As' have never disappeared and have kept influencing the ways in which energy security has been approached. In particular, certain conservative policy and academic environments have been sceptical about the idea that market measures could neutralize the inherently geopolitical and inherently military nature of the problem. According to them, the uneven geographical allocation of oil and gas is a reality that market regulation cannot change and remains an important and persistent cause of conflict, a tool of political and diplomatic leverage, and a strategically important component of national security. When energy security is inserted in national security, it absorbs a conventional geopolitical culture, which is avowedly state centric, cares almost exclusively about oil and gas, and prioritizes a view of security in terms of military significance. At the heart of this rendering of energy security lie Westphalian ideas of power, sovereignty and the state: energy security is treated as a matter of balancing different national security interests in the international environment – which is understood as innately anarchic and conflictive – and makes states prone to secure their resources or access to supplies through military calculations and defence strategies. After 9/11, a considerable body of the energy security literature has embraced this defence-oriented approach to energy security. Especially in military environments, energy security has been coupled with rising concerns over terrorism and the connected risk of armed attacks and sabotage against oil and gas infrastructure. This way of problematizing energy security has led to a focus on the physical security of energy, which has promoted and normalized the deployment of military and paramilitary units in the energy sector. Whereas this points to the colonization of the energy sector by security, it needs to be acknowledged that it does not happen without contestation. As previously outlined, conventional conceptions of energy security, especially its inclusion in national security, have been challenged on multiple fronts. More recent accounts of energy security have welcomed renewed attention and care towards the environment. Aware of the cost of global warming and climate change, a branch of energy security studies has recalibrated the predominant interest in oil and gas security and in national security by positioning the environment and its protection as the drivers and the referent objects of energy security. These studies warn that orthodox definitions of energy security are not only unsatisfactory but also counterproductive and potentially dangerous: their persistent focus on fossil fuels has long hidden the multiple forms of insecurity that oil and gas create in relation to the environment and human health. Rather than looking for the security of the state and the stability of the market, these scholars suggest shifting attention to the environment as the main reference object. Because hydrocarbons are major contributors to rising temperatures, environmental degradation and pollution, energy security should foster policies that aim at reducing emissions and decreasing reliance on fossil fuels through diversification of sources, efficiency in use and sustainability. Mulligan (2011) understands energy security as a fundamentally ecological concern; Pascual and Elkind (2010) recommend reformulating energy security with a view to sustainability and global warming. By changing the definition of the threat and the referent object, also security acquires a different meaning. These studies reframe energy security in terms of responsible use of fossil fuels, sustainable patterns of energy consumption, energy efficiency and the protection of the natural environment.

Against the variety of energy security concerns, most literature tends to privilege one specific perspective of energy security – economic, environmental, geopolitical or physical security – or combine multiple factors through an add-and-stir logic. However, despite the diversity of approaches, most of these accounts share the underpinning assumption that discovering the *real* nature of energy security is possible and aim at resolving the inner diversity of the concept through a definition that responds to clear technical requirements or normative principles. Nonetheless, the broad semantics of energy security and the heterogeneity of its policy principles pose several theoretical and practical challenges: for instance, energy security indexes – based on tens or hundreds of variables – fall into conceptual traps, lack theoretical integrity, can lead to policy inaction, and empty the term of any *actual* significance. As such, due to its ambivalence and broadness, the concept of energy security raises more questions than it answers: what energy is a security concern? What security does energy security require? Is it an end or a means? Is energy a security target, a referent object, a source of danger or a security domain? What security measures – military, political, economic, environmental, etc – should be taken to achieve it? Who should provide energy security: the army, the diplomats or the energy, financial and economic stakeholders? What needs to be secured? Whose security should be prioritized: that of the state, the importers, the producers, the users, the companies, the workers or the infrastructure?

Scholars have recognized the slippery character of energy security. Dannreuthers (2017, p 10) acknowledges that 'there is no single, comprehensive definition of energy security'. While some scholars focus on the polysemic and multidimensional nature of energy security (Chester 2010; Vivoda 2010; Sovacool and Mukherjee 2011; Mansson et al 2014), others see its plasticity as a form of ambivalence, which makes the phrase an often ambiguous and fuzzy label (Ciuta 2010; Valentine 2011). Energy security as a concept is constantly in flux. It opens questions of politics, identity and sovereignty, among other dynamics, and highlights that how we make sense of energy security depends not only on concrete spatially and temporally defined conditions, but also on cultural, social, political and ideological factors.

The original sin of energy security lies precisely in the juxtaposition of these two terms – energy and security – which escape easy conceptualizations and are semantically ambiguous, discursively extensive, materially fluid and own a primordial, ontological attachment to the question of life and death. It is, however, possible to escape the illusory trap of catching the *truth* of energy security without falling into absolute relativism and transforming it into an object of endless meanings. This can be done by considering energy security as a relational, intersubjective, historically and socially situated concept, which does not describe an external, immovable and universal reality but interprets *one* reality. Energy security is neither a self-evident, objective, brute fact nor a subjective perception based on totally relative, personal feelings. Rather, it emerges as intersubjective: what energy security means is socially mediated, based on collective understandings and beliefs, and formed through mutual interactions, meaning-making processes, and intelligible and discursive practices, which are embedded in a specific historical, cultural, social and material context. That is to say that definitions of energy security are inextricably linked to specific perceptions and representations of the problem. Ideational and material factors intertwine to such an extent that the two cannot be separated from one another. As Côté (2016, p 541) explains, 'intersubjective beliefs are a product of social and group interaction and provide meaning to the social and material world through the creation of shared meanings, norms, values, and identities'.

This approach draws upon the poststructuralist tradition of (critical) security studies and the ways it has abandoned the mission of defining what security is in absolute terms and moved away from an understanding of security as 'a noun that names things' (Dillon 1996, p 16). Poststructuralists favour an understanding of security as a (re)production that, simultaneously, (re)produces things, creates an order and establishes a certain regime of truth about that issue. In other words, security is inevitably tied to and dependent upon the historical, social, economic and cultural context in which it is formed: what security *is* varies based on concrete and contextually situated variables; the reiteration of that knowledge has ontological effects. Claims about security cannot be objective or neutral but always rely upon how we represent security and insecurity, threats, and referent objects. The same is true for energy security: definitions of energy security cannot be separated from specific forms of knowledge and representations about it. Poststructuralism places considerable attention on the relationship between the ways a subject represents a problem (including a security threat) and their identity, understood as a socially and discursively constructed perception of the self against the other. Against the well-established rationalist tradition of energy studies, a growing body of literature analyses how perceptions of energy security threats vary across states depending on ideational factors, in particular their national identity, and become fundamental to energy choices and policies. Of particular interest is the way in which energy systems are influenced by collective social norms and values and larger imaginaries of progress and technology, which sits within larger ideas of national identity, namely the perceptions of who we are as a society and what we want to be.

Acknowledging the constructed nature of energy security is, however, only the point of departure of our intellectual inquiry. Poststructuralists pay attention to what security *is* in a specific context to understand what it does: definitions of security – as well as of energy security – have implications for how to intervene, the identification of the subjects and the objects to protect, and the threats that need to be neutralized. Concomitantly, every time energy security is enacted in a certain way, it reiterates the very conceptualization of what it is. This points to the performativity of energy security. Early understandings of performativity developed from the work of Judith Butler, who introduced the term to denote 'the reiterative and citational practice by which discourse produces the effects that it names' (1993, p 2) and, again, 'an act, which brings into being or enacts that which it names' (p 6). Progressively, the original emphasis on the discursive dimension of performativity has been narrowed down, leading to defining performativity as the 'vehicle through which ontological effects [such as the effect of a doer behind the deed] are established' (Butler in Osborne 2013, p 110). A certain problematization of energy security assumes particular performances – from behaviours to practices – which are expected to bring certain security outcomes; the reiteration of these behaviours cements the impression of what energy security *is*. We act as though *being* of energy security is a simple fact, but in reality, it is a phenomenon that is produced and reproduced over time; that ontological formation that comes from reiteration is its performativity. In this sense, energy security is relational and performative because its ontology is socially constituted and through that social construction, enaction and reiteration, energy security consolidates and delimits specific ways of doing, thinking and being.

Recognizing the relational, contextual and performative nature of energy security implies challenging and problematizing the claims to its universality and, by doing so, also acknowledges its political nature. Performativity and relationality point to the ability of energy security to draw the boundaries of political, legal, institutional and even social actions, and as such, they reveal that behind the allegation of objectivity lies a certain arrangement of political, economic, social and cultural power. This is particularly relevant for my research: if we accept that the securitized rendering of energy security is not inherently given but rather results from a complex configuration of practices, power and authority, then we need to divert attention towards the circumstances that make energy securitization and its modalities possible. This requires a critique of the political that dissects the relationship between energy, security and power. Since its early days, the critical security scholarship (Der Derian and Shapiro 1989; Fierke and Fierke 1998; Huysmans 1998, 2006, 2011; Bigo 2002, 2005; Balzacq et al 2010) has eloquently exposed how and why security is political: it embodies specific ideas and normativities about what is right or wrong, and legitimate or illegitimate, important or irrelevant. Huysmans, framing a now widely accepted idea, conceives security as a political technique that situates the logics of survival at the heart of the political process and mobilizes fear to order societies. The work of Neocleous (2000, 2007, 2008, 2011; Neocleous et al 2013) has been particularly enlightening to situate the critique of security within a much larger critique of power. While still problematizing security and its contemporary hype, Neocleous teaches us to limit our gaze to security and the state as isolated problems but to reinsert them in their larger political and economic context imposed by the neoliberal order.

Critiquing security tells us that exploring what security is and does is particularly important because of the peculiar, priority status ascribed to it, which originates from its ontological bond with the question of life and death: security has traditionally been associated with the conditions for survival and, as such, for the possibility of existence and against the threat of death. Security is the necessary prerequisite for life to develop; without security, everything else wavers. Taking a step further, security can be said to be not only the external imperative of life but the equivalent of life itself. While there are extensive reflections on the thickness, pervasiveness and stickiness of security because of its bond to life, less has been said about the ways in which the peculiarity of energy adds up to the peculiarity of security. In fact, a very similar attachment to life can also be found in the way energy is conceived and understood. While energy is a broad and chameleonic concept, it often emerges as both the expression and the possibility of life itself. As for security, energy also appears to enable the existence of society and the individual. For instance, at the micro level all living organisms require energy as it is the vital force that allows a being to grow, reproduce and maintain its existence; at the macro level, energy has come to be understood as the lifeblood of contemporary societies and the main form of their sustenance: energy sources are the engine that has propelled and keeps propelling progress, not only in terms of modernization, but also in terms of existential evolution. Burke (2002, p 6) notes that the power of security is tied to its relation to modernity and 'the imagination of "progressive" forms of modern political and economic subjectivity'; for him, security is constitutive of and foundational to modernity. While I agree with this proposition, I also argue that energy itself has had an enormous impact on how we have materially and ideationally shaped the very possibilities for our futures. Not only have specific understandings of energy emerged through security, but also the renderings of security have been affected and mediated by energy, both ideationally and materially. The technological, economic and scientific developments at the base of our political and social order, which impact how we problematize security, are both symbolized and materially enabled and built by energy. Understanding the co-constitutive relationship between the technological and the social world provides us with a tale of how we dream about our future and how we narrate our past and present. Science and Technology Studies tell us that how societies imagine and use technology reconfigures authority and performatively creates power (Jasanoff and Kim 2015). Thus, analysing energy security gives us a chance to think about the ways in which energy and security reciprocally mediate and intersect in a bidirectional relationship. Finally, energy security needs to be approached as a concept that acquires signification only from a specific position within a particular discourse and in relation to particular practices of governance. As I have previously clarified, this book zooms into a particular force-oriented notion of energy security in Azerbaijan, which is framed as energy securitization. The following section delves into the specificities of the theoretical framework.

From energy security to energy securitization

The perspective on energy security developed in this book recognizes the importance of setting up a theoretical and epistemological framework that centres around the relational, contextual and political nature of energy security and its implications. In view of the complexity of energy security and drawing upon the growing influence of anti-foundationalist and critical accounts of International Relations and Security Studies, the energy security literature has shifted its attention away from its early explanatory and defining tasks. Recent research, principally nested in the social sciences, has sought to balance the technical jargon and endeavours of energy security with a perspective attentive to political, societal and cultural dynamics. In this context, an alternative pathway and major source of philosophical innovation has been offered by securitization theory.

Securitization pertains to the construction of security; it denotes the strategic, pragmatic and deeply political process that designates what and who constitutes a threat, what measures need to be applied and who retains the power to do so. Conventionally, three main features have denoted the process of securitization: first, the identification of a threat to the existence of a specific referent object; second, the creation of emergency measures to address the danger; third, the prioritization of security and the interruption of normal politics (Buzan et al 1998).

Generally speaking, securitization exposes the ways in which, by situating energy in the security realm, it becomes an object of existential importance and critical vulnerability, which, consequently, enacts traditional logics of security and requires emergency security measures. Albeit still a niche in energy security studies, securitization theory puts the emphasis on the constructed and political character of energy security and introduces a more critical sensitivity towards 'security'. Motivated by scepticism towards security and security politics, securitization theory helps problematize the stickiness, thickness and alleged neutrality of security, as both a philosophical concept and a political practice. This requires exploring what happens when energy becomes and is dealt with as a security concern, including its paradoxical and parasitical relation with multiple forms of insecurity. Energy securitization covers the proactive, constant and diffuse deployment of force in the energy sector by security techniques of control, prevention and coercion, with the aim of protecting certain energy objects from identified threats.

Securitization theory contributes to exposing the social and political dimension of energy security, rejecting aprioristic notions of the concept in favour of an appreciation of its intersubjective and contextually contingent dimension. With the existing literature of energy securitization, my book shares a harmony of intents and an epistemological constructivist sensitivity: current works on the securitization of energy recognize the influence of social dynamics, including identity, cultural and historical variables against the long-standing positivist tradition of energy security studies. As Suzanne Risley (2006, p 30) notes, all processes of securitization belong in 'broader political projects and visions, ... which contributes to the construction of political authority as well as of political identities and subjectivities'. The social, political, cultural and economic context and the dimension of the ideational become central: Janeliūnas and Tumkevič (2013, p 67) conclude that 'the very essence of [energy] securitisation varies' and Philips (2013, p 17) argues that energy security is primarily a matter of governments' subjective perceptions, stressing that the decision to securitize energy is foremost a political choice. Christou and Adamides (2013, p 510) situate the securitization of energy in wider political processes and as part of widespread political, economic and even military threat discourses that solidify a certain understanding of energy threats and security solutions. Leung et al (2014) conclude that the securitization of energy in China is influenced by institutional interests, policy preferences and capacities, historical memories, governance paradigms and examples of other countries experiencing energy security pressures. Kratochvíl and Tichý (2013) explain that European attitudes towards Russia, especially the way the EU perceives Moscow as a security threat, deeply affect their energy relationships and facilitate processes of securitization.

Early formulations of securitization theory, often related to the School of Copenhagen, describe securitization as a speech act, used by an actor to claim that a specific object – considered to be vitally important – is existentially threatened and in need of extraordinary actions to respond to the threat. Rooted in language theory, securitization theory assumes that the linkage between the word 'security' and *real* things is less important than the utterance itself. In this original conceptualization of the theory, the emphasis is put on language: securitization refers to 'a specific way of framing an issue' (Wæver 1996, p 108), placing the fabrication of a security concern in the sphere of discourse and claiming that its existence depends upon its utterance. Paraphrasing Wæver's argument on security – namely that 'by saying the word [security], something is done' (1993, p 55), we can affirm that by saying energy security, energy security is created and done. Language has the power to evoke, create and transform what security *is*; in other words, security is ontologically discursive and its utterance affects how a specific issue is approached. In securitization theory, it is the act of labelling that creates a security concern; in doing so, that speaking of security creates an opportunity for the state to establish extraordinary measures, special powers and whatever instruments are deemed necessary to respond to that threat.

Most of the literature on energy securitization develops from this early approach to securitization theory and centres the analysis on language, looking for the threads of 'national security' in energy security discourses. While still recognizing the essentially contested and contextual nature of security, securitization points to a specific way of problematizing an issue *through* security, which is rhetorically centred around military force, evokes politics as exceptionalism, equates security and defence, and understands the state as the referent object and the provider of security. More importantly, securitization recognizes the power of security to elevate an issue above normal politics and, as such, to escape limitations to authority, checks and balances, and a democratic exercise of power. Energy securitization stops seeing energy security as a reaction to self-evident, *real* external threats; by recognizing its constructed nature, the framework has been applied to examine and explain the conditions under which energy security becomes an object of security, able to activate exceptional policies.

Together with an emphasis on language and discourse, most of the energy securitization literature conceptualizes securitization *as* and *through* the rhetoric of the extraordinary. Even recent attempts to move beyond the emphasis on the speech act and to recentre the analysis on practices have analysed energy securitization through policy decisions that are understood as breaking with ordinary policymaking. They may also hinder democratic participation, limit the possibility for open debate and bypass well-established channels of decision making. Attention is mainly given to the ways in which energy policies are defined by a politics of exception. In this sense, resorting to the security sector is often assumed to be extraordinary in itself, given the peculiar aura that surrounds the military and national security. However, as I explain in the following section, not all security practices belong in the exceptional; in turn, they often entail a wide set of normal, banal, even repetitive activities that share little with the spectacular imaginary of security as a life and death situation and are not confined by the narrow temporalities of an emergency.

Often understood as a negative process (Aradau 2004), securitization has been associated with the spread and normalization of forms of antagonism, control and oppression. This is because the logic of securitization and its practices is essentially conflictive, exclusionary, coercive and controlling. In the processes of securitization, security emerges in its conventional connotation as *mors tua vita mea*: the construction of a securitized threat identifies a dangerous 'other' and develops through processes of exclusion and othering. Moreover, as securitization is motivated by an aspiration to manage the threat, it materializes in politics that merge forms of control and coercion. Attention to securitization has helped reveal the damaging side of security, especially the multiple forms of insecurity it paradoxically produces. This has also concurred to problematize the blind faith in security and show the ideal of security as a good-for-all solution, not only as utopian and counterproductive, but also as a silencing device. A disillusion with security has allowed the countering of a culture of security that sees the greatest benefits in the maximization of security and securitization. Rather than assuming that more security is less insecurity, a critique of securitization points to its negative effects: securitization is seen as a failure of normal politics, but also as a mask for multiple forms of oppression, violence, coercion and, finally, insecurity.

There have been efforts to redeem securitization and understand it as a process able to raise attention and allocate resources. This potentially can help better address energy problems – especially lack of access and sustainability – conferring an emancipatory potential upon securitization. Nonetheless, most securitization scholars who have focused on energy share a pressing concern over the entanglement of energy and national security because of the conflictive and militaristic logic it enacts. Jonna Nyman (2014, p 49) contends that energy security reinforces and reproduces state-centric understandings of security, rival logics of state competition, and national security-focused policies. Similarly, Phillips's (2013) study on energy security in Asia claims that energy securitization interacts negatively with existing alignment patterns and has aggravated pre-existing regional tensions.

With regard to the undemocratic exercise of power connected to securitization, Janeliunas and Tumkevič (2013, p 67) recognize that 'the formal designation of energy issues as an object of concern for national security ... justifies the breaking of established rules in order to respond to an existential threat'. This literature has also exposed the ways in which a totalizing attention to national security has relegated energy to a corollary of security. In particular, this has resulted in poor energy choices, especially due to a misuse of energy resources, a neglect of clean energy, and the detrimental effects of hydrocarbons on the environment.

Studies on energy securitization agree that the process elevates the importance of fossil fuels by constructing oil and gas as vital to the security of the state and its survival and making them a political priority. Energy securitization enacts a synecdoche: the use of the term 'energy' most commonly indicates oil and gas. As a result, scholars (Christou and Adamides 2013; Nyman 2014, 2018a, 2018b; Judge and Maltby 2017) have noted that energy securitization increases policy attention on fossil fuels to the detriment of alternative energy sources: energy securitization exalts the role of oil and gas in the energy mix and their contribution to the economy, downgrades the importance of renewables, neglects the possibility of energy transition and green policies, and dismisses environmental concerns as security issues.

Most criticism of energy securitization has focused on its effects on environmental security. The critique of energy securitization has built on the larger literature that has analysed security and securitization with regard to the environment and the climate. A central contribution comes from Deudney's work (1990), which problematized the association between national security and the environment. While noting that war and violence have little in common with environmental degradation and habitability (p 465), he observed that the logic of national security permeated environmental politics. According to him, security was used to attract public attention and mobilize political action but ended up introducing a military-focused mindset that would distort environmental policymaking and orient it towards the use of force (pp 465–9). Since Deudney's article, multiple studies have warned against the nexus between security and the environment. Taken together, these works have also concurred to reveal the inappropriateness of military-oriented approaches of security to protect the environment: Trombetta (2008, p 586) signals that security brings a specific logic that relies on 'confrontational practices associated with the state and the military'; Gilbert (2012, p 4) argues that the military approach 'do not lend itself to addressing fundamental social structures that perpetuate environmental degradation'; Lunstrum (2014, p 817) documents processes of 'green militarisation' based on 'the use of military and paramilitary actors, techniques, technologies, and partnerships'; and Dalby (2013, p 185) warns against 'the political dangers of invoking climate change as a matter of military security'.

I have already made clear that I share the concern about coupling energy with national security and I agree its militarization is a central problematic. However, current works of energy securitization have not engaged in depth with an analysis of the modalities of securitization, overlooking intrinsic and profound diversity of security practices and their wider implications. In particular, the attention on the military obfuscates the diversity of security practices; the focus on the state negates agency to non-state actors; the emphasis on security shadows alternative logics, rationality and structures; the centrality of language dismisses the role of practices and the relationality between the ideational and the material. As such, the diversity, complexity and heterogeneity that characterizes energy securitization is lost in the traditional analytical approach. The rigid and exclusionary emphasis of securitization theory on language, national security and the extraordinary has hidden the importance and influence of materiality, practices, the ordinary and non-state actors on energy securitization. This gap creates multiple loopholes that concern not only the epistemology of energy securitization (as anticipated in Chapter 1), but also its ontology. Current literature tends to understand energy securitization as a monolithic process, driven by the state and for the state through a rhetoric of the extraordinary. This view of securitization exercises a metaphysical abstraction, which portrays a simplified and dichotomized understanding of the world: its focus on national security assumes the state is a unitary actor and neglects the interaction of the 'national' with different *others*, belonging in the international and the private spaces of energy security. Energy securitization points to a multiplicity of actors, practices, discourses, interests and bodies of knowledge that sustain it; these processes may share the same impulse to securitize, but they have distinct focal points that should be taken into consideration. Far from being purely national, energy securitization implies a constant engagement of the 'national' with the non-national, especially as an expression of the international and the private dimensions of energy security: international organizations, energy companies and security contractors are at the forefront of energy security. Acknowledging energy security as an assemblage of multiple and diverse elements reconfigures the role, capability and legitimacy of the state in securing energy and challenges the conventional image of the state as the holder of the monopoly on the use of force and defence. The assemblage of energy securitization stretches across social universes – assembling defence and enforcement, national and international, public and private – encompassing security institutions, security logic, neoliberal rationales, policing technologies, practices of risk management and policing, strategies of defence, maritime security and counterterrorism, and patterns of international cooperation, to name only a few of its elements.

A look at the ontological diversity of energy securitization exposes the fallacy of seeing it as a mere subset of national security: the centrality occupied by the state in the securitization literature wavers against the reality of a heterogeneous constellation of securitizing actors and institutions. This research demonstrates the complexity of energy securitization and its multiple configurations beyond a metaphysical and abstract vision of the process as the exercise of state power. In the face of this diversity, this book argues that energy securitization lacks the unitary and homogeneous character that its ideal type aims to achieve and needs to move away from a state-centric ontology and towards the analysis of actually existing energy securitization(s), which reposition security in its broader context. While security has definitely become sticky and omnipresent in contemporary politics, its analysis should not make invisible the embeddedness of energy securitization in a context marked by larger economic, political and social regimes and struggles, especially the influence of the liberal, capitalist order on the formation of security. Securitization theory has not only neglected the problematic interaction between security and the capitalist, neoliberal order, but it has also accepted it as a necessary component of a desirable order. This is evident in those works that discuss the de-securitization of energy – that is the process to free issues from the constraints of securitized logics and practices and relocate them in the realm of ordinary politics – in (neo)liberal terms of market liberalization, deregulation and global environmental governance (Kuzemko 2013; Nyman 2014; Kustova 2018).

This book recognizes the intellectual force of the securitization framework and its contribution to the growth and innovation of the study of energy security. This section has acknowledged securitization theory as an extremely valuable conceptual tool and reified some of the important lessons learnt from the securitization of energy. Nonetheless, a clear awareness of the limitations of the theory underlies and informs this book, which emerges also from a dissatisfaction with some of the foci of the existing literature of energy securitization. Since its first formulation, securitization theory has experienced several evolutions and transformations; yet these have only partially been learnt, absorbed and developed with regard to energy. Energy securitization remains principally anchored to a conventional reading of the theory, based on the early work of the School of Copenhagen. These insights are used in the following section to put forward, in a more systematic way, an alternative approach to energy securitization, which is embedded in the theoretical and empirical tradition of IPS. This marks a clear departure from securitization theory and requires a different conceptualization of energy securitization. As such, energy securitization demands refreshed thinking. The following sections insist on the importance of paying attention to the heterogeneity of energy securitization and put forward five theses of energy securitization.

Actually existing energy securitization

What I call energy securitization refers to the fabrication of energy as a security concern through discourses and practices that enable and normalize the proactive, constant and diffuse deployment of force in the energy sector. The securitization process is, therefore, about the construction and management of energy security threats and contains an idea of security which is fundamentally aggressive; this aggression presupposes protection and controllability and emerges through a combination of coercion and control. While this book is primarily concerned with those practices that imply the actual or potential use of force, its findings also point to a diverse set of corollary programmes that stretch the contours of security, defence and enforcement in uncharted fields. In Azerbaijan, energy securitization materializes through manifold security practices, which include patrolling energy infrastructure, legislating on land management, conducting due diligence on energy workers, establishing international best practices or participating in security training. It is not only the nature of labour that varies considerably, but also the strategic objectives that drive these practices, the mandates that regulate them, the discourses around them and the typology of professionals involved. This heterogeneity, which is at the centre of the processes of energy securitization, needs also to be kept at the analytical level and demands an alternative theoretical approach which moves beyond the ontological and epistemological contours of securitization theory. Current renderings of energy securitization do not account for the diversity, inconsistency, fragmentation and contestation that characterize energy securitization as any other social phenomena. Willing to encompass the *actually existing* complexity of the social, a growing branch of IR scholarship has taken a stark interest in understanding international politics and security as a multi-layered space where manifold processes intertwine and unfold, assemble and disassemble. It is in the relationality among those elements that power emerges and governance is formed.

In this context, theory does not aim to provide a simplifying tool to make sense of the reality and reduce complex phenomena to a single unit; rather, it seeks to grasp the changeable and complex character of world politics, acknowledge its determinative irreducibility, and problematize the apparent stability and coherence of social phenomena by paying attention to the conditions under which they are created, reproduced and even fixated. This serves to reflect upon the power dynamics that fabricate and sustain a particular way of doing and thinking of politics and security. Solid philosophical progress in this direction has been made in certain areas of Critical Security Studies; for example, studies on border security and surveillance have reshaped how we empirically approach security with a view to grounding the theory in the diversity and complexity of the empirical. These developments have only lightly touched the fields of energy security and energy securitization; as noted before, energy securitization has worryingly remained confined to state ontology and speech act theory and has questioned securitization only as an expression of the power of the state. Accordingly, what falls outside traditional categories of international politics has remained unseen, silent and ignored.

This book is willing to encompass the complexity and vibrancy of energy securitization as a heterogeneous sociotechnical process. Thus, the first argument that it puts forward contends that energy securitization should be understood as a sociotechnical assemblage, generated from the entanglement and disentanglement of ideational, material, social and technical elements. To cite a few, the assemblage of energy securitization interlaces internal security with external security, military with civil, defence with enforcement, coercion with control; it relies on surveillance and policing technologies as much as on maritime defence and counterterrorism; it intertwines the national and the international, as well as the public and the private domains; it builds ties amidst different security actors and institutions that belong in different social universes; it merges security logic and neoliberal rationales, as well as security techniques and neoliberal modi operandi; it intersects energy security with local dynamics, power structures and histories while also encircling into patterns of international cooperation and corporate strategy.

This book has inherited the idea of assemblage from Gilles Deleuze's work and enriched it by integrating and drawing upon Michel Foucault's oeuvre – including Deleuze's own reading of Foucault – especially his idea of security assemblage as a technology of power (see thesis number 4), and the copious critical security literature that has applied assemblage thinking to different security fields. Multiple definitions have been given to the concept of assemblage, all of them reflecting a specific philosophical sensitivity; nevertheless, the conceptual essence and power of the assemblage as a theoretical approach lie in its ability to encompass the complexity, diversity and plasticity of sociotechnical processes like energy securitization. Deleuze (1988, 1992; Deleuze and Guattari 1987) emphasized that the function of the assemblage is to link heterogeneous elements together. This diversity is expressed also by Latour's (2005) famous definition of the assemblage as 'an unstable and contingent collection of heterogeneous elements'. The notion of the 'assemblage' derives from the Foucauldian concept of the 'dispositif', which was introduced to indicate a 'thoroughly heterogeneous ensemble' (Foucault 1980, p 194) of institutions, discourses, laws, practices and materiality, which retains the ability to create a specific order and ordering of the social. The ability to create and impose a specific order on the social has been the primary focus of most engagements with the concept, which stress the power of the apparatus to manage, control and influence people and behaviours.

Deleuze introduced the idea of the assemblage to inquiry reality in its complexity and variety, emphasizing that social phenomena are processes, rather than fixed objects, made of heterogeneous elements and their contingent and ever evolving relations. Another way to put this is following Foucault, who wrote that this way of ordering the social is formed 'at a particular time, in a particular country, to satisfy certain needs' (2000,p 292). Assemblage thinking implies reflecting about 'relations, heterogeneity, and differences rather than parts, homogeneity, and similarities' (Kamalipour and Peimani 2015, p 404). Hence, with reference to this research, assemblage thinking is particularly useful to include elements and relations that are often overlooked by securitization theory, providing a more accurate ontological and epistemological account of the process of energy securitization. More explicitly, the inclusion of practices, materiality and non-state actors allows the limitations of speech act theory to be overcome. In his analysis, Schuilenburg (2017, p 68) explains that securitization makes it clear that the pursuit of security takes place in a plethora of practices and environments. The use of the term 'plethora' here is emblematic: it underlines the depth and extent of the multiplicity of elements within the securitization process; it points to the widespread variety of forms, dynamics, factors and possibilities that underpin security. The assemblage is therefore introduced to grasp the diversity and variety behind energy securitization. The starting point is the appreciation and acknowledgement of energy security in its heterogeneity and complexity: the assemblage accounts for the assortment and richness of discourses; the wide range of practices and the diverse networks of practitioners; the changes in the governance of energy security, intended as temporal, spatial and institutional changes; and the multiple ways in which its space is enlarged, distorted and (re)constructed. The emphasis on the expansive spatiality of energy securitization is contained in the idea of assemblage as 'diverse hybrid structures that inhabit national settings but are stretched across national boundaries in terms of actors, knowledge, technologies, norms, and values' (Abrahamsen and Williams 2016, p 251).

To approach energy securitization as an assemblage means that it is no longer meaningful to look for the exact significance of energy among the multiple possibilities of its meanings but to embed each specific rendering within the relations that form it. In this sense, the assemblage grasps *actually existing* energy securitization. I have borrowed the phrase 'actually existing' from Brenner and Theodore (2002, p 349), who used it to identify 'the contextual embeddedness' of social processes, 'insofar as they have been produced within national, regional, and local contexts defined by the legacies of inherited institutional frameworks, policy regimes, regulatory practices, and political struggles'. *Actually existing* energy securitization aims to make explicit its distance from the abstract ideal type of securitization as defined by the traditional, speech act-oriented theory and its state ontology, and to account for its inner heterogeneity.

The ontological and epistemological importance of practice and materiality in the analysis of energy securitization has been explained in the introduction of this book. Here I emphasize why it is important to stress the social diversity of actors and how it impacts the ontology of energy securitization. Approaching energy securitization as an assemblage requires allowing for the role of different actors and their interrelations across the wide spectrum of governance. The state certainly occupies a decisive role in the securitization of energy; nonetheless, it is far from being the only actor in securing energy. In particular, energy companies and security companies provide services and conduct operations that were previously within the exclusive remit of national armies and law enforcement agencies. Similarly, international organizations are reinventing themselves in ways that affect the power of the states and are embodied in forms of transnational governance that challenge the realm of national security: international security organizations, for instance, are enlarging their capacities; extending their powers of action; defining security strategies, goals and modi operandi; establishing certain knowledge about security concerns that were once perceived as purely 'national' issues; and asking the states to adapt to their regimes of truth. In this complex configuration, non-state actors operate alongside the state to provide energy security: whether it be the contribution of intergovernmental security organizations to address global threats, or the emerging opportunities for energy and security businesses, states' role as exclusive providers of security falters. Securitization as a theoretical framework must, therefore, account for encroachment of the private and the global into the national, the entanglement of state and non-state security actors in *doing* energy security, and the relationality of the commingling of public-private, global-local, international-national. The ways in which the state exerts its securitizing ability is largely influenced and subjected also to its interactions with the other, non-state agents that operate in the field: energy securitization is made of the constant assembly and disassembly of these relational configurations. The point here is not to prove whether states are more or less powerful but to capture the density of reality through an exploration of its multiple actors, dynamics and relationships and the ways their relationality creates order and space. The relationality that sits at the basis of these processes is, therefore, of fundamental importance. Assemblage as a concept points to and underlines the connections among the parts, their assembly and disassembly, including the process of (dis)entangling and shaping claims for identity, security and insecurity. While the fixation on force and the previously mentioned emphasis on coercion and control entangles the heterogeneous elements of the assemblage, the strategic objectives might vary as the normativities, the particular interests, and the culture that underpin energy securitization often lack coherence and harmony across actors.

Five theses on energy securitization

The multiple elements and relations that constitute its assemblage emerge from a spatially and temporally contextualized historical conjunction, which creates the conditions for both their possibility and change. As such, the first thesis of this book maintains that energy securitization – as an assemblage – is constructed and performative. I have already explained that energy security is not based on purely material and technical evaluations; it is not simply a matter of ensuring a certain number of supplies. Securitization relies on claiming knowledge of a threat, of the target, of ways to 'block' it, and of how to persuade the audience to accept it (Frowd 2018, p 60). What energy matters and how to secure it embodies values, expectations, imaginaries and even assertions of one's own self; as security scholars often underline, security and identity are inextricably linked. This is not entirely in opposition to the long tradition of securitization studies and its emphasis on securitization as the social and intersubjective construction of a threat. However, IPS takes a step forward and challenges how the School of Copenhagen understands 'the social', for the purpose of placing, once again, the heterogeneity and complexity of world politics at the centre of the inquiry. In this framework, the constructed nature of social phenomena should be seen not as the product of 'one natural world called society' but of multiple professional, social and cultural universes. In energy securitization, discourses, practices, knowledge and forms of governance emerge in and through the relationships of different authorities. The interaction among all those elements holds a performative power, producing and reproducing the discourses, practices, normativities and forms of governance of energy securitization. Energy securitization is performative because each of its practices establishes specific problematizations of energy and security, which invest them with specific signification and manifest their ontology.

The socio-genesis of energy securitization is dependent on and subjected to the positions of power of the different securitizing actors. In questioning the fixation on a particular notion of energy security in Azerbaijan, the sociological approach to energy securitization shifts attention towards the social forces that have the ability to impose specific bodies of knowledge to show that energy security is a political and cultural practice; this is the second thesis of this book. Energy securitization is cultural to the extent that it embodies cultural and ideological sensitivities, a specific *Weltanschauung* that determines the judgements about energy security threats and solutions. As a cultural practice energy securitization can be taught, passed on and even inculcated. Behind the multitude of actors and practices that share the impulse to securitize energy lie a wide variety of rationalities, interests, logics and forms of knowledge that constantly interact with each other. How actors securitize energy delimits and guides the practices, defines interventions, mobilizes resources and capital, and generates a regime of truth about energy (in)security and how to manage it. Energy securitization is, therefore, both a process and a product of that knowledge. Thus, securing energy is, foremost, a cultural practice, reflective of specific beliefs, imagination, education and cultural predisposition. Discourse analysis reveals Azerbaijan's state security actors, NATO and BP conceptualize energy security in dissimilar ways: they are motivated by different normativities and institutional cultures, connect energy security to specific imaginaries that reflect their cultural baggage, and do not always share the same strategic objectives. However, as the assemblage entangles and disentangles manifold elements, specific cultural assumptions – they have emerged in localized social universes – are made 'standard', normalized, diffused and even indoctrinated through the definition of best practices, joint training, technical assistance and the spread of interoperability as a shared strategic objective. The 'assemblage' approach renders visible the spaces of contestation and negotiation that coexist in energy securitization, stressing that energy securitization emerges from both opposition and harmony, change and fixation.

Energy securitization is also political: it presupposes political judgements about legitimacy, freedom, ownership, mobility, past and future, and progress. Attempts to depoliticize energy by masking it under an alleged objective technicism are also political. The rationalities behind energy securitizations are always political. As explained in Chapter 1, this book is particularly interested in understanding why, regardless of its inner diversity, energy securitization remains centred around a specific rendering of the problem. This question pertains to the formation of certain regimes of truth about energy securitization; in other words, the construction of energy security at the base of the process of energy securitization produces certain knowledge about the problem and its solution. Reminiscent of Foucault and his ideas on the power/knowledge nexus (1990), this argument explains how certain ways of thinking of and doing energy security become predominant and how their epistemic foundations reflect power structures, while also assigning power and authoritativeness. It is the symbiosis of power and knowledge that determines who retains the epistemic authority and has the ability to speak and act, the positions that can be legitimately voiced and performed, the actors that channel and spread that knowledge across sites. The ways elements (dis)assemble are not neutral but deeply political: in the assemblage, the articulations of energy and security depend on what meanings different actors attach to energy and security; these meanings are an expression as well as a catalyst of power. This implies that the empirical inquiry should not focus on what energy securitization is – this could fall in misleading abstraction and essentialism – but on what energy securitization does, how it works, where, and why. The transformations and the conservation of meanings depend on the ways the elements of the assemblage entangle and disentangle; their mobility is not neutral. In particular, the flexibility of the conceptual and practical boundaries of energy security practices does not jeopardize the criticality and centrality given to both energy and security; it has the power to maintain a universal appeal while pointing to very different orders. Scholars (Balzacq et al 2010) have seen in securitization a specific technique to govern, impose political agendas and develop political programmes that determine what/who is in need of protection and what/who is a threat and subjected to control and coercion. Through the comparative analysis of three different actors – Azerbaijan's state agencies, NATO and BP – this book notes that energy securitization is not purely an expression of national security: while it relies on and expands the use of sovereign power, it is not justified exclusively in terms of state security and framings. In turn, it raises questions of global governance and business profits, more specifically in relation to liberal values, interests and practices, which do not centre necessarily on national security and prioritize a liberal, economic sensitivity towards cooperation, interconnectedness and interdependence. Through my exploration of energy securitization in Azerbaijan, I came to notice that the rendering of energy security as a global threat or as a business concern, or the presence of foreign experts and private security contractors, were not readily visible if I looked at the problem exclusively through the conventional lens of security and its focus on the state.

This book suggests that the assemblage of energy securitization is partly shaped by (neo)liberal rationalities, market logics and economic interests that assemble with security; the success of energy securitization in colonizing governance is also ascribable to its fit with the liberal project. There is a whole liberal universe connected to energy securitization in Azerbaijan, which is rendered visible in both discourses and practices, for example through the special attention to energy corridors, the protection of integration and interconnectedness, the recognition of a legitimate interest and role in securing energy for private companies and transnational organizations, and an enlargement of the responsibility for the provision of energy security towards 'new "responsibilized," "localized," and "enterprised" agents and agencies' (Lippert and O'Connor 2003, p 334). Energy securitization implies paying particular attention to the energy market, with the goal of making it more reliable and flexible. As such, energy materializes as a (physical) space in need of military and policing. This has eventually led me to formulate the third thesis of this book: there is a whole universe, entangled with energy security, which is explicitly about building and consolidating a liberal order through making energy more interdependent, interconnected and profitable; this fosters securitization.

Energy securitization has not only increased the number of actors involved, but also the need for coordination among them, establishing institutional channels and harmonizing practices. However, while the encroachment of the global and the private into the national is often seen as being in opposition to and to the detriment of the state, an embedded analysis of actually existing securitization points to a different outcome. For instance, the proliferation of international and private actors in the provision of energy security does not weaken the state but offers it a chance to reshape its role, refine its tools and increase its resources, while boasting the support of private and international actors in maximizing the security machine.

In its fourth thesis, this book argues that the spatiality of energy securitization blurs conventional configurations of space. Most literature on energy securitization lacks attention to its spatiality and imposes limits that are rarely reflected in the actual securitizing processes. Energy securitization has traditionally been constrained by the conceptual and empirical boundaries of national security: the centrality of the state organizes space according to Westphalian territorial configurations, centred around borders. Yet, the empirical space of energy securitization in Azerbaijan points to a much more complex and (dis)entangled terrain, which escapes traditional dichotomies. In particular, the spatiality of energy securitization needs to be reconsidered on two levels: one that accounts for transnational arrangements and a larger, more encompassing view of space and scale; the other that is attentive to the mobility of the contours of the national and the blurriness of its internal and external confines.

With regard to the first aspect, it needs to be recognized that the ideational and material expressions of energy security are transversal, transnational, trans-sectorial and trans-border. As a lesson learnt from the wider IPS scholarship, the focus on an apparently secondary and often overlooked dimension of security practice allows reflection on the relation between the localized area of security practice against the universal and objective aspiration of security and its effects on governance. For instance, the patrolling of energy infrastructure, which is one of the primary energy security practices, cannot be understood through the prism of territorial sovereignty: Azerbaijan's state security professionals who patrol energy facilities tend to perform their tasks following NATO's best practices and guidelines, and as they operate on BP's energy sites they do so under the company's rubrics. This is reflective of the complex configurations that underpin energy securitization as a multi-scale and multi-layered process, where local practices, global governance and private businesses assemble and disassemble. Assemblage thinking helps emphasize the alternative spatial configurations of security, revealing that the provision of security in a specific national territory is rarely confined to its physical borders. The assemblage, as a conceptual tool, contains a reflection on the peculiar transnational spatiality of energy securitization and its ability to cut across the false binary lines of national-international, global-local and private-public.

Energy securitization is also indicative of the inner complexity of the national and the opacity of its spatial boundaries. The space of the state, marked by its national borders, has traditionally defined the space of its security: threats come from the outside; security is guaranteed in the inside. This understanding of the space has also determined a division of labour between two realms of security: 'one of war, defence, international order and strategy on the one hand, and crime, internal security, public order and police investigations on the other' (Bigo 2007). As noted in other security fields, energy security practices do not maintain this distinction and tend to conflate the two dimensions of security, promoting the coexistence of the national army, the police and the intelligence services. The hybridity of energy security entangles the social universes of policing and defence, embedding the military into the civil and vice versa, merging internal control and law enforcement with defence and warfare. In Azerbaijan, energy securitization has extended the participation of the military sector in internal security and civil matters, while also legitimizing the deployment of military personnel during peacetime and outside war zones. Conventional representations of space along topography and national boundaries impose a false cohesion to the social space of the state and dismiss the endless mobility of social reality. The convergence of external and internal security underpins a different conceptualization of the space of security and affects the ways the division and realization of security labour: as Bigo (2006, p 171) noted, 'external security agencies are looking inside the borders in search of an enemy from outside. ... Internal security agencies (national police forces, police with military status, border guards, customs) are looking to find their internal enemies beyond the borders.' It is not only security that marks the mobility and flexibility of energy securitization; its space is defined and affected also by energy, whose ontology is materially and ideationally vast and mobile. Through assemblage thinking, the spatiality of energy securitization is understood as formed by the interaction of all its elements; its boundaries are therefore flexible and incoherent.

The fifth and final thesis of this book contends that security has a paradoxical and parasitical relation with insecurity. The considerable expansion of security practices has facilitated the proactive, constant and diffuse involvement of security and military professionals into and beyond Azerbaijan's energy sector, which has fuelled a system of fear, violence, oppression and control. This book reveals that energy securitization in Azerbaijan creates and exacerbates the different forms of insecurity that exist in the country and confirms that 'any attempt to obtain maximum security always provokes maximum insecurity' (Balzacq et al 2010, p 13). Energy securitization enables and normalizes a way of doing politics that is abusive and coercive and curtails the possibility to imagine and enact alternative energy and security solutions.

3

Energy Securitization in the Land of Fire

In Azerbaijan, oil and gas pipelines draw a parallel topography, running across and beyond the national territory. Around the capital city of Baku, onshore and offshore drilling platforms shape a singular skyline. In the Absheron peninsula, Baku's region, oil-well derricks in succession populate the dry, semi-desert steppe, creating suggestive lunar landscapes. There lie the largest oil and gas deposits. One can smell exhaust gas even from the city. The soil in the Absheron peninsula is so rich in gas that it generates spontaneous fires every time it leaks to the surface. This inspired the country's brand: Azerbaijan, 'the Land of Fire'. On the hillsides, particularly on the Yanar Dag mountain, flames blaze continuously due to natural combustion. In the surrounding areas of the Absheron peninsula, it is not rare to spot oil ponds, residual barrels, and sewage; these are signs of the pollution that contaminates large parts of Azerbaijan's territory. Driving 50 kilometres south of the capital city, in a dusty, rocky and sandy area, the highway passes by the Sangachal terminal, a vital link of the country's oil and gas industry and one of the world's largest oil and gas terminals. The terminal, which – at the time of writing – is still under expansion, currently covers about 550 hectares and is connected to the four main gas and oil pipelines that cross the land. Among them, the Baku–Tbilisi–Ceyhan pipeline is the second-longest pipeline in the world and runs along 1,760 kilometres from Azerbaijan to Turkey through Georgia, more than half of it underground. Called 'the pipe-dream' throughout the 1990s, the construction of the BTC finally began in 2002; it was inaugurated in 2005 and started operating the following year. Other pipelines include the Western Route Export Pipeline (WREP), which since 1999 has transported oil from the offshore Chirag field in the Caspian Sea to the Supsa terminal in western Georgia, and the Baku–Novorossiysk pipeline (NREP), which was inaugurated in 1997 and runs north for 1,330 kilometres from the Sangachal Terminal to the

Novorossiysk terminal on the Russian Black Sea coast. The South Caucasus Pipeline (SCP; also called BTE – Baku–Tbilisi–Erzurum) exports gas from Azerbaijan Shah Deniz to Georgia and Turkey, following the BTC oil route. The trajectory of the SCP and the BTC pipelines has long been a matter of controversial debate about their exposure to *terrorist* threats: passing close to Nagorno-Karabakh and the border between Georgia and South Ossetia, the two pipelines are considered to be potential targets of sabotage and armed attacks by the region's militants and separatists.

Off the coast, energy facilities have conquered the Azeri section of the Caspian Sea. One of the most remarkable examples is the city of Neft Daşlari, where an offshore oil platform built in 1947 has developed into a massive industrial settlement. Built in Soviet times, the main artificial island covers more than 7,000 hectares and connects to a network of 2,000 platforms through about 300 kilometres of roads and bridges. At its peak, Neft Daşlari hosted around 5,000 people, mostly workers and their families. Today Neft Daşlari is a functional, although decrepit, urban centre in the middle of the sea, where Soviet-style apartment buildings rise next to oil rigs and pipes. In the city, defence and enforcement measures are high: security agents patrol the site and its access; surveillance and digital technology such as satellite images are used to control mobility; and access to the city remains forbidden to non-residents. Safety, health and environmental protection, on the other hand, do not seem to be on the government's radar. Neft Daşlari perfectly exemplifies the paradoxical status of energy and security in the country: the field has achieved record figures over the last decades, producing more than 175 million tons of oil, and yet its infrastructure suffers from severe neglect and lack of investment and maintenance. The dream of an oil city with cafes, cinemas, shops and parks clashes with the reality of a place in decay. The floating city might be an engineering miracle of Soviet times but most of its facilities are now broken, leaking, rusty and half-submerged. Most of its oil rigs are inoperative and only one third of the connecting roads are still accessible. Living in the isolated oil city is hard and work unsafe: explosions, fires and shipwrecks have caused several deaths and injuries among the oil and gas workers. The housing buildings, where energy workers live with their families, have partially collapsed into the oily waters that surround them or become condemned due to the frequent floods. After years of reckless industrial contamination, Neft Daşlari and other areas of the Caspian Sea record worrying levels of water and air pollution. The country's efforts in maximizing extraction and production have destroyed extensive portions of Azerbaijan's land and water.

I begin with these contrasting images to anticipate a major theme of this chapter, as well as of the book: the definition of what energy deserves security and what security should be provided to energy is not only inherently political, but also it reflects a constant process of inclusion and exclusion to determine what matters and what does not. To understand energy securitization in Azerbaijan, this chapter first explores the national security discourse and responds to these questions: how is energy securitized in Azerbaijan's national security discourse? What contextual dynamics facilitate energy securitization? What consequences of energy securitization can be first seen through discourse analysis?

This chapter argues that Azerbaijan's national security discourse securitizes energy by conflating it with the security of the state. Energy security has become an overriding political interest, intrinsically linked with the construction of the nation and the legitimation of the Aliyev family regime. Based on the findings of the discourse analysis of Azerbaijan's National Security Concept, Military Doctrine and Maritime Security Strategy, the following sections put forward three main arguments. First, in the national security discourse, energy security is constructed as a function of state security, which follows three main rhetorical lines: (i) the physical protection of energy infrastructure symbolizes the protection of the country's territory and sovereignty; (ii) energy security emerges as Azerbaijan's integration and participation in the western, (neo)liberal economic order; (iii) energy security is about defending a certain idea of the nation and its history. Second, this analysis signals that the construction of energy security and the fabrication of national identity are co-constituted in an ontological but also political way. Energy security is embedded in the country's process of nation building; it hinges upon specific representations of two main historical events – the Contract of the Century and the war in Karabakh – and personality – the former President Heydar Aliyev– that hold the highest emotional charge and symbolic power in the nation. The discourse mobilizes the national sentiments of pride and victimhood, out of which Azerbaijan's sense of self and belonging has developed. Building on this point, the third argument explains that energy securitization validates processes of militarization and power centralization, legitimizes the Aliyev family's regime, and instils a political culture of obedience.

The four axes of the national security discourse

The history of Azerbaijan tends to be told together with the history of its energy industry, which is also seen as the starting point of the history of world oil development. In the early 9th century Arabs travelling in the Absheron peninsula were intrigued by how local communities were using oil for heating; in the 13th century, a similar fascination was reported by Marco Polo, who praised Baku's petroleum, its multiple usages and its commercial potential. In 1844, when Azerbaijan was still part of the Russian Empire, the world's first drilling occurred in the field of Bibi-Eybat, putting the country at the forefront of oil development worldwide. Only a few decades after its first drilling, Azerbaijan's oil sector boomed. The country tried to capitalize on its black gold by attracting foreign tycoons: at the beginning of the 1870s a change in the legislation opened resource management to foreign investors and allowed for long-term commercial lease to replace state-granted concessions. In those years, the Nobel brothers arrived in Azerbaijan and established the Nobel Brothers Oil Extracting Partnership, which soon became a global oil leader and pioneer. Their investment in the country brought capital and resources: they introduced modern technologies, built transport infrastructure, introduced railway and maritime tanks, and ameliorated storage techniques. Seeing the many opportunities for profit offered by the oil industry, French businesspeople from the Rothschild family and the British company Shell entered the market and contributed to the financing of Baku's oil industry. The three foreign corporations soon accounted for more than half of the country's oil extraction and production. Some scholars (Heradstveit and Strømmen 1999; Cornell 2015) explain that Azerbaijan's government was more willing to open its industry to western oil tycoons than to local, mainly Armenian, businesspeople, who were perceived as competing threats to the ambitions of the native Azerbaijani industrialists. By the end of the 1880s Baku's oilfields became the most productive in the world, amounting to more than 100 million tons per year – more than ten times US production rates – and representing 30 per cent of the world's exports. Following oil development, Baku itself went through a first process of urbanization, which made it the only city to experience industrialization in a largely rural land. In a decade, the businesspeople, engineers, geologists, chemists and factory workers who arrived in the city seeking their fortune increased its population tenfold. The construction industry flourished and outside the Muslim fortress of Baku, new urban areas and rich neighbourhoods mushroomed, where local and foreign oil magnates – the famous families of the Rothschilds and the Nobels, as well as the nationally known industrialists Musa Naghiyev, Murtuza Mukhtarov, Zeynalabdin Taghiyev and Shamsi Asadullayev – built mansions and residential edifices. The oil industry created important social divides: as ownership and management were mostly in the hands of foreign magnates and skilled workers, Azerbaijanis were cut out from the gains brought by the development of the national energy industry. The largest share of its native population remained in the countryside and kept working in agriculture, seeing almost no change in their lifestyle.

During the last years of the Russian Empire and after the 1905 revolution, oil production in Azerbaijan began marching towards a steady decline; oil exports fell to 8 per cent and production rates kept dropping until the 1990s. In the aftermath of the 1917 October Revolution and the establishment of the Russian Soviet Republic, Azerbaijan's oil industry was nationalized and put under the centralized control of the Soviet regime; private companies were expropriated, and foreign owners thrown out of the country. In 1918, Azerbaijan declared its first independence. Founded in the middle of the Russian civil war, the Azerbaijan Democratic Republic (ADR) survived for only two years: in 1920 the Bolshevik troops took over Azerbaijan and annexed it to the Soviet Union. Yet, the ADR achieved important objectives: the leadership strove to establish a pluralist and democratic government, managed to establish the first secular republic and was the first country in the Muslim world to allow women to vote. While the ADR was a short experience that lasted for only two years, during that time the oil industry was denationalized again, and properties returned to the private, foreign magnates that had invested in the first years of oil development. When the Soviet state reoccupied Azerbaijan and ended its autonomy in 1920, it also restored the nationalization of the oil industry and dismantled all joint ventures with foreign companies. With the intent of boosting production and growth, the Soviet government put Baku at the centre of its energy strategy, pushing oil production to record levels and building export corridors towards mainland Russia. The centrality of Azerbaijan's oil in the Soviet energy strategy lasted for only a few decades, until oilfields were found in western Siberia, and investments were redirected away from the province and towards the newly found sites on Russian territory. Having lost its priority status, Azerbaijan's oil industry suffered from serious lack of investment; between the 1960s and the 1990s production rates dropped dramatically and Azerbaijan's contribution to Soviet oil production went from over 70 per cent in 1940 to just 2.4 per cent in 1980. The industry timidly started to reopen to foreign investors in the years of perestroika; in early 1991, offshore exploration in the Azeri-Chirag-Gunashli fields was assigned to a foreign consortium. Yet, those years were marked by political, social and economic instability and turmoil, which affected the development of the energy industry. The war in Nagorno-Karabakh in 1988 shook the country and mobilized Azerbaijanis against the Soviet leadership, who were blamed for being complicit in the conflict with the Armenians. The year 1991 was marked by a determined intent to gain autonomy from the USSR. Organized in the newly founded Azerbaijan Popular Front (APF) and capitalizing on the looming collapse of the Union, Azerbaijanis declared their independence in December, a few weeks before the formal dissolution of the Soviet bloc. Independence led to years of political and economic instability: the first administrations were marked by continuous overthrows and power changes; the high costs of the war and inflation were eroding the economy of the newly born republic. Azerbaijan, like the other newly independent republics, was enormously affected by the end of the USSR, when political instability worsened the country's dire economic circumstances. The disintegration of the Soviet Union brought major macroeconomic uncertainty and accounted for the stark decline of the region's economy due to the collapse of the integrated market, the breakdown of the supply chains, and the fall in trade volumes and production outputs. In the first half of the 1990s, Azerbaijan experienced a severe devaluation of the Manat, soaring inflation and a fall in its GDP of over 60 per cent. The first democratically elected president, Abulfez Elchibey, an admired leader of the APF, sought to reinvigorate the national oil industry through foreign investments as a way to exit the country's economic recession. However, his presidency was fairly short-lived – from June 1992 to September 1993 – and after only a little more than a year he was forced to resign, blamed for Armenians' military gains in Karabakh.

When Heydar Aliyev took power in 1993, he had learnt the lessons of his predecessors and understood that to achieve success he had to bring substantial change to the country's economy and the situation in the Karabakh region. Aliyev's efforts to overcome political and economic instability revolved around the negotiations of the ceasefire in Karabakh and the liberalization of the oil industry; both moves allowed him to centralize power in his hands and attach it, symbolically and institutionally, to his authority. To Aliyev, access to the international market offered a lifeline: in his words, hands over oil and natural gas would protect the regime. Aliyev signed a first agreement on production and exploration with a consortium of 11 oil corporations to develop the offshore Azeri-Chirag-Gunashli fields through a newly established Production Sharing Agreement format.

Celebrated as the Contract of the Century, the deal responded to a clear political strategy to reinforce Aliyev's regime: the coalition with foreign companies gave the President the possibility to create enormous financial resources. As he became the prime and only interlocutor with foreign investors, he could bypass political opposition, gain political legitimacy and finally reinforce his leadership. To do so, Aliyev strove to create a favourable, flexible and liberalized market for foreign investments. He established the Azerbaijan International Operating Company (AIOC) to establish a partnership between the recently established national oil company, SOCAR, and foreign energy giants, like BP, Exxon, Unocal, Amoco, Russian Lukoil and Turkish Petroleum Company. The AIOC would facilitate the access of foreign investors to the country's oil market.

Sahin (2018) explains that in the 1990s Azerbaijan introduced a set of laws, such as the Law on Protection of Foreign Investments, the Law on Investment Activity, the Law on Privatization of State Property and the Law on International Arbitration, to provide foreign investors with currency convertibility, a stable legal framework, the right to repatriate funds, and free access to international arbitration. The openness to foreign investment transformed Azerbaijan's energy industry from a state-run sector into a peculiar form of liberalized industry, which, even if under state control, was almost completely dependent on foreign investments (see Chapter 6).

This marks a significant difference in the way Azerbaijan developed its oil industry compared to its oil-rich neighbours, like Uzbekistan, Turkmenistan or Russia, which vowed to nationalize national resources, controlling the oil and gas industry, and curtailing the presence of foreign oil companies. Against foreign, especially western, expectations, liberalization did not decentralize power in the country. Conversely, the contractual regime introduced in Azerbaijan in Aliyev's years to attract and regulate foreign investments, especially the introduction of Production Sharing Agreements (PSAs), reflected Azerbaijan's political system of centralized power: Bayulgen (2010) notes that on the one side, decision making was restricted to the President's office and its close collaborators, representing a convenient 'one-stop shopping' platform; on the other, as PSAs are ratified by the Parliament, they acquire the status of law and 'prevail over any other existing or future law or decrees whose provisions differ from or are in conflict with the contract' (p 95). This system, based on the interpenetration of politics and business, makes it impossible to distinguish private interests from public affairs. In Azerbaijan, as the political elite corresponds to the business elite, the management of energy is inherently political. The oil contract regime created a favourable investment environment, which brought enormous cash inflows in a relatively short amount of time. Revenues spread an almost religious faith in the energy sector as the country's primary magnet for growth. Azerbaijan's economic boom helped transform Baku into a rich, cosmopolitan business hub. As an homage to and an icon of Azerbaijan's energy wealth, a major architectural complex, the Three Flame Towers, was built in Baku in 2013 in an effort to revamp the capital. The Flames, three skyscrapers that overlook the medieval Old City, have transformed the skyline and modernized Baku while restating the importance of oil and gas in the country's national imagery. Yet, the unimaginable wealth brought by the national energy industry has remained inaccessible to most Azerbaijanis. The capital's luxury and opulence conceal the reality that lies behind the 'Belt of Happiness', a concrete wall that runs across the capital to seclude its poorest neighbourhoods. The paradoxes brought by energy wealth do not emerge in the national security discourse, which focuses exclusively on a rhetoric of economic and political success. As this chapter further explains, energy securitization has important political implications: the merger of energy with security helps centralize political power in the hands of the local elite, multiply the overlaps between business and politics, and deepen the socio-economic divide within the local population. The analysis of the national security discourse illustrates that the peculiarity of security – particularly its ability to become a thick signifier that brings an issue to the forefront of politics – transforms energy into a definitive component of elitist state power. The specific cognitive logic that underlies energy security in Azerbaijan points to securitizing processes that not only produce knowledge of what energy (in)security is, but also determine who holds power. Energy securitization reinforces the existing power poles that rule in Azerbaijan, namely the ruling family, the military warlords and the business elites. In Azerbaijan, the oil and gas sector and the state's leadership are not independent worlds but overlap consistently, to the extent that the process of nation building, and the development of the national energy industry are intertwined. By hinging on pressing and highly emotional symbols of national identity, energy securitization endorses how politics is conducted in Azerbaijan, legitimizing the leadership and normalizing the centralization of political and economic power around well-established centres.

In the three national security strategy documents, the national security discourse is highly securitized. Its rhetoric, centred on the extraordinary and critical character of energy and security, seems a classic textbook example of securitization: through discourse, energy is constructed as a special security concern and tied to the survival and success of the country. The national discourse depicts security as a mix of coercion and control, requiring widespread deployment of military and law enforcement.

The national discourse insist on the importance and vulnerability of energy criticality. The emphasis on energy criticality can be seen in the recurrent use of adjectives such as 'crucial', 'integral', 'vital' or 'indispensable'. Attention to energy vulnerability emerges in the numerous calls for security actions, including 'defending', 'protecting', 'controlling', 'banning' and 'patrolling'. The National Security Concept puts it clearly: energy security is a priority of Azerbaijan's national security. However, the strategies of argumentation used in Azerbaijan's security discourse are diverse and rhetorically rich. In particular, the national discourse constructs energy security as a national security following four main lines of arguments, defined as rhetorical axes, which are used to present the findings of the discourse analysis. While these four lines of arguments have distinct narrative foci – the first one is military security, the second economic interests, the third geopolitical interests and the fourth economic protection – they share the same aggressive security rationale that characterizes processes of securitization. As this analysis shows, sometimes this logic is explicit and other times it is hidden. In the securitarian axis, the security logic is unequivocal. The securitarian line of argument connects energy security with the use of force, especially with defence and enforcement. It ties energy security to the protection of the national interest and while the referent object is finally the state, it centres around the physical security of energy infrastructure. The threats are clearly identified in conventional military concerns: the securitization rhetoric specifically evokes the war and the risks of terror, sabotage and armed attacks. As the term 'military security' is occasionally used, the securitarian axis renders the overlap between energy and the use of force obvious. Throughout the three documents, energy security interventions are explained in tactical and operational terms, with references to 'interoperability', 'compatibility', 'military-strategic assessment' or 'favourable operating conditions'. In the national security discourse, energy security belongs in the security of the state. The National Security Concept includes all possible actions against the country's energy infrastructure within the primary threats to national security. This mirrors a widespread perception among Azerbaijan's public, media and policymakers, who see the possibility of armed attacks against the country's energy infrastructure as a realistic threat, as documented by Azeri media, official government speeches, policymakers' declarations and the national think tanks. The particular salience given to terrorism is confirmed in the Maritime Security Strategy, the latest published strategy of national security, which compiles a list of threats and classifies them according to their priority, impact and probability degree: 'international terrorism and sabotage' score 'high' in all three categories. Only three among the other maritime threats obtain the same evaluation: 'illegal use of hydrocarbon resources', 'territorial claims of coastal states' and 'violations of military balance'. All the highest threats are put in relation to energy deposits and infrastructure in the Caspian Basin. However, the strategy pays most attention to terrorism, which is the most repeated threat throughout the text. Compared to the other dangers, which remain imprecise, terrorism is contextualized and explicitly tied to Armenia. Even regarding potential energy attacks, terrorism is traced back to the hostile relationship between Azerbaijan and its neighbour through specific reference to the conflict in Nagorno-Karabakh. Azerbaijan and Armenia have been claiming sovereignty over the Nagorno-Karabakh region for a century: while the region belongs formally to Azerbaijan, most of its population is ethnically Armenian. Altstadt (2017) explains that the roots of the conflict are not 'ancient' but belong in the aftermath of World War I, as population displacement changed the ethno-geography of the region and influenced Azerbaijan's and Armenia's respective claims over the territory. During Soviet times, Karabakh was considered an *oblast*, namely an autonomous region, together with the areas of Nakhjivan and Zangezur. While these two eventually became part of Azerbaijan and Armenia respectively, Karabakh and its autonomy remained disputed. In 1988 the controversy escalated into an intense and bloody six-year war, which was halted in 1994 when, under Aliyev, Azerbaijan agreed with Armenia on a ceasefire. Following the war, Azerbaijan lost a significant part of its territory, including areas that were ethnically homogeneously Azeri; it was estimated that over a million people were displaced due to the conflict. While large-scale fighting ended, tension remained high: a profound and almost irreconcilable acrimony characterized – and does even nowadays – the relationship between Azerbaijan and Armenia. Since the first war, the two states have constantly been building up their military capabilities and, as of today, Armenia and

Azerbaijan are among the top ten most militarized nations in the world. During the early 2000s, several clashes happened and, although controlled and restricted to sniper warfare, from time to time they escalated from low-intensity warfare to direct confrontation. In 2016 violence exploded in a war that lasted for only four days and led to an inconclusive ceasefire. At the time of writing (winter 2020), the tension is high. In October 2020 intense fighting flared up again, multiplying civil casualties, tearing up villages and forcing displacement of the people living in the region. While discussing the complexity of the war is not within the scope of this analysis, a brief introductory remark on the conflict is essential to understand, contextualize and problematize. In Azerbaijan's security discourse, energy security is constructed in relation to wider narratives of national identity, nationhood and security. In particular, it is important to highlight that three security strategies firmly and explicitly define Armenia's presence in the Karabakh region as an occupation and, as such, illegal. That is why terrorism tends to convey a declaration of hate towards Armenia: as Armenia's armed interventions are illegitimate, they are often labelled as acts of terror. The pairing of energy with terrorism needs to be read in connection with this widespread anti-Armenia sentiment. In 2012, the Presidential Administration Officer Tahir Suleymanov stated that the main danger to the country's energy security comes from Armenia and alleged that Armenia had repeatedly conducted suicide attacks against energy assets in Azeri provinces close to the BTC, BTE and Baku–Supsa oil pipelines. The former Head of the Department of Energy Infrastructure Protection at the former Ministry of National Security, Cavad Tinayev, affirmed that the first threat to oil and gas transport is the proximity of Armenian armed forces to the pipeline, and the penetration of terrorist and extremist organization in these areas, both onshore and offshore. The juxtaposition between energy security and Armenian terror is a persistent theme and, as I explain later, a persuasive rhetoric; however, it is not free of ambiguity: most deposits and facilities lie far from the border with Yerevan and there is very little evidence of attacks carried out by Armenians against Azerbaijan's energy facilities. To question this narrative further, I refer to the Maritime Security Strategy, which shows an even higher degree of ambivalence: the document opens with a long statement on the prominence of energy in Azerbaijan's national security and maritime security, suggesting that offshore deposits are the most critical asset of the Caspian Basin and anticipating that the whole strategy develops around the need to secure energy. This is a common idea among energy stakeholders, who usually consider the country's offshore projects to be more strategically important than the onshore ones. The second article of the Maritime Strategy further develops this idea by merging, in an unclear way, energy (maritime) security with the war in the Karabakh region:

> 1.2. The main threat to the security of our country in the XXI century is the existence of the conflict in and around the Nagorno-Karabakh region of the Republic of Azerbaijan. 20% of Azerbaijan's territory is under occupation, and most of the national defence resources are spent on resolving the conflict. At the same time, Azerbaijan's economic and energy security is mainly related to ensuring maritime security and, in particular, the protection of offshore energy infrastructure. In this regard, maritime security is important for Azerbaijan.

Although the war against Armenia is a fundamental piece of Azerbaijan's security, this provision sounds bizarre: it lacks coherence and focus, especially considering that the article belongs in a *maritime* strategy and Nagorno-Karabakh is, as its name says, a mountainous land with no access to the sea. Yet, the juxtaposition of energy security and the question of Armenia enhances the securitizing power of the securitarian line of argument because it intertwines energy security with the sensitive question of sovereignty and territorial integrity, which are fundamental pieces of national security. The insistent emphasis on the war with Armenia seems to target clear political purposes. Karabakh is not the only territorial controversy faced by Azerbaijan; the country is also involved in a dispute over the division of the Caspian Basin with the other littoral states of Turkmenistan and Iran. The question is not a secondary one, especially for energy security: the partition of the Caspian Sea directly affects the allocation of the subsoil energy resources among the littoral states. In particular, Turkmenistan and Iran claim ownership over some important oilfields currently under Azeri control, the Kyapaz/Serdar field and the Araz-Alov-Sharg exploration block, respectively. Yet, unlike the conflict in Karabakh, the dispute over the division of the Caspian Sea is rarely mentioned. References to the dispute tend to avoid representing disagreement as a conventional security threat and try to emphasize the legal dimension of the issue against potential military ramifications. There is only one mention of a more traditional view of security: the Maritime Security Strategy calls for an 'effective security system' of the Caspian reservoirs, but emphasizes shared business interests and the need for cooperation to grant economic success. This belongs to the second line of arguments established by the national security discourse: the economic axis. The main referent object remains the state and its national interests, but the economic axis shifts from the previous focus on energy infrastructure to an emphasis on energy trade. This economic rhetoric values the enormous amount of capital that the oil and gas industry has generated in the country since the late 1990s. It constructs the criticality of energy security by pointing out its contribution to the nation's prosperity, growth and welfare. This rhetoric builds on hard data: oil and gas are, as a matter of fact, Azerbaijan's economic backbone and a magnet for foreign investment. The two industries make the largest contribution to Azerbaijan's export-oriented economy: in 2017 they accounted for 87.4 per cent of all the country's exports (Statistical Committee of the Republic of Azerbaijan 2017).

In the national security discourse, Azerbaijan's integration into the western, neoliberal and globalized market is celebrated as both a successful historical moment and a central political strategy in the country's processes of state and nation building. The Contract of the Century and the consequent opening up of the energy sector allowed for and boosted the transition into a market economy and the integration into the global neoliberal system, deemed as decisive transformations of Azerbaijan into a modern state. In Azerbaijan's imaginary, the country's integration in the global market economy was crucial to ensure the newly born republic membership in the international community, especially to develop close ties with the EU and NATO. National data show that between the mid 1990s, when the industry started opening to foreign investments, and 2010, Azerbaijan received around USD 60 billion. By 2004 foreign investment accounted for 97.6 per cent of total investments in the oil sector. Between 2001 and 2017, the State Oil Fund of Azerbaijan (SOFAZ) received over USD 126.68 billion of investment to finance the development of the Azeri-Chirag-Gunashli oilfield, which is the largest in the country. According to figures from 2013, 32.7 million tons of oil were produced in the Azeri-Chirag-Gunashli field, of which 22.3 million tonnes were destined for export. That means that in 2013 Azerbaijan's profits amounted to 68.8 per cent of produced oil. Moreover, it was estimated that the construction of the BTC pipeline totalled USD 150 million investment. As previously mentioned, the national discourse attributes to the oil industry Azerbaijan's economic recovery after the recession that followed the dissolution of the USSR. Oil wealth fed an unprecedented economic boom, which reached a long peak between 2003 and 2009, when the average annual growth was of 27 per cent a year (World Bank 2019). By 2000, oil accounted for more than 40 per cent of government revenues (Wakeman-Linn et al 2003). The country's growth can be ascribed to a sustained situation of strong oil and gas production gains, high international oil prices and sharply higher public spending. In 2006 Azerbaijan was the country with the highest GDP growth – up to 34.5 per cent – worldwide. Trade turnover reached USD 31 billion in 2014, which was 24 times higher than in 1995 (Gurbanov et al 2017, p 19). By 2000, oil already accounted for more than 40 per cent of government revenues (Wakeman-Linn et al 2003). Between 2005 and 2008 oil revenues increased more than predictions, due to the spike in oil prices on world markets. The rise in prices expanded the country's currency reserves up to USD 18 billion by the end of 2008 – twice its foreign debt. In that year, the oil sector accounted for 42 per cent of the value-added (as a percentage of the GDP); in the following year, it was estimated (Ciarreta and Nasirov

2012) that it represented 90.7 per cent of total gross exports and 83.9 per cent of total foreign investment. Due to the 2014–2016 global oil price crisis, the country's production experienced a decline of 1.7 per cent in 2016 alone. As oil went from USD 110 a barrel to an unprecedented low of USD 50 in 2017, Azerbaijan was forced to devalue its currency by 30 per cent in February 2015 and by a further 50 per cent in December 2015. In 2016 Azerbaijan's GDP fell by 4.5 per cent year on year, and non-oil GDP fell by 6.8 per cent year on year, causing the first economic recession in 20 years. In the same years the trade surplus disappeared and the booming trend in the construction industry, which was fuelled by high oil prices, stopped after a 35.5 per cent annual decrease.

The economic and industrial decline proves that Azerbaijan is not only oil rich, but also oil dependent. While economic overdependence on oil is mentioned in the National Security Concept, there is no reference to potential mitigation strategies; this is also confirmed by a lack of related policies (see Chapter 7). Up to 2017 many non-oil industries, as well as non-oil GDP more broadly, depended upon the oil revenues. The discovery of the large gas reserves in the Absheron-Pribalkhan field and the South Caspian Deepwater Basin in the mid 2000s revamped the national gas industry. While still at an early stage of exploration, the Deepwater Basin is estimated to contain around 75 per cent of Azerbaijan's commercial gas reserves. In the basin lies the giant field of Shah Deniz, which is the largest gas field in Azerbaijan and the ninth largest in the world, with reserves of around 1.2 trillion cubic metres (Ciarreta and Nasirov 2012, p 286). While exploration is still ongoing, a trade agreement is already in place, binding Azerbaijan to deliver significant volumes of gas (10.9 bcm/a) to European customers for the next 25 years for a total contractual value of USD 100 billion (Statistical Committee of the Republic of Azerbaijan 2017). Recent estimates calculate that further developments in the Shah Deniz Field, as well as the minor fields of Absheron, Nakhchivan, Shafag, Asiman and Zafar-Mashal, Umid and Babek, could increase the country's gas exports by up to 30 billion cubic metres.

The importance of the oil and gas revenues emerges clearly in the energy security discourse; as endorsed by the Maritime Security Strategy in its opening article, 'rich oil and gas fields will continue to ensure the interests of Azerbaijan'. In fact, untapped onshore and offshore reserves keep feeding international interests: it is calculated that Azerbaijan's proven oil reserves amount to around 7 billion barrels, almost 0.4 per cent of the world's oil supply, while gas proven reserves, reaching 35 TcF, represent 1 per cent of the world's gas supply. The economic axis favours the emphasis on energy criticality to the analysis of energy vulnerabilities and threats and welcomes the importance of foreign investments in the energy sector for the nation, as they 'play a vital role in the long-term sustainable and balanced development of the Republic of Azerbaijan'. What is interesting is that the attention on the economy is still translated into conventional security practices, which put an emphasis mostly on the physical security of energy objects. The forms of economic insecurity to which the texts make most reference refer to the economic reverberations caused by potential disruptions to energy production and transport, alluding mostly to the damage to the physical assets and the disruption that creates to international trade.

Often intertwined with the economic and securitarian rhetorical axes is the geopolitical line of argument. The state remains the referent object, but this time it is the idea of the nation and its position within the international system that needs to be protected. In this sense, energy emerges as a potential source of security. The national security discourse, expressed in the three documents, ties energy security to regional interstate dynamics and builds its argument on a deterministic understanding of geography, seen both as a blessing and a curse for the country. Geography emerges as a key defining element, which determines the degree of (in)security of the country and condemns it to the risks of potential interstate conflicts. In a mix of realist and liberal arguments, Azerbaijan's geographical position is described as an asset to gain strategic advantage, by acting as a 'bridge between the West and the East', as well as a vulnerability, as the Caucasus is seen as a potential powder keg, a dangerous and politically unpredictable region of bellicose and revanchist states. Its geographical position is an important imaginary of Azerbaijan's national identity, reflective of the country's history.

A hub of hubs, Azerbaijan has always been a vibrant agora at the centre of prosperous commerce. In medieval times, Azerbaijan was a transit point along the Great Silk Road for goods passing from China and India through the Black Sea to Constantinople. Azeri carpets, raw silk, dried fruits, precious stones, jewellery, sturgeon and caviar were traded across the west and the east. Today, the country is at a nodal point of the commercial corridors that traverse the Eurasian landmass, including in the energy trade: the BTC already transports Kazakhstan's oil to the European market; the Baku–Novorossiysk pipeline and the Baku–Supsa pipeline connect the Caspian Basin to the Black Sea; the proposed Trans-Caspian Pipeline will transport Turkmenistan gas to Europe via Azerbaijan. The geopolitical line of argument accentuates the criticality and the vulnerability of energy. While it reiterates that the importance of energy lies in its economic value, it does so by recognizing the highly political nature of the economic order and affirming the foreign policy dimension of energy trade. All documents propose a west-oriented narrative that cherishes cooperation with the Euro-Atlantic area and stresses the contribution of Azerbaijan to European and global energy security. The National Security Concept sees energy projects as a means to promote security by facilitating the integration of Azerbaijan into European and Euro-Atlantic security structures. This alludes mostly to

NATO's and Azerbaijan's ambition to provide more decisive support from the Alliance, including with respect to the war in Karabakh.

In the national discourse, energy can facilitate the integration of the country into transnational forms of security governance, offering common ground to develop multilateral dialogue. This dialogue, as the discourse confirms, embodies (neo)liberal principles, typical of western politics: it positions energy security under the rubric of multilateralism, free trade and global cooperation. In particular, Azerbaijan's discourse emphasizes energy and economic interdependence with Europe. In the three texts, attention to European energy security – intended in terms of access, availability and affordability of oil and gas supplies – remains a predominant and pressing concern, even when compared to the meagre references to the national energy needs. The National Security Concept remarks that Azerbaijan took several steps to contribute to European efforts to diversify their supplies. While this seems to suggest that European energy security offers an economic advantage to Azerbaijan, in line with the national interest, poor data on the country's access to, availability and affordability of energy contradicts this idea. The pursuit of European energy security negatively affects domestic trends: in the past decades, Azerbaijan has not been able to cover its internal energy demand given that most energy production is due for export. To face internal demand, the country has been forced to import electricity and gas from Russia, Iran and Turkmenistan; as a result, domestic prices and tariffs have skyrocketed (see Chapter 7). Poor energy trends in the country are neglected in the national security discourse; in other words, they do not constitute a form of insecurity. Instead, the focus of security remains on the idea that investing in and developing transnational energy projects serves the national interest more than fixing the national energy deficit. At the end of the 1990s, a French journalist, Anna Nivat, interviewed then Minister of Foreign Affairs Hasan Hasanov. In an article titled 'Oil Is Our Destiny', Hasanov affirmed that oil determined not only the country's foreign policy but also other states' attitudes towards Azerbaijan. This is endorsed by a more recent study (Tokluoglu 2012) on Azerbaijanis' public opinion; the article argues that there was a widespread expectation among the population that oil would not only bring international wealth, but would also develop international relations, and as a direct consequence, political stability, and democracy.

The geopolitical axis of the national discourse does not contemplate any alternative to international dialogue but conflict: the Military Doctrine warns that 'interstate tensions are growing because of competition for access to natural resources, primarily energy resources'. This echoes the fourth line of argument used in the national security discourse, that is the environmental axis. This rhetoric pays significant attention to resource management and environmental degradation as security problems; it identifies the main threats in resources depletion and pollution. Compared to the other lines of argument, the environmental axis has a secondary importance: references to energy security as part of a broader interest in the environment are marginal in the National Security Concept and the Maritime Security Strategy and are completely absent from the Military Doctrine. It is, however, important to notice it and include it in the analysis because despite its novel referent object, it allows understanding the diversity and broadness of securitization of energy. Rather than moving towards environmental care, security remains heavily focused on conflict, terrorism and traditional security thinking. The exceptionality of the threats lies in the unusual association between the environment and the risk of terror: the focus on the environmental impact caused by potential armed attacks against oil and gas pipelines and terminals. Like the other three lines of arguments, the environmental axis presents several ambiguities. A strong accusation has been made against Armenia and the Soviet Union, which are considered responsible for environmental degradation:

> The environmental problems in the Republic of Azerbaijan are a result of the decades-long old-fashioned oil production methods mainly in the Absheron Peninsula and in the Caspian Sea in order to meet the Soviet Union's energy needs in disregard of environmental consequences. Furthermore, mass destruction of the flora and fauna in the territories of Azerbaijan occupied by Armenia, including the wide-scale fires on these lands, has become one of the acute environmental challenges for the country. (Azerbaijan National Assembly 2010)

Resource depletion in Nagorno-Karabakh is a recurring argument that traces back to what Altstadt (2017, p 37) defines as 'an emotional and psychological turning point for Azerbaijan' in the conflict: in late 1988 Armenians proposed to deforest the Tokhana natural reserve to build a factory; while Gorbachev welcomed the project, most Azerbaijanis were angry, disappointed and scared of the impact that the project would have on the forest, which was considered a national treasure of great sentimental value. The Tokhana issue is considered to have further motivated Azerbaijani to take up arms. Yet, restricting attention to resource management by the Soviet Union and Armenia removes responsibility from the Azeri government and their mild policy actions in environmental protection, some of which have not changed since Soviet times. While pollution and environmental degradation are acknowledged as threats, mitigation and adaptation measures are not prioritized; clean energy sources are absent from energy security discourse and practices, as Chapter 7 shows and argues.

Energy security and Azerbaijan's sense of self: building the nation through securitization

The national discourse is full of symbolism that can only be understood if situated in relation to the process of national identity building started with Heydar Aliyev's leadership. The 'nation' and the 'national' occupy a key role in the construction of energy security of Azerbaijan's national security discourse. Energy securitization involves a symbolic and emotional process, which traces back to the pressing question of national identity and consciousness in Azerbaijan's post-Soviet era. With the collapse of the Soviet Union, Azerbaijan had to tackle not only the question of state building, but also the process of nation building and the creation of a sense of belonging to the new republic. Nation building has not been a straightforward process in the ethnically and culturally diverse state of Azerbaijan. Over the centuries, the country has been shaken by different waves of identity building: the processes of Turkification, Islamification, Russification and Sovietization have multiplied Azerbaijan's historical and cultural roots and diversified its ethnic and social fabric. The Persian and the Ottoman empires left a religious legacy, gradually imposing Islam over ancient Zoroastrian practices. The arrival of the Russians in the 19th century and the process of Sovietization of the 20th century brought a gradual centralization of power through political and economic unification and increased ethnic diversity due to government-sponsored immigration. Migration flows have been a defining factor in the demographic composition of contemporary Azerbaijan. Armenians and Russians have gradually left the country to return to their motherlands and the large influx of Azerbaijani refugees from Armenia and of Azerbaijani internally displaced persons from the Karabakh and adjacent territories have given a more homogeneous character to the country. The primary ethnic group, the Azerbaijani Turks, represents 91.6 per cent of the country's population and holds a strong presence also in neighbouring Iran and Turkey.

Accepting that national identity is a construction, I argue that there is a mutual performative relation between energy security and national identity. In the brand 'Land of Fire', oil and gas are not only Azerbaijan's material spine and economic backbone, but also a quintessential part of the country's national identity. As such, Azerbaijan's energy security discourse acquires signification only when embedded in the country's process of nation building and historical trajectory. In particular, the national security discourse hinges upon specific representations of those historical events and personalities that hold the highest emotional charge and symbolic power in the nation. As previously outlined, the national security discourse indicates that Nagorno-Karabakh and the Contract of the Century have a special role in merging energy with security. They do so by accentuating, simultaneously, both the vulnerability and the criticality of energy and security. Constant references to Nagorno-Karabakh and the Contract of the Century serve to alternate the perception of fear with a validation of the efforts to securitize energy. This see-saw between security and insecurity, solace and danger, parallels the dual spirits of Azerbaijan, a nation divided between and built on the contrasting sentiments of pride and victimhood. These sentiments shape the national security discourse too. Azerbaijan's energy industry is a key piece in building the idea of national success. In particular, the Contract of the Century, which is cited multiple times in the National Security Concept, the Military Doctrine and the Maritime Security Strategy, is seen as an exceptionally glorious moment of Azerbaijan's history: the agreement brought economic growth, facilitated technological and infrastructure development, and improved international reputation. As Guliyev explains (2014, p 2), the Contract of the Century has 'instilled a sense of national pride'. The economic success that has raised so much national pride is tied to Azerbaijan's decision to join the liberal order, as a specific western-oriented project. After his first visits to Europe in the late 1990s, various media outlets questioned then President Heydar Aliyev about his radical liberal economic reforms and large privatizations. More specifically, journalists asked Aliyev whether he was giving priority to the west and its interests; surprisingly, the President responded with a firm 'yes'. This propensity to please their foreign, western interlocutors, from investors to policymakers and even journalists, can be understood as an integral component of Azerbaijan's processes of nation and state building, including the formation and definition of its polity in relation to the 'international', especially the western world. While domestically the leadership rejected the western models of democratic governance, internationally it strove to be recognized and accepted into western institutions, especially by conforming to their economic rules.

Energy has been a key piece of this process. Overall, it has brought economic, international, political and diplomatic achievements and it has facilitated a process of modernization. Of course, modernity is understood in western neoliberal terms. In the national security discourse, the pathway to economic, social and technological progress passes through Azerbaijan's participation in western (neo)liberal institutions and free markets. Stressing its view to modernity in neoliberal terms, the national security discourse constructs a positive imaginary of the country's future through its assimilation into western structures. This incorporation is ideational but also material: political and economic alignment has passed through institutional ties, shared infrastructure and a common energy market. The centrality of the liberal order is repeated throughout the National Security Concept, where energy projects are repeatedly associated with practices of 'cooperation' with and 'integration' into the western system. This is not a purely diplomatic issue of alliances and agreements but a deeper transformation in the way Azerbaijan sees itself and the world. The Contract had an impact on the country's process of nation building. Beyond its business dimension, the tie with the west emerges in the national security discourse as a strong political and moral affinity, based on 'European and Western values', which are defined as 'an inalienable component of the Euro-Atlantic security architecture'. The Contract has contributed to transforming Azerbaijan's sense of self, primarily by marking a farewell to its Soviet past and its cultural, historical and economic models. Azerbaijan's aspirations to use energy security to be part of the west should be understood as a larger attempt to define its own self; yet this emerges as a construction based on its relationship with the other. Scholars explains that postcolonial nations, including the specific cases of former Soviet countries (Moore 2001; Ringmar 2002; Ismayilov and Tkacik 2009; Ismayilov 2015), tend to aim for recognition through practices of imitation and conformity, which become constitutive of their sense of self in the process of nation building. According to Ismayliov (2015, p 215), post-Soviet nations have built their *new* identities based on 'the notion of international legitimacy as widely understood at the time'; this means that following the disappearance of the USSR, the criteria for political authority that internationally determined 'legitimacy' were set by the west and its institutions. Moore (2001, p 118) also argues that in the post-Soviet region, 'postcolonial desire from Riga to Almaty fixates not on the fallen master Russia but on the glittering Euramerican MTV-and-Coca-Cola beast that broke it'. The emphasis on the west has two major implications for the securitized construction of energy security. First, by consolidating a representation of itself as a modern and western-oriented state, Azerbaijan steers its energy system towards a neoliberal, export-driven model. This has undesirable consequences in terms of domestic consumption, especially hindering energy availability and affordability, producing electricity and gas shortages, and facilitating price spikes (see Chapter 7). Second, through its western rhetoric, the national security discourse enhances energy securitization, primarily by intertwining energy with questions of sovereignty and independence. The Military Doctrine maintains that foreign investments have been an integral part of the process of reforms and reconstruction after Azerbaijan's independence. In his memoires, Hafiz Pashayev (2006), Deputy Minister of Foreign Affairs and former Ambassador to the US between 1992 and 2006, writes that the Contract did not bring only western money, but also 'an insurance policy for our new-found independence'. Azerbaijan hoped – and still does – that western interests in Azerbaijan's oil and gas would grant the country a form of protection in case of any aggressive move from Russia and Iran. Azerbaijan's increasing fear of potential revanchism from its neighbours, especially Russia, emerges in the Military Doctrine: the document took three years to be published as the text was amended in the light of the Russia–Georgia war in 2008. The Military Doctrine is in fact heavily focused on the questions of national integrity and independence, and harshly denounces any form of external aggression by a third state. Among scholars, there is widespread agreement on Azerbaijan's cautious regional relationships: Flegel (2015) makes reference to 'a persisting fear of Russian influence that is deeply seeded in national history', while Ismayilov (2015) notes that Azerbaijan sees with concern the historical and ethnic ties with Iran, where a third of the population is Azerbaijani. At the first stage of negotiations with the west, Azerbaijan was also hoping for some sort of protection or support in Karabakh from either NATO or the US and other European states. In 1994, during his first official visit to the UK, then President Heydar Aliyev explicitly tried to link oil development with the war and declared that great powers' oil companies had to show an interest in the political situation of the republic. In her memoires, Elmira Akhundova (2003, p 32) recalls that when in London Heydar Aliyev met Margaret Thatcher, then UK Prime Minister, and explicitly demanded more active assistance from the UK government to help settle the Armenian–Azerbaijani conflict. According to Akhundova, Heydar Aliyev would make foreign investments in Azerbaijan the principal topic of discussion during his diplomatic meetings, transforming energy trade into his principal foreign policy strategy. More generally, Aliyev hoped that by opening the energy market and signing a deal with large western companies he would find some political support among the governments of the signatories. Today, these hopes have been largely lost, but in the popular imaginary the idea remains that Aliyev saved the country from economic despair by concluding the 1994 agreement. The deal became the contract that marked the century and the country's prosperity. The image of Aliyev's grandiosity shines in the national security discourse: the development of the national energy industry, the Contract of the Century, the construction of the BTC pipeline and the openness to the west are described as Aliyev's personal successes. The Maritime Security Strategy clearly states that 'the successes of our country are the result of the oil strategy founded by national leader Heydar Aliyev and successfully continued by the President of Azerbaijan Ilham Aliyev'. Likewise, the National Security Concept explains that under Aliyev's leadership, Azerbaijan gained an indispensable role in the realization of regional energy and transportation projects, which helped the country 'overcome all difficulties' and become 'an economically and politically dynamic modern State'. The three documents rename the BTC pipeline after the former President and always call it 'the Heydar Aliyev Baku-Tbilisi-Ceyhan pipeline', never the BTC. In all the texts, when discussing the country's energy policies established between 1993 and 2003, the emphasis on the 'national' is abandoned in favour of a personalized designation of the policies as 'Heydar Aliyev's oil strategy'. Heydar Aliyev's leadership is portrayed as the condition behind the development of the energy industry: under his regime, Azerbaijan lived an age of splendour. Aliyev himself is depicted as a successful businessperson with an exceptional acuity of mind. The description of the President as a wealthy entrepreneur has also been inherited by his successor, his son Ilham Aliyev, who nationally is principally seen by both his allies and opponents as a tycoon rather than a political mastermind. It is interesting to note that this emphasis on business success and business skills alters the relationship between security and energy. When the national security discourse frames the leaders' economic success in terms of business, it shifts the attention from the national dimension of the economy to the more private dimension of business affairs. Business, unlike the idea of the economy, especially as a national activity, is usually discussed behind closed doors and is not necessarily subjected to public scrutiny. 'Business' as a concept differs from the notion of energy as a public good. The use of the term 'business' reorients policy priorities towards individual profits, instead of collective gains. This acquires specific importance in the context of Azerbaijan, where politics, private business and personal profits often overlap (see Chapter 4).

The national security discourse uses Aliyev to bridge a view of the future and a related idea of modernity with a nostalgic rhetoric of the past, anchored to an ancient splendour. The past, however, is never grounded in the country's pre-modern historical roots but in the relatively recent and circumscribed time period of the post-independence era. This focus implies that the sense of belonging to the nation depends on the process of state building that inevitably began only with the second declaration of independence in 1991. In the national security discourse, Heydar Aliyev is a powerful and fundamental piece of Azerbaijan's processes of nation- and state building. He has become an idealized, heroic and worshipped figure, whose successes include political stability, economic growth and, more importantly, the creation of a sense of unity. Heydar Aliyev's photos, statues and portraits can be found in most Azeri towns. Like the BTC pipeline, also Baku's airport and numerous buildings, avenues and parks are named after him. It is common to see his face on billboards across the country. An official quote from current President Ilham Heydar says that the state's security machine protected the great leader in the most difficult days for Azerbaijan and by doing so, they protected the independence of Azerbaijan. Scholars note that the cult of Heydar Aliyev hinges on three main issues: Aliyev's ethnicity, which makes him the only true representation and protector of the *original* national identity (Babajew 2009; Bolukbasi 2011); his role in the first years of newly independent Azerbaijan, which gives him the name of 'Father of the Nation' (Hug 2012); and his political achievements, especially in the oil industry and Karabakh. The war and Ilham Aliyev's business interests in the energy sector have been used to legitimize his son Ilham Aliyev as the *natural* political successor, the only one who could restore the country's territorial integrity and ensure economic prosperity, political stability and a good relationship with the west.

At the centre of energy securitization lies a specific historical construction of the political, which, while focusing on the construction of the 'national', locates the sense of the collective self in relation to the leader. According to some scholars, Heydar Aliyev has filled a vacuum in the national memory, whose cultural foundations were weak and divisive and were reminiscent of the political fragmentation of the process of state building. Marina Ottaway (2013, p 53) writes that the history of the first Azerbaijani republic is for many 'a source of division, since the short-lived republic was torn asunder by strife between nationalists and socialists'. Aliyev emerges as a symbol of unity among social division, the glue that holds an ethnically and politically divided nation together.

This hyper-personalization of Azerbaijan's politics has significant repercussions also for how security is conceived: if the president *is* the state, then *his* security is the state's security. The cult of personality around Heydar Aliyev is the most typical manifestation of the country's authoritarian style of government. Shannon O'lear (2007) reminds us that in Azerbaijan real political power and legitimacy are linked to a strong personality who constitutes the foundations of political power. While the unrestrained discretion of the political elite, loyalty to the president, and a mix of fear and economic benefits have favoured patrimonialism in contemporary Azerbaijan, the cult of the leader is rooted in a longer cultural tradition that goes back to Soviet times and Stalin's leadership. The propensity towards a strong leader, to the detriment of democracy – in western terms – was reinforced during the chaotic first years of the country's independence and became the main political ideology of the ruling elite. A plural political system based on large participation was perceived as synonymous with political weakness and instability. The idea of democracy was, first and foremost, embedded in the existential struggle for sovereignty and independence of those years. As Bolukbasi (2011, p 214) writes, 'democracy was perceived rather as the will of the people to get rid of Russian dominance, defeat the enemy, and restore Azerbaijani rule over the NKAO [Nagorno-Karabakh Autonomous Oblast]'.

According to International Crisis Group (2010), in Azerbaijan 'the cult of personality has become a method of control, [... which] ingrains a political culture of obedience and servility'. This cult hinges on a revision of history which sets Heydar Aliyev as a saviour who rescued Azerbaijan from the chaos of democracy. Following the collapse of the Soviet Union, Azerbaijan lived through years of disorder: before Aliyev took power, Azerbaijan experienced four overthrows of power which led to four different Presidents – Ayaz Mutalibov, Yagub Mamedov, Isa Gambar and Abulfaz Elchibey – in just three years, from 1991 to 1993. In the last months of Elchibey's government, the threat of a military coup worsened a context marked by social turmoil and widespread anger towards Elchibey's incapacity to achieve immediate economic recovery. Aliyev's rise to power and his ability to maintain control over the opposite factions built him a winning reputation. His capacity to survive a series of failed coups and eliminate his rivals during his two first years in office made him popular among the public and the country's elites. It needs to be stressed that under Aliyev, power in Azerbaijan went through a process of personalization, which was not only ideological, but also institutional and material: democratic institutions and pluralism were progressively replaced by a centralized government and personal loyalties, as Chapter 4 documents. In the first decade of independence in Azerbaijan, democracy was perceived as a volatile and failing system, which only brought economic recession and military defeats; thus, many Azerbaijanis were supportive of the establishment of a strong regime. National propaganda emphasized that, unlike his predecessors, Aliyev managed to broker a ceasefire with Armenia, sign a multibillion contract with foreign companies, and project Azerbaijan in the international sphere as a politically and economically successful country. As shown earlier, this interpretation of Azerbaijan's history during the first years of its second independence emerges clearly in the national security discourse and its construction of energy security.

Along with the sense of pride in the country's success, largely linked to Aliyev's grandiosity, the national security discourse also has a more bitter side. In the discourse, pride and hope coexist with a strong sense of victimhood, which rises from a common and internalized reading of national history, especially the war in Karabakh. While energy and the war are both highly emotional issues in the country, the latter is associated with a negative sentiment of failure and disappointment. In the nation, there is a widespread and profound sense of abandonment, attributed to the international community, blamed for betraying the political promises of support raised during the negotiations of the Contract. Compared to Armenia, which has built a more successful narrative around the defence of the principle of peoples' self-determination, Azerbaijan has largely failed to raise international empathy: by constantly displaying an image of strong military power and aggressive leadership, Azerbaijan has not conquered the hearts and minds of the international audience and, despite its political and diplomatic efforts and its propaganda, struggles to be recognized as a victim.

Azerbaijan's self-victimization has also had several repercussions on energy securitization: it has facilitated and justified a securitized view of security, validated processes of militarization and power centralization, created and sustained a shared desire for retaliation, and offered an opportunity to blame external actors, especially the west, locating accountability and responsibility outside the government. According to Blum (2018, p 33), the war has been the 'most powerful source of social cohesion and state legitimacy'. Wars are also fought through propaganda, especially the use of cliché and stereotypes to describe the enemy against one's own sense of self; according to Baghdasaryan (2013, p 105) in Azerbaijan these narratives have helped 'maintain a high state of alert and concentrate resources' in the hands of the rulers. The conflict has long been used to normalize a growing internal security machine. The sense of victimhood can be grasped in the energy security discourse and its numerous references to the possibility of terrorism: victimhood, resentfulness and the sense of injustice evoked by the war merge with the fear and anxiety connected to the unpredictability of terrorism. This process of self-victimization has influenced and legitimized a view of security in terms of military as self-defence.

Finally, the energy security discourse hinges upon widespread sentiments and images of the nation's sense of self; it appropriates Azerbaijan's cultural symbols and collective interpretations of the country's history. The ways in which the discourse presents the threats to energy security and the suggested solutions are not only meaningful but also *natural*, almost self-evident and justifiable (if not justified a priori). The naturalness of energy as a security concern normalizes and sediments a securitized understanding of energy security. Rather than being just one possible interpretation among many, energy securitization becomes the common way for thinking about energy and its security. The strong ties between energy security and the 'national' – expressed through the sense of self, the sentiments of pride and victimhood, or the historical account of nation building – point to the performative effect of energy securitization and its ability to determine, frame and assert national identity. Energy securitization in Azerbaijan is not only about identifying and addressing security threats, but also about creating a sense of 'the political', which, in this case, is informed by and concurs with the country's construction of nationhood. The analysis shows the relationality and mutual performativity of the process. Energy securitization fabricates national identity by endorsing a distinctive and shared understanding of national history and identity that unites Azerbaijan's society against a clearly identified *other*, namely Armenia. Simultaneously, the distinctive imaginary that revolves around Azerbaijan's national identity, its symbols and sentiments, gives a special place to energy in the nation's security, defining what energy needs to be secured, why and how.

Building on these findings, the next chapter reflects on energy security practice to move beyond the rhetoric of the exception and expose the ordinary aspects of energy securitization.

4

Everyday Practices of Energy Security in Azerbaijan

In Azerbaijan, the creation of a highly institutionalized structure to deal with energy security started at the beginning of the 21st century, when investments transformed the national oil industry, and the newly gained independence initiated the process of state building. Interviewees recalled that until the late 1990s it was mainly police officers who patrolled energy facilities, especially to avoid oil thefts. After the signing of the Contract of the Century, the presence of military and paramilitary professionals in the country's energy sites proliferated. In the very early days of the negotiations for the BTC pipeline, security concerns drove much of the talks between the corporations, their countries of origin and Azerbaijan's government. To western investors, the short life of the republic, the political instability of the region, and the fresh memories of the Cold War tension raised serious concerns, especially regarding energy transport and the physical protection of the pipelines. The deal not only established the criteria for oil extraction and production, but also posed the question of the physical security of the growing industry and defined the state commitment to grant security. Investors requested the local government to provide more security guarantees. Since then, the government of Azerbaijan has set up a rich legislative corpus that defines and regulates the provision of security in and around the energy sites. This legislation has expanded the role of law enforcement agencies, enabled the deployment of military forces in and around all those energy sites that are deemed *critical*, and established ad hoc security bodies that are exclusively responsible for oil and gas security.

This chapter begins by mapping the national security actors that secure energy in Azerbaijan; it outlines their organization, structure, activities and tools to identify how energy security practices are performed in Azerbaijan. By focusing on the practices, this analysis moves beyond the rhetoric of the exception and recentres its focus on the everyday as the ordinary and routine aspect of energy securitization. The first argument that this chapter puts forward is that energy securitization has created a crowded sector of professionals with military, paramilitary and enforcement expertise. While the range of security practices is multiple and diverse, it is not always possible to draw clear boundaries between different institutions, mandates and even activities. This chapter continues with the analysis of what subtends energy security practices, including the political dynamics and contextual idiosyncrasies that have favoured energy securitization. By doing so, it advances three main arguments. The first and central argument contends that energy securitization interlaces with Azerbaijan's process of state building and, over the years, has contributed to consolidating the power of the ruling family and the country's elites. Energy securitization confirms this tie: the creation of a highly institutionalized security machine to secure energy cannot be understood outside the process of state building that began with Heydar Aliyev in 1993, after the years of political turmoil that came before him.

In the previous chapter, it emerged that energy securitization belongs in the process of nation building: it centralizes the construction of energy security around the image of the leader and hinges on the national sentiments of pride and victimhood to gain legitimation. By shifting the attention from nation- to state building, this chapter points to the interaction between energy securitization and the creation, operationalization and consolidation of the country's governmental institutions. In other words, its focus moves from the imaginary of power to its concrete expression. According to this analysis, the prioritization of energy security and the corollary enlargement of the military and paramilitary machine – enacted by energy securitization – have provided the elites with abundant financial resources, larger mandates, increased responsibilities and, finally, greater political power. The findings confirm the centrality of the leader but also point to a more fragmented space, where power is constantly mediated and contested among elites. In this context, loyalty becomes a tool to (re)produce power: loyal practitioners that faithfully conduct their security practices grant fidelity to a specific way of thinking and doing energy security and exercise authority; energy security offers a pretext for reinforcing patronage and exchange favours between the ruler and the country's energy tycoons and security warlords.

Another important argument advanced by this chapter concerns the spatiality of energy securitization. The extension of energy security practices and the lack of geographical, temporal and sectorial boundaries affect its practices, in term of ontology but also with regard to their political, legal, strategic and operational nature. This research shows that the disordered regulatory framework that regulates energy security practices has created a more expansive role for law enforcement agencies, which now have competencies in defence and military affairs, and has enlarged and normalized the involvement of the operational arms of Azerbaijan's defence forces in civil matters.

This chapter introduces an important issue for this book, that is how energy securitization as a project expands security intersects and contributes to a specific economic model that favours private business and profits.

Who does energy security in Azerbaijan?

The army

In Azerbaijan, energy security practice involves the three branches of the military, namely the land forces, the navy and to a lesser extent the air force; these are all under the Ministry of Defence. The navy with both its regular troops and its special forces, deploys both its warships and its small patrol boats around energy sites. Within the special forces, the surface vessels brigade is one of the most active bodies in securing offshore sites. The special forces are organized and structured in five ad hoc and highly specialized divisions: the guard division, the landing vessels division, the mine-sweeper division, the search and rescue division, and the training vessel division. Together with special forces, the navy deploys the national waters security brigade, the marines battalion and the coastguard units to patrol the energy fields of the Caspian Sea. The special assignment and intelligence centre collects data and intelligence and provides operational support. The forces of the navy protect offshore energy infrastructure in the Caspian Basin, primarily in the two fields that sit in the disputed border waters of the Caspian Sea: the Kyapaz/Serdar field, located on the median line between Azerbaijan and Turkmenistan, and the Alov-Sharg-Araz field on the Azerbaijan-Iran border. In those areas, the prime responsibilities of the maritime naval forces are defending offshore oil and gas installations and ensuring sovereignty, territorial integrity and border security. The importance of securing energy in defining the operational remit of the naval forces emerges in the target of their training preparation. For instance, in 2020 the maritime forces participated in tactical drills centred on the protection of energy infrastructure along the Caspian Sea border, with a focus on improving responses in the event of direct military combat.

Growing responsibilities in securing the Caspian energy fields have brought larger investments in the navy, which had historically been the least developed sector of the armed forces, and it has now become the second-largest fleet in the Caspian Sea after that of Russia. Since the mid 2000s, the navy has undergone a steady build up, which has provided its forces with advanced weaponry and equipment, including Gabriel-5 missiles, Barak-8 air-defence systems (advanced anti-ship cruise missiles), a Green Pine missile-defence radar system, and Searcher and Heron drones. Azerbaijan's maritime energy security interventions have been designed in close cooperation with the US special forces, whose structure and remit were used to establish the Azeri counterpart. Over the years, US forces helped Azerbaijan form and establish its maritime energy security programme. In many aspects, this was done by replicating the model of cooperation that the US had previously established with Turkey to strengthen its navy by launching a close interagency cooperation. US forces provided and installed a wide range of control and communication technologies, including a joint command-and-control centre for the navy and the coastguard, an interoperable command, various communication networks and sensors, and a long-range, round-the-clock radar capability that provides continuous and wide-range coastal surveillance over the city of Baku.

The presidential agencies: the Special State Protection Service, the State Border Service and the State Security Service

Onshore, the lightly armoured infantry works alongside numerous law enforcement and paramilitary agencies to patrol energy sites that are deemed of critical importance. The mandates and level of engagement of the paramilitary and enforcement agencies vary. Most paramilitary agencies report to the president but in a few cases, they are subordinated to either the Ministry of Interior or the Ministry of Emergency Situations. Those agencies that respond directly to the president include the Special State Protection Service (SSPS – the former National Guard, *Milli Qvardiyası*), the State Border Service and the State Security Service. The primary responsibility of the SSPS is to provide security for the president and other high-ranking government officials. Essentially, the SSPS agents are bodyguards in charge of personal security; they also conduct intelligence and counterintelligence operations. However, in 2003 the mandate of the SSPS was expanded to include the protection of the country's energy assets, particularly oil and gas pipelines, including the pump and the measuring stations and other surface facilities. Today, the SSPS is in charge of patrolling energy sites and providing immediate armed interventions; the nature of their duties is paramilitary and excludes more traditional enforcement duties like arresting or prosecuting. The institutional and bureaucratic structure of the SSPS was enlarged with the creation of an ad hoc energy security office, which is the Export Oil and Gas Pipeline Security Department. The department has nine regional subdivisions and deploys thousands of agents across the territory. Depending on the terrain, these armed agents move on foot, by vehicles or on horseback. The number of horseback patrollers increased by more than four times in 2013, reaching a total of 38 units, and was expected to grow in the following years. Originally, the SSPS was meant to cover only the BTC pipeline area but, given that 443 kilometres of the BTC is close to the existing WREP and the South Caucasus Pipeline, the geographic scope of the service has been extended further. Today, the SSPS is responsible for all Azerbaijan's export pipelines. The SSPS operates through its local headquarters: initially, these were based in those areas closed to the BTC (Baku, Sangachal, Hajigabul, Ujar, Yevlakh, Shamkir and Agstafa), but progressively new bases were opened, covering areas that are on the trajectory of the Baku–Novorossiysk and the Baku–Supsa export pipelines. Today, the SSPS permanently operates also in the areas of Sumgayit, Siyazan, Khachmaz, Nefahi, Erkand and Garacemirli.

In spite of its extensive presence, there are, however, some limitations to the SSPS mandate, which pertain to the private ownership of the energy sites they patrol: governmental forces need to come to terms with BP to conduct their operations and get access to BP owned sites. The SSPS is very active around the Sangachal Terminal, which is a critical node in oil and gas collection and transport; nonetheless, its patrol competencies concern only the territory outside the terminal, as access to Sangachal can be permitted only by BP's Security Department and is usually requested for *extraordinary* situations. According to a confidential document (US Embassy in Baku 2008), governmental forces can request access through a direct phone line between BP's Security Department and the local detachment of the SSPS. Another document (Safiguliyev et al 2008) indicates that BP oversees the access of the SSPS agents to the protection zone, a strip of land closed to the BTC and the SCP pipelines, which cannot be accessed otherwise. When patrolling BP facilities, the SSPS has also to comply with the regulations established by the energy company, especially the Voluntary Principles regulation. These were introduced to raise attention on the way security operations were conducted and to make sure they did not violate civil liberties and human rights. Yet, despite the Voluntary Principles, patrollers often behave violently and abuse their power. These are outlined in Chapter 7, which explores the multiple forms of violence and insecurity caused by energy security practices; here it is important to note that patrolling practices are subject to very limited public scrutiny. This points to the broader lack of accountability that characterizes energy security practices: energy security mandates, which are defined by presidential decree and subjected to contractual law, exclude parliamentary oversight. Moreover, since regulations are loose, energy security practices expand through informal praxis, have created a grey legislative area and, consequently, rarely face sanctions. Expansive interpretations of the mandates are common – it is not just the case for the SSPS; most security agencies have been expanding their remits – and are generally tolerated if they do not breach other stakeholders' interests. Energy security has given to Azerbaijan's law enforcement agencies a motive to expand their paramilitary activities, equate their operations to defence, and equip their personnel with heavy weapons. Similarly, Azerbaijan's military forces have been progressively engaging with civil matters and they have become embedded in the territory, during peacetime and outside war zones.

The second presidential agency, involved in securing energy, is the State Border Service (SBS), whose main responsibility is the protection of Azerbaijan's borders. The SBS was created after the Ministry of National Security (MNS) was dissolved; its institutional formation sheds light on how power is managed in the country and how security has a fundamental role in allocating, or not, authority. The MNS was the direct successor of the Soviet State Security Committee, namely the KGB, and the country's main intelligence body. In October 2015, in the midst of clan struggles over power, the MNS was dissolved; the Minister, Eldar Mahmudov, and around 250 officials were dismissed and many other officials were arrested following accusations of corruption, abuse of power, illegal interference in business, and treason. The two agencies created on the ashes of the MNS were put under the direct control of the president to avoid the possibility of emerging, alternative power poles. The first agency, the SBS, was established to ensure the protection and inviolability of the state border. The structure of the agency is extremely broad and includes several specialized units, such as the border troops, the coastguard, the riot police, the paramilitary aviation unit and the offshore paramilitary unit. As for the SSPS, the original mandate of the SBS did not specify any responsibility with regard to energy security. While the mandate has not been revised, the agents of the SBS de facto conduct operations of critical energy infrastructure protection. The SSPS has been patrolling and guarding oil and gas pipelines, especially the BTC and BTE, along their whole trajectories and even beyond the border zones. With the support of the US government, the SSPS has instituted a marine force, namely the coastguard, which has become the main maritime patroller of Azerbaijan's offshore energy sites in the Caspian Sea. One of the main responsibilities of the coastguard is granting security in the two-mile area surrounding the oil and gas platforms. Coastguard units are permanently deployed in that radius where navigation is forbidden. Unlike the navy, the coastguard has enforcement duties and can, therefore, interdict and search any ship that approaches the area. The coastguard is supplied with advanced technology devices and military equipment, including missiles, radar, torpedoes and military vehicles, such as point-class cutters and other high-speed patrol boats, Tufan ships and a 62-metre-long frontier guard ship furnished with boats and a helicopter.

The third agency under presidential authority is the State Security Service (SSS). Like the SBS, it was formed following the dissolution of the MNS and has retained most of its duties. The SSS is responsible for internal order and the suppression of domestic dissent. It conducts espionage and counterespionage operations, with special attention to Armenian citizens – and the possibility of their working as spies – but also inspecting and controlling Azeri citizens. Energy sites have become a critical area of engagement for the SSS; there the service uses its sophisticated surveillance technologies to control workers and conducts covert intelligence operations as part of its preventive counterespionage strategies. In my research, evidence emerged around some tactical characteristics of how intelligence operations are conducted in energy sites: agents from the SSS are usually in charge of conducting due diligence and monitor energy workers, especially when of foreign origin and low skilled. The SSS agents work undercover, mostly in the local areas where they are originally from, as this is considered more effective for gathering sensitive information.

Law enforcement and civil defence: the Ministry of Interior and the Ministry of Emergency Situations

Azerbaijan's law enforcement agencies – the national and local police forces and the Internal Troops, all under the Ministry of Interior – have been the first bodies responsible for the energy assets since the 1990s. They were first employed in oil refineries and storage places to prevent oil theft and diversion. Today they still patrol the Baku–Guzdek and Baku–Sumgayit pipelines, Baku oil refineries and other oil storage facilities to prevent theft of oil products. The Ministry of Emergency Situations (MES) also has a presence on the energy sites, with its paramilitary troops, the civil defence police, which has central and local executive authorities. They operate *whenever* there is an emergency, but this is considered in broad terms; consequently, the nature of the engagement of its agencies tends to favour prevention, rather than risk response: the troops of the MES are permanently deployed on the ground. For instance, its civil defence police regularly patrol the oil and gas production and refining facilities, the pipelines and their terminals, the electric power stations and also the hydro-technical installations.

SOCAR Department of Security

While SOCAR does not formally belong in Azerbaijan's national security infrastructure, I have decided to include its Department of Security in the map of national security actors involved in the energy sector for several reasons. First, SOCAR is state owned and state controlled and, as such, it is fully integrated in Azerbaijan's state institutional architecture. Second, the company is equipped with security professionals, who have a quasi-military character. Since its early days, the company has enlarged its corporate structure to host a security department, which operates through paramilitary units that patrol the secondary export system of oil pipelines and some domestic pipelines, two domestic refineries, the Soviet-era offshore derricks and platforms, and SOCAR administrative buildings. Third, SOCAR works closely with the Ministry of Defence Industry, especially since energy-focused military procurement has become the centre of recent national investments in the indigenous defence industry. Since the mid 2010s the Ministry of Defence Industry, which oversees military manufacturing, and SOCAR have invested in the production of automation systems for monitoring oil and gas production, as well as warships and a shipyard to protect the facilities. The cooperation between the Ministry of Defence Industry and SOCAR – especially the involvement of the company in the manufacturing of military products – speaks to the interpenetration of business logics in national security. The company's view of energy security mirrors the securitized narrative that has emerged in the national security discourse (see Chapter 3): as Flegel notes (2015, p 284), the company's energy security strategy puts the emphasis on the physical security of energy from external threats, exalts the country's resource abundance, and overlooks the lack of energy efficiency, safety and general industry development. In particular, SOCAR is an interesting case, which points to the merger of energy business and national security and confirms the political nature of energy security in the country. The company is a textbook example of the encroachment of private interests into the public sector, the implications of which are analysed later in the chapter.

Energy securitization, state building and power consolidation

The concurrence between the formation of the new Republic of Azerbaijan and the growth of its energy industry reveals a deep connection and mutual influence between the state and the oil and gas sector. Energy securitization confirms this tie: the creation of a highly institutionalized security machine to secure energy cannot be understood outside the process of state building that began with Heydar Aliyev in 1993, after the years of political turmoil that came before him.

Looking at the consolidation of energy securitization over almost three decades allows us also to see how energy securitization intersects with the consolidation of power, (re)producing the existing political order. There are multiple theoretical approaches to state building; here I use the term to refer to the formation of governmental institutions and reflect upon its effects on power distribution among political bodies. The following analysis examines energy securitization in relation to different aspects of Azerbaijan's political context, state building and power consolidation. In particular, the early processes that securitized energy came from a series of initiatives that Heydar Aliyev undertook to enhance his authority and shape the state, namely the creation of a strong executive power, a political system that depends on his institutional and symbolic authority, and the establishment of a loyal military entourage and trustworthy bureaucracy.

In Chapter 3, the analysis explained that energy securitization in Azerbaijan hinges on the most emblematic symbols of national identity to leverage on collective emotions, unite the nation, mobilize it in favour of the security project, and legitimize energy security practices. In the process, the role and image of the leader Heydar Aliyev have emerged as one of the most fundamental drivers of energy securitization. Building on those findings, this section shows that the former leader, as well as his successor and son Ilham Aliyev, occupy a special place also in defining the actual security practices that have concurred to securitize energy in the country. In Azerbaijan, there is an intimate relationship and an evident overlap between the process of nation building and the centralization of power as a reflection of the process of state- and regime building that started after independence and was consolidated with the Aliyevs' takeover. The ruling family and the country's elites set the national identity, defining and (re)producing the elements and symbols that mark the nation.

In almost two decades, the body of legislation that allows for the deployment and use of force in and around the energy fields has grown extensively. Most laws have been established by presidential decrees, determining de facto the president's monopoly over the decision-making process regarding energy security. This should not be seen, however, as an extraordinary move that breaks with normal politics; rather, it follows Azerbaijan's ordinary policymaking: in the country, the legislative power is subjected to the executive; the Parliament has very limited initiative and acts as an accessory branch, mainly responsible for approving presidential decrees. The dominance of the executive power was established by Heydar Aliyev in the Constitution, which was a milestone in Azerbaijan's state-building process. In theory, Azerbaijan's Constitution institutes a democratic, republican system, provided with checks and balances to ensure that the executive is accountable to the judiciary system and the legislature. De facto, the power of the executive grants the president control over the whole system and the president exercises his power beyond his constitutional rights. In practice, the president's office dominates the legislative process: he can circumvent Parliament to legislate, and presidential decrees become law on the day of their publication and are not subject to rescission by Parliament (Articles 113, 149). As Jody LaPorte (2016, p 102) observes, 'Azerbaijan's Constitution lays out a semi-presidential regime with a strong presidency, a weak prime minister, and some autonomy for the legislature'. Progressive amendments to the Constitution, also under Ilham Aliyev, have reinforced the president's grip on power. Azerbaijan's regime has been defined as a regime of semi-presidentialism (LaPorte 2016), marked by a strong presidency, a weak prime minister and a limited legislature, which coexist in the larger context of authoritarianism. Other scholars have emphasized the semi-authoritarian nature of the regime, defined by a lack of power transfer, weak institutions, and a limited civil society (Ottaway 2013, pp 14–19), and its sultanistic character, based on a boundless personal rulership, the elites' loyalty based on a mixture of fear and rewards, and no commitment to any ideology or value system (Chehabi and Linz 1998). Guliyev identifies an overlap between semi-authoritarianism and sultanism in the case of Azerbaijan, expressed by 'the extreme personal presence of the ruler in all elements of governance' (Guliyev 2005). In the process of state building, decisions about how institutions are formed and shaped tend to mirror the dominant configuration of power, especially at the time of writing the Constitution (Easter 1997). The case of Azerbaijan seems to confirm this argument and the central role of Heydar Aliyev not only in drafting the text but also in allocating and defining authority. According to Kamrava (2001, p 229), the President, acting as 'the dominant power-broker', moulded the Constitution 'to ensure that those institutions on which the state relied for power were not only pliant but, indeed, supportive of his own hold on power'. Within this context, the president has enormous authority to establish the legal boundaries of energy security practices, as most mandates and agencies are established by presidential decrees. This mirrors not only his ability to influence the legislative domain, but also his discretion in allocating power and determining what institutions can exercise force, when, where and how. As the previous analysis has shown, most security agencies involved in energy security are under the direct jurisdiction of the president. Similarly, even those that respond to other ministries are still under the strict control of the leader, given that, according to the Constitution, the president's decision to appoint or remove cabinet ministers is not subjected to any legislative oversight. The first years of Aliyev's leadership were essential in the definition of Azerbaijan's model of government. Heydar Aliyev aimed to build a system made of controllable institutions that would grant the president's hold on power. Loyal officers were appointed to the most important offices, in the bureaucracy, in the Parliament and especially in the armed forces, which following the dissolution of the USSR had emerged as one of the most powerful as well as potentially threatening institutions. In the first years of his presidency, a few attempted coups and assassination plots were used by Heydar Aliyev to reinforce his control, get rid of any potential adversary, and ensure his grip also over the military.

A look at energy security practitioners indicates that energy security practices are in the hands of Azerbaijan's most influential, close-knit elites: the presidential family, the military warlords and the energy tycoons. International Crisis Group (ICG) identifies three main factions within the elites, a categorization that corroborates the prominence of energy and military in the country's power structures. According to ICG, the first faction refers to the Aliyevs' extended family; the second belongs in the military and security tradition and is led by the 'old security guard' Ramiz Mehdiyev, who is the President's chief of staff; the second includes the oligarchs who are Aliyev's business protégées and with whom he shares business interests. Azerbaijan's elites are organized as a tight series of networks, which revolve around the President and whose connections favour tribal kinship and long-lasting intimate relationships. Clans based on regional identity are an enduring aspect of Azerbaijan's politics. Contemporary Azerbaijan has still inherited the social and territorial divisions created by the khanate system of the 17th and 18th centuries, which, rather than building a sense of national unity, grouped the communities along their tribes, villages, cities and, to a lesser extent, ethnic ties (Tokluoglu 2005). During Soviet times, economic hardship, despotic control and prosecution reinforced the presence and activities of these groups: Huseyn Aliyev (2015) notes that traditional extended families and local communities acted as focal points for networking and support. The solidification of familiar and territorial networks formed more consolidated institutional structures, the so-called clans, which shared a sense of kinship and loyalty and constituted the base for the country's social, political and economic organization. The Nakhicheveanis were the first established clan in Azerbaijan, together with the Yerazis, to set a practical modus operandi which aimed at strengthening their ties through marriage and clientelism and using their internal network for political and economic gains. When Heydar Aliyev took power, he selectively chose his collaborators from among his regional clan, filling the government with loyal members from the Nakhichevan region and eliminating his rivals. Cornell (2015, p 43) observes that most of Heydar Aliyev's 'new hires' had backgrounds in the security services and hailed from the same region, the enclave of Nakhichevan. Heydar Aliyev and most of the inner circle of his regime, especially the members of the old guard, also shared a past in the highest ranks of the Communist regime and active participation in the early years of the war in Nagorno-Karabakh. In her book, Bayulgen (2010, p 100) explains that in the country 'policy making is restricted to a close circle of senior ministers, advisers and aides to the president, [... who] are recruited on the basis of personal loyalty to the leader ... and regional tribe'. Reinforcing this argument, Valiyev (2011, p 12) shows that in the country 'personal trust prevails over professionalism'. During Heydar Aliyev's presidency, the Nakhichevan clan consolidated its power and as such, clientelism and regionalism became chronic features of Azerbaijan's political system. This also helped Aliyev gain, maintain and solidify his leadership: apart from protection from political opposition and possible coups, the elite (re)produced and spread pro-government discourse and culture. Coming from the Soviet political tradition, the Nakhichevan clan defended traditional ideas of power and leadership and concurred in spreading the narrative of a strong, charismatic statesman with renowned experience in state affairs as the only salvation for the country. This culture translated into the legitimation of a controlling executive authority, whereby the president acts as the power broker mediating among competing interests and determining power configurations (Bertelsmann Stiftung 2012, 2016; Cornell 2015). Loyalty to Heydar Aliyev contributed to sustaining the glorification of his figure and consolidating the idea of what the Aliyev family represented for the nation, especially through the reminiscence of Heydar Aliyev's successful years as the Chairman of Nakhichevan's Supreme Assembly, the first secretary of the Communist Party of Azerbaijan and an important member of the Politburo. In exchange for their support to Heydar Aliyev, the members of the clan benefited from extensive leeway for conducting their businesses and making profits, while also holding public office. The arrival of Ilham Aliyev to the presidency partially changed the composition of the elite: unlike his father, Ilham Aliyev lessened the power of the regional clans and moved closer to the new and growing oligarchy, that rose out of the oil bonanza and showed 'more capitalist-like management qualities and profit-oriented skills' (ICG 2010, p 4). Studies (eg Schlichte 2005) show that the inclusion of magnates into political institutions and the consequent 'privatisation of the state' might intensify competition among groups competing for political and economic power. Even in this context, loyalty remains a central factor in the allocation and management of political authority. Azerbaijan confirms this. With the intent to suffocate intra-elite conflicts, reinforce loyalty to him – rather than the government – and secure his grip on power, Ilham Aliyev resorted to some drastic moves to oust those ministries and top leaders that he felt he could no longer trust. The dissolution of the MNS in 2015, for instance, led to the dismissal of hundreds of generals and high-ranking employees and the arrest of prominent representatives of the government. The former minister Eldar Mahmudov was a police colonel, native of the Sharur district of Nakhichevan, the clan led by Ramiz Mehdiyev, and played a key role in strengthening Heydar Aliyev's regime. In the 2010s, as clan rivalry and the threat of uprising increased, Mahmudov became a thorny figure, whose loyalty to the old guard was greater than his loyalty to Ilham Aliyev. In 2019 Ramiz Mehdiyev himself was demoted as part of a purge that, as Guliyev (2020, p 8) notes, 'disproportionately targeted political heavyweights from the Mehdiyev-led "old guard"'. In a similar move, in 2017, another prominent figure, Ziya Mammadov, then Minister of Transport, was fired after 15 years in the job. Mammadov, one of the closest allies of Heydar Aliyev, had gained enormous power over the years: not only he was responsible for the whole oil and gas pipeline network and its security, he also established his private holding, through which he won numerous government transport projects and established a near-monopoly on niche transport services. Some of the most influential personalities of the Nakhichevan clan have survived the passage of power between Heydar and Ilham Aliyev, managing to increase their power too: Kemaleddin Heydarov (Minister of Emergency Situations since 2005), Baylar Eyyubov (Head of the SSPS), and Rovnag Abdullayev (CEO of SOCAR) have had some of the most influential roles in domestic policies during both Heydar Aliyev's and Ilham Aliyev's regimes.

Despite the reshuffling, the system has upheld its most fundamental characteristics: according to Guliyev (2011, p 585), across the two regimes, power concentration, a neo-patrimonial public administration and the use of a patron–client network act as the principal institutional mechanisms for wielding political power. Following in his father's footsteps, Ilham Aliyev preserved and even reinforced patronage and clientelism to ensure the elite's loyalty and discourage antagonism and conspiracy. While the elite still retains strong interests in keeping Aliyev in power as the stability of his government works as a guarantee for retaining its profits and benefits, Ilham Aliyev has tightened his grip on power and showed his firm intention to suffocate any dissent through all possible means. This has increased the rigidity of the system, normalized patronage and made corruption chronic. Chayes (2016) explains that the elite in Azerbaijan is horizontally integrated through 'massive holding companies that are composed of subsidiaries in a variety of lucrative economic sectors' and vertically integrated through 'a bribe-pooling system', whereby bribes and extorted fines are pooled centrally and partially redistributed back down as salaries. In this system, energy has played a key role and has contributed to an obscure and intricate encroachment of the energy business into the management of political power: oil and gas generate revenues that are used as a currency to gain political power; political power is used to manage energy wealth and make sure it keeps feeding the oligarchy.

While most scholars agree that politics and economics interweave in Azerbaijan and that government officials manage large sectors of the country's economy, there is a tendency to overlook security as the third fundamental piece of the power puzzle. Historically, the Azeri military leadership, especially the most active division belonging to the Nakhichevan clan, has played an enormous role in bringing and maintaining the Aliyevs in power. Heydar Aliyev put members of the Nakhichevan clan in the most strategic ministries and offices: the army, the Ministry of Internal Affairs, and the MNS, which allowed him to govern unchallenged and, in the first years of his presidency, prevented potential coups. It is well established in the literature that non-democratic political systems such as Aliyev's regime also need legitimation (Holm 2004; Vuori 2008). The mere use of force, fear and terror can undermine the legitimacy of a regime and mobilize resistance against the validity of public institutions and their authority (Fraenkel 2018; Linz 2000; Pfister 2004). Security works as an effective source of legitimation: it speaks to a collective sense of belonging, hinges on shared sentiments and believes and creates a common mission. In this sense, security serves to amplify loyalty and support to the government, ensuring and consolidating its legitimacy. Energy securitization in Azerbaijan is no exception: the prioritization of energy security and the corollary enlargement of the military and paramilitary machine has provided the elites with abundant financial resources, larger mandates, increased responsibilities and, finally, greater political power. In the context of Azerbaijan, where political offices are allocated through intra-elite bargaining with little accountability to the civil society (Finkel and Brudny 2012), energy security offers a pretext for reinforcing patronage and exchanging favours with energy and security magnates. The purges that have occurred under Ilham Aliyev in the security sector, especially the dissolution of the MNS and the replacement of untrustworthy security officials with die-hard loyalists, confirm the strategic importance of controlling security offices to ensure the stability of the regime. The collusion of the oligarchs, the police, the judiciary courts and the top security officials has created a system of shared interests between the security and the business sectors that capitalizes on the connivance of the regime. Over the years, security mandates have also enlarged the power of the most loyal elite members. For instance, Kemaleddin Heydarov, from the Nakhchivan clan, joined Heydar Aliyev's government as the Chairman of State Customs Committee. After Ilham Aliyev took power, he was one of the few who benefited from the change of regime as he was appointed as the Minister of Emergency Situations. The minister was created especially so that he could be upgraded; its original responsibilities focused on environmental risks, with special attention to the danger of fires and natural disasters, but its remit was soon expanded to include energy security and the protection of critical infrastructure. This also allowed a paramilitary structure to be put in place: with the enlargement of its responsibility towards energy security, the MES has been equipped with heavily armed brigades, which, rather than acting during emergencies, are deployed permanently around *critical* sites. Its transformation into a paramilitary organization has come with larger financial resources: the MES has the largest budget across the government. Heydarov has become one of the most powerful people of Azerbaijan and has won the nickname 'the Minister of Everything Significant' from the ministry's acronym (ie MES). Energy securitization has, therefore, helped maximize power within offices and factions, as well as the whole government: it has served as a power amplifier for Heydar and Ilham Aliyev's regimes, an effective legitimator and a glue that allowed the different and competing interests that emerged in the country's complex political context to be held together.

Loyalty to the president has emerged as a fundamental piece in the construction and maintenance of the system, including the energy security project: loyal practitioners reproduce the energy security discourse, faithfully conduct their security practices and, finally, show fidelity to the specific way of thinking and doing energy security. As power is not only centralized but also personified in the president, loyalty to the regime translates into celebratory devotion to the Aliyevs. The previous chapter has shown that the national energy security discourse hinges on and reproduces narratives of leadership that glorify the ruling family and contributes to forming a specific understanding of Azerbaijan's history and identity. This has also confirmed previous works (eg Shaffer 2006) that noted how Azerbaijan's elite would engage with identity language in the attempt to reinforce legitimacy and achieve political mobilization. The analysis of energy security practitioners further illuminates how loyalty embeds energy securitization in the fabrication of Azerbaijan's national identity: loyalty to the regime is, in fact, also loyalty to its security project. Discourse analysis (see Chapter 3) has made clear that energy securitization in Azerbaijan mobilizes national identity; through practices, it emerges that it is also loyalty that grants the reproduction and reiteration of energy security, including by activating identity and identity discourse. The nexus between security, loyalty and identity is eloquently discussed in the work of Mark Neocleous, who sees loyalty as 'a key political technology for gauging identity and reaffirming security' (2008, p 108). He concludes that the triad helps 'organise the political imagination around the state' (p 141). Building on the work of Neocleous, I want hereby to emphasize that the way security, loyalty and identity intertwine does not have only ideational implications but also affects practice and brings material consequences. Identity and loyalty determine who has access to resources and is given responsibilities and a mandate to govern; they also affect how security is *done* on the ground, informing the cognitive and epistemic logic that sustains the practice. In turn, security practices offer an opportunity to loyal practitioners to increase their material capability, exercise power and affirm their identity. Moreover, looking at the triad in relation to energy securitization in Azerbaijan, it appears that energy itself emerges as a fundamental piece of that complex, which sustains the configuration of power, ideationally and materially: its physical vastness, its ownership, the wealth it creates, its centrality in the national economy, its symbolism, and its attachment to national identity are all functional to the reproduction of the political order.

Energy securitization in Azerbaijan shows the tie between energy, politics and business. For instance, SOCAR security activities are managed autonomously, reflecting the high degree of independence that the company boasts. More broadly, SOCAR's institutional structure and its decision-making process exemplify the ways in which political power in Azerbaijan is managed and distributed among established poles. The company is not an independent entity but an extension of the government. When founded in 1992, SOCAR formally acted as the country's Ministry of Energy and its president as the minister who reported directly to Azerbaijan's president. Over the years, despite changes in the management of the company, SOCAR top-level executives have always been chosen from among the closest allies and supporters of Heydar and Ilham Aliyev. In fact, prior to replacing his father as Azerbaijan's president, Ilham Aliyev acted as SOCAR vice president from 1994 to 2003, the years following the Contract of the Century. With the establishment of the Ministry of Fuel and Energy in 2001 (renamed Ministry of Industry and Energy in 2004), SOCAR lost only part of its governmental responsibility and authority: while the newly established ministry is formally in charge of energy policy and regulation, SOCAR managed to keep its monopoly over the oil and gas industry, including its exclusive authority in the exploration, development and production of oil and gas fields, transportation, and processing and sale of crude oil, gas and oil products. SOCAR also kept its ability to influence the decision-making process, manage and supervise the implementation of the contracts, oversee export pipelines, settle investments autonomously, regulate licences, and act as the state representative in international negotiations and the signatory to all PSAs. The PSAs – which constitute Azerbaijan's legal regime of oil development, define the commercial, legal and fiscal conditions behind the participation of international companies in Azerbaijan's energy industry and, as such, regulate their relationship with the government – can only be agreed by SOCAR and once they are signed, they are routinely ratified by the Parliament and become law. Commenting on Azerbaijan's PSA system, Hoffman (1999, p 16) noted that 'oil contracts tend to operate outside normal regulatory channels .... Parliament, irrespective of the constitution, exercises virtually no oversight powers, and there is a distinct lack of a horizontal distribution of state power within the government, resulting in a heavily deformed regulatory and legal regime.' As SOCAR and the president have a close special relationship, the company has the ability to bypass legislative and bureaucratic processes, including the scrutiny of wider political stakeholders and the limits imposed by the state's law on monopolies. Ilham Aliyev has deepened the ability of the president to interfere in the management of the company and has criminalized the spread of business information through corruption and nepotism. The flexibility given to the government and SOCAR business elite to administer the company includes lax mechanisms to administer energy revenues, which remain at the government's disposal: wealth redistribution among the wider society is limited and the government boasts total discretion in managing energy revenues. Direct cash contributions to the government are routine practices in Azerbaijan. Similarly, despite the domestic energy industry remaining largely in the hands of the state, oil and gas have provided manifold opportunities for business people and privately owned companies to profit from partnering with SOCAR. Global Witness (2013), an NGO, found out that newly established companies, which act as proxies for the ruling family and whose ownership, experience and activities remain opaque, have gained ownership stakes in SOCAR and other oil and gas utility companies. In recent years, SOCAR's funds have also been used to build public infrastructure, including hospitals and schools. While this largely aims at whitewashing how energy wealth is managed by both the government and the company, the way revenues are spent still points to the commingling of private and public interests and the overlaps between public structures and private entities. SOCAR funds are in fact managed and allocated through third parties and organizations that are loyal to the President, including the Heydar Aliyev Foundation, a charitable organization named after Azerbaijan's former leader and headed by the First Lady Mehriban Aliyev. SOCAR exemplifies how energy, politics and business intertwine in Azerbaijan, to the extent that distinguishing between the public and the private sector is not always possible. In particular, the management of public goods is often directed towards the creation of private gains. Energy securitization reinforces this linkage. What emerges out of the analysis of energy security discourses and practices is that the creation and expansion of the security project through energy securitization becomes a tool to protect private interests while enlarging and reinforcing the power of the state and its leadership. Energy security ultimately aims at maximizing both security as securitization and energy in terms of energy business and wealth.

Energy securitization: a fragmented terrain of multiple security practices

Legislative scholars have suggested that these initial provisions to secure energy, especially those established in the light of the construction of the BTC, have 'created a thousand-mile swath of militarised corporate sovereignty running from Azerbaijan's Caspian shore to Turkey's Mediterranean' (Reyes 2006, p 879). This is true, but limited; in fact, we should not conceptualize the deployment of forces as a line that follows transnational corridors to protect them from external enemies; rather, energy security provisions are a disperse, extended and disorganized assemblage that blurs the distinction between the internal and the external space of security. This reflects and is reflected by the practices that are carried out on the ground. What is usually less underlined in the idea of energy as a securitized space is that military forces work together with civil and paramilitary bodies in an effort to address threats that come from within and outside borders. The military, militarism and militarization coexist with policing, enforcement, surveillance, intelligence and control. As the division between external and internal security blurs, the traditional separation between military and civil security is distorted too. In Azerbaijan, this is not a novelty but intensifies a peculiarity of the country's military and security apparatus. Nationally, the distinction between military and enforcement is historically not neat: on the one side, law enforcement agencies, civil defence bodies and military forces all operate in similar ways and according to analogous paradigms that lean towards military structures, modi operandi and mindsets; however, they also embrace a desire to enforce domestic control and discipline through close vigilance of the population, which is passed on to military personnel who act as vigilantes.

Azerbaijan has kept enlarging and investing in its military sector, partially because of the war in Nagorno-Karabakh, but also because of the highly militaristic nature of the state, rooted in its historical trajectory but also in the authoritarian nature of the Aliyevs' regimes. Since Ilham Aliyev took office in 2003, Azerbaijan's military spending has increased 15-fold. Today the country has around 67,000 military and 15,000 paramilitary forces currently operating. Azerbaijan has not been able to fully transition from the militaristic model of the Soviet era and struggles with a changing security environment that would require more unconventional operations. Rather than rethinking its military, Azerbaijan has progressively instilled a militaristic approach to law enforcement, transforming civil agencies into de facto paramilitary forces. As a result, while agencies' statutory and administrative principles are regulated separately from military forces, most enforcement agencies have quasi-military models: they have adopted hierarchical bureaucracies, organize around a neat chain of command and are equipped with high-powered weapons, rather than the more conventional light weaponry of civil bodies. In December 2018, the government revised the 1993 Law on the Armed Forces with the aim of clarifying mandates and further distinguishing between defence and enforcement; yet the results are still very mild. On the ground, the legislative distinctions remain blurred, especially with regard to less conventional, so-called hybrid, security issues like energy security, where military, paramilitary and civil forces have all found a space for intervening. There are significant overlaps in terms of responsibilities and practices and the mandates in energy security remain very similar among different forces. According to the three strategic documents, namely the National Security Concept, the Military Doctrine and the Maritime Security Strategy, and the more tailored decrees that regulate specific agencies – such as Presidential Decree No 873 dated 31 May 2003 on the Special State Protection Service; Presidential Decree No 706 dated 14 December 2015 on the State Security Service; Presidential Decree No 740 dated 31 July 2002 on the State Border Service and the Coast Guard; the Law of the Republic of Azerbaijan on the Armed Forces dated 9 October 1991 and its revised version of 2018; Order No 132 of the President of SOCAR dated 23 December 2005, based on Presidential Decree No 844 dated 24 January 2003 on the creation of paramilitary forces within the national energy company – military, paramilitary and civil forces all participate in and conduct similar operations of energy security. In particular, they are all permanently deployed on the ground to prevent and counter any physical attack to energy infrastructure. As a result, on the one side, energy security in Azerbaijan has created a more expansive role for law enforcement agencies, which now have competencies in defence and military affairs; on the other side, energy security has enlarged and normalized the involvement of the operational arms of Azerbaijan's defence forces in civil matters, as well as the presence and deployment of military personnel on the ground even during peacetime and far from the conflict zone.

Despite multiple interagency training and capacity building programmes, energy security practices remain disentangled and fragmented. As energy security emerges as a hybrid security concern, the field is overpopulated by security and military professionals from the police forces, the army, and the emergency and civil defence forces. The disordered regulatory framework creates confusion and overlaps, and generates spaces for interinstitutional competition, which is exacerbated by the inclusion of transnational and private actors. At the very dawn of the BTC project, the government enacted a decree on the security of the of oil and gas export and pipelines (President of Azerbaijan 2002), which instituted a National Commission to start dealing with the security of the oil and gas export routes. Since then, the Commission has been one of the main bodies responsible for taking decisions regarding the protection of energy facilities. It unites 15 governmental bodies and consists of members of the Ministry of Energy, the Ministry of Ecology and Natural Resources, the Ministry of Transport, the SSPS, the SSS, the Border Service, the Ministry of Defence and the MES. Its wide membership reflects the heterogeneity of the actors involved in the country's energy security, whose expertise ranges from energy engineering to defence and enforcement. Moreover, Azerbaijan's enforcement agencies often conduct interagency training, especially joint exercises and simulations, such as those carried out in Quba, a large city close to the Russian border, the BTC, the SCP and the Baku–Novorossiysk pipeline (NREP), with the participation of the internal troops, the local police forces of Quba, the Khachmaz region and Qusar, the SBS, the civil defence police from the MES, as well as the state road police inspectors of Kuzun in Şirvanovka. Drills to increase combat readiness among the air force, the SBS, the coastguard and the navy often focus on the protection of submarine export oil and gas pipelines and platforms.

Nonetheless, there is a severe lack of clarity regarding the management of intersecting practices. These include those activities that have similar tactical and operational scope, such as energy-critical infrastructure protection and counterterrorism. Likewise, it is unclear how different security agencies manage their information-sharing activities. The significant duplication of effort among forces speaks of high inefficiency, fragmentation and a profound lack of coordination among security agencies. Azerbaijan's law enforcement, military, and intelligence agencies share the same mission and conduct similar operations on the ground: they patrol, guard, control and defend physical assets. Due to this fragmentation and lack of clarity, energy security practices have been able to enlarge the space of energy security: no line can easily be drawn to define their territorial, temporal and professional configuration. During my fieldwork, concerns were raised over the overlapping responsibilities between the different agencies operating offshore, which share similar duties: there is no clarity in relation to the division of responsibility between the coastguard and the navy. Interviews also mentioned that despite recent military build-ups, offshore forces remain poorly equipped and suffer from inadequate training. This is a widespread concern: despite its huge military and paramilitary machine, Azerbaijan's forces are often considered inadequate, still reliant on the outdated military industrial base of Soviet times. Although energy wealth has given Azerbaijan an enormous advantage in terms of military acquisition, its armed forces remain relatively weak, especially when compared to its Armenian counterparts or its neighbours Iran and Russia, and it remains unclear if modernizing its artillery has improved Azerbaijan's operational capability. In particular, Azerbaijan's armed forces have long suffered from the low technical-cultural level of the workforce base and a lack of modern technology, which has jeopardized Azerbaijan's effectiveness, particularly as regards the requirements of modern warfare. In the last decade, significant military investment has aimed to improve and enhance the country's technological capability. While the war in Nagorno-Karabakh has long driven the country's military capacity building, recent purchases point to the increasing emphasis on energy security: military procurement has favoured weaponry and technologies that, rather than targeting the conventional tactical and operational needs of combat operations in Karabakh, have responded to the strategic and operational needs of securing energy assets. For instance, Azerbaijan has heavily empowered its naval and dual-use maritime security facilities, with the explicit goal of protecting the oil and gas fields in the Caspian Sea. This has led to the acquisition of large numbers of patrol boats, warships, fighter jets, unmanned aerial vehicles (UAVs), drones, long-range missiles, ballistic missile systems, and operational-tactical missile systems. Nonetheless, it needs to be pointed out that, while these recently acquired security systems have long-distance capability that goes beyond the contested territories of Nagorno-Karabakh, Armenians have been reporting increased activity from unmanned technology close to the line of contact that separates rival troops. Energy securitization – as a set of diverse practices – does not work in isolation but constantly assembles and reassembles with existing military strategies and operations in such a way that distinguishing between distinct security objectives is not feasible. The assembly has the ability to decontextualize and create a sense of coherence and belonging among different projects, despite the heterogeneous and disentangled nature of its practices. The next chapter continues the exploration of energy security practices, particularly the interplay of energy, defence, enforcement, economy and identity, and builds on the theoretical framework used here by paying attention to the global dimension of energy securitization.

5

Beyond the National Borders: NATO and Energy Security in Azerbaijan

The oil and gas industry is one of the most globalized sectors in the world. Its processes of extraction, production and trade cannot prescind from the collaboration of national governments, international organizations, local firms and multinational corporations. Foreign actors and their interests coexist and interact with their national counterparts; the global energy markets make the non-national a prime interlocutor of domestic energy politics. The internationalization of energy has progressively bent the space of its security and created multiple opportunities for foreign and international security interventions. Due to the growth of the energy industry, resources, infrastructure and markets flow and are not restrained by borders, stretching the spatiality of energy security outward. This has important consequences for energy security, which are both material and ideational: energy security threats are dealt with, perceived, understood and even imagined as global concerns. When Heydar Aliyev liberalized Azerbaijan's oil and gas sector in 1994, he not only opened the industry up to foreign money, but also facilitated the presence and participation of a wide variety of foreign actors in the local energy sector. To accelerate and intensify extraction and production and to develop an international transport network, Azerbaijan partnered with several overseas companies; neighbouring countries, particularly Turkey and Georgia; regional and non-regional states, such as the US and most European consumer states; intergovernmental organizations, such as the European Union and NATO; and several stakeholders that had an interest in the country's energy potential and related lucrative opportunities. By collaborating in the energy projects, all these actors have developed a direct interest in Azerbaijan's energy industry and its security, creating a space for themselves to influence the decision-making process of the country's energy and security politics. The stakes they have in Azerbaijan's oil and gas affect how these actors perceive and feel about energy security; notably they tend to deal with Azerbaijan's oil and gas as one of *their* own security concerns. Increased salience and attention to energy security by international organizations and third states have intensified the political focus on the international dimension of energy (in)security.

These preliminary remarks serve to introduce the main question that drives this chapter: what happens when energy security is embedded in discourses and practices of global security? My task in this section is to account for the global dimension of energy securitization, here intended as an analysis of its ontology – the nature of its threats – and political – the forms of governance it creates. The emphasis on the global character of energy security threats elevates the scale of the danger and asks for a new vision of how to manage it. The global ontology of energy security implies a new form of polity and governance based on international solutions. This chapter explores the particular vision of order, the forms of authority and the patterns of social organization around which this specific problematization of energy security as a global issue coheres. Couched in discourses of cooperation and security support, the global rendering of energy security has formed a space for international interventions in small energy producer states like Azerbaijan and covered securitizing practices with a legitimizing and normalizing gloss that has largely remained unquestioned. This analysis aims to unpack these processes by exploring the case of NATO, as one of the most prominent and active security organizations involved in energy security in the country. In particular, it examines how NATO securitizes energy in Azerbaijan through discourse and practices of global security.

This chapter begins by providing a first glance at the internationalization of energy security in Azerbaijan, outlining the many security actors and initiatives that operate in the country to secure energy through bilateral and multilateral cooperation. This section serves to contextualize the overall institutional and political landscape in which NATO has started operating, offering a view of the global circuits of energy security and an introduction to the historical roots of the security partnership between the Alliance and Azerbaijan.

This study then moves to present the findings of discourse analysis and mapping. Overall, the empirical analysis brings forth three main salient points. First, NATO energy security discourse and practices securitize energy by insisting on the exceptional, critical, global and novel character of its threats. As such, energy securitization legitimizes NATO's interventions, the creation and sustained proliferation of its energy security programmes, as well as the enlargement of its institutional architecture through the formation of ad hoc energy security-oriented units. This normalizes the proactive and widespread presence of military and security professionals in and around energy sites and also positions energy security under the rubric of global security, global cooperation and global interoperability. Building on this first argument, the second point explains that energy securitization renovates NATO's security mandate, proves its continuing relevance, and enlarges its authority to the extent that it positions the Alliance as *the* global expert in energy security. NATO's energy security discourse and practices are motivated by a pedagogical intent: by virtue of its (self-)established expertise, NATO determines and spreads strategies, techniques and knowledge through best practices, training, interoperability and capacity building. The third claim reflects on how the principles of harmony, cooperation, alignment and integration that undergird energy securitization concur to (re)produce and cement liberal norms and values as the only possibility for and pathway towards global (energy) security.

This chapter also makes a theoretical contribution to the understanding of energy securitization. First, it confirms the relational and performative tie between securitization and identity: in the case of NATO, energy securitization not only hinges on specific representations of the self and the other (Azerbaijan), but also responds to a specific strategy of being. Azerbaijan is, therefore, socialized into western-defined norms of security via interoperability, best practices, training and joint drills.

The second contribution of this chapter lies in its novel approach to securitization within a global dimension. Energy securitization has long been theorized as a national phenomenon, driven by the state *for* the state. Yet, energy securitization is a much more complex and heterogeneous process compared to its ideal type. In response to the abstraction and distortion of Securitization Theory (ST), this chapter offers a more encompassing picture of energy securitization, focusing on its actual complexity and intricacy. To do so, it builds on the view of energy securitization set out in Chapter 2, which establishes it as a heterogeneous and (dis)entangled practice. This chapter builds on those theoretical reflections to look beyond the state as the prime analytical unit and the sole empirical terrain of securitization.

International actors and energy security in Azerbaijan

One of the implications of the liberalization of Azerbaijan's energy market has been the proliferation of foreign, international and multilateral initiatives to ostensibly secure oil and gas – especially flows and infrastructure; as a consequence, the manifold interests connected to the energy business have come to the surface. In the rush to secure Azerbaijan's oil and gas treasure, the US soon took the lead and started cooperating with the country from the early days of the energy negotiations in the mid 1990s. Motivated by broader foreign policy interests and strategies, US administrations realized that Azerbaijan could help diversify American energy imports, moving away from its excessive dependence on the Middle East, while gaining influence in the ex-Soviet space. At the beginning of the 21st century, under the George W. Bush administration, Azerbaijan's energy security formally became an issue of US national security: then-Secretary of Defense Donald Rumsfeld declared that the US Department of Defense was directly responsible for the security of the transportation of Caspian oil and the BTC oil pipeline. US interest in the Caspian region had risen after 9/11, making the Caspian Region a priority of US foreign policy. Azerbaijan's proximity to Iran and Chechnya put it in the spotlight. Since the early 2000s, the US has acted as a major military and financial supplier for Azerbaijan, led bilateral initiatives of capacity building in critical energy infrastructure protection, and encouraged US-based oil companies to invest in the country. In 2003, the US European Command (EUCOM) launched the Caspian Guard Initiative and inaugurated the Coast Guard Training Centre and the Caspian Maritime Security Cooperation programme to coordinate the security cooperation activities in Azerbaijan and Kazakhstan with those of CENTCOM and other US defence departments. This initiative has a clear pedagogical imprint: it aims at fostering Azeri expertise in securing energy sites. Since 2003, within the Caspian Guard Initiative, military troops and border guards from both the US and Azerbaijan have conducted a large number of joint training exercises and drills. The programme has trained combat units, provided military equipment and helped Azerbaijan establish a network of technical checkpoints near offshore facilities. In 2007 the remit of the Cooperative Threat Reduction Program – which was originally launched to secure and eliminate nuclear, chemical and biological weapons in the former Soviet Union by providing and assisting in the safe disposal of the material – was expanded to include the protection of energy sites, particularly as part of the mission to manage threats in the maritime realm. Since then, Azerbaijan's navy's special forces have joined the US Marines Corps in exercises and simulations around offshore platforms. The US also provided aid to support the expansion of Azerbaijan's Maritime Domain Awareness system. These examples show that energy security has been a driver, a major focus and an abiding force in the US–Azerbaijan relationship. Energy security has also been used to circumvent the three-decade ban on US aid to Azerbaijan, enforced by Section 907 of the 1992 Freedom Support Act, which blocks assistance to Azerbaijan as a result of the war in Nagorno-Karabakh. Despite the ban and with a view to securing its energy and foreign policy interests, the US kept investing in the country. Between 2004 and 2006, financial aid to Azerbaijan's security and military soared; a USD 2 billion investment allowed the purchase of a number of drones, anti-terrorism patrols and American aerial radar surveillance systems to control the BTC pipeline and the other energy corridors. According to the US Financial Report on Foreign Military Training (2007–2014), US forces have been involved in conducting joint training and capacity building activities, aimed at preparing Azerbaijan's forces to prevent and respond to terrorist attacks and sabotage.

Nonetheless, Azerbaijan has long claimed that its security needs have been 'left unmet' by the US, as well as by the other European states. Cooperation with Europe on energy security has remained centred on the economy and trade, focusing on the contribution of Azerbaijan's oil and gas supplies to the EU market. While some initiatives to open dialogue on security exist, these are marginal and mainly outsourced to third security platforms and organizations, such as the OSCE and NATO. Israel has fulfilled part of Azerbaijan's security desires that the EU and the US have not satisfied, by supplying advanced military weapons. In February 2012, Azerbaijan signed an arms agreement with Israel that allowed the acquisition of sophisticated military technology – including drones, Gabriel-5 missiles and a missile-defence system – which has mostly been deployed to secure the Caspian offshore sites. In the same year, a joint venture was established in Azerbaijan to produce drones for military use (Göksel 2015). The military trade with Israel has also offered an opportunity to overcome the voluntary arms embargo against Azerbaijan, which was requested by the OSCE in 1992 as a response to the war in Nagorno-Karabakh and has not been removed yet. Azerbaijan has a complex relationship with the OSCE. Although it is one of its 52 member states, Armenia's membership of the OSCE is a problem for Baku, which has limited the involvement of Azerbaijan in OSCE energy security initiatives. Today, Azerbaijan participates in some of the organization's energy security initiatives: the OSCE has an Energy Security Unit that fosters cooperation in energy trade and an Anti-Terrorism Unit and a Transnational Threats Department that promote joint training on the protection of energy infrastructure. As a result, Azerbaijan has been reluctant in participating actively in the OSCE's security initiatives, including in the energy sector. Moreover, in the early 2010s, the organization began to accuse Ilham Aliyev's regime of violating civil liberties and human rights; as a response, in 2015, the government shut down the OSCE's office in Baku.

Regional energy projects, such as the BTC and the BTE, have encouraged cooperation with Turkey and Georgia. With the vigorous support of the US, which has facilitated multilateral dialogue and created platforms for joint activities, Azerbaijan, Turkey and Georgia have put in place a multilateral, defence-oriented initiative centred on energy security. Motivated by shared security concerns over the oil and gas pipelines, the three states launched the Trilateral Cooperation. In its early years, cooperation happened mostly on a bilateral basis, with Turkey acting as the leading interlocutor between Azerbaijan and Georgia. In the late 1990s Turkey provided Azerbaijan with considerable financial support – up to USD 3.5 million in 1999 – and military equipment. While formally this aimed at securing energy facilities, it also helped Azerbaijan modernize its forces and offered leverage against Russia's assistance to Armenia in Karabakh.

A few years later, in 2002, Azerbaijan signed a military agreement with Georgia to cooperate on pipeline security, pushed by a shared apprehension about the risk of terrorism and sabotage. In the 2010s, the collaboration took a more institutional turn and a clearly defence-oriented character: with a view to developing military preparedness to protect energy infrastructure, the Trilateral Cooperation now provides for regular consultations among the three ministers of defence and top military officials. The partnership has launched a series of cooperation initiatives for capacity building, military education and exchange of know-how and best practices, often with the support and cooperation of NATO, of which Turkey is a member. Although Azerbaijan does not aspire to become a member of NATO, it perceives a close relationship with the Alliance as a necessary component of its foreign and security policy and a leverage against the regional powers of Russia and Iran. This decades-long partnership has deepened and broadened through the development of joint energy cooperation.

Today, NATO is the most involved foreign actor in the security of energy in Azerbaijan. Over the years and despite its previous distance from the energy sector, the Alliance has managed to build a reputation as the pre-eminent expert in the field within the broader constellation of energy security actors. NATO's purely military character, especially its focus on the use of force and the uniformity of its personnel's background and know-how, has concurred to establish its privileged status and authority in energy security. Its energy security cooperation with Azerbaijan happens within the framework of the Partnership for Peace (PfP), a programme launched in 1994 to establish military cooperation on a bilateral basis with non-member partner countries. The 1994 PfP Framework Document committed Azerbaijan to developing 'cooperative military relations with NATO, for the purpose of joint planning, training, and exercises' and transforming its forces according to NATO's principles and guidelines to be 'able to operate with those of the members of the North Atlantic Alliance'.

Within the PfP, Azerbaijan's military and paramilitary forces have participated in frequent joint military forums; trained at western military facilities; enrolled on courses at the NATO School in Oberammergau, the NATO Defence College in Rome, and the PfP Training Center in Ankara; and transferred and spread their know-how locally upon their return. The PfP has offered NATO a tool for educating on how the Alliance *does* security, prompting other states to adopt its modus operandi. In doing so, NATO has acquired a leading role in forming knowledge, setting expectations, and defining security and military practices. It is important to notice that the PfP has marked the transition of NATO from a purely defensive transatlantic alliance to a much wider and diversified security-community institution based on cooperative-security practices (Adler 2008). In the Caucasus the programme has been the main vector to strengthen military cooperation with a view to harmonizing partners' security organization and practices with NATO's standards. Reflecting the overall sentiment behind the PfP framework, NATO's energy security programmes embody and diffuse a *consciousness* and a modus operandi to deal with the related threats. The pedagogical function that underpins NATO's energy security intervention has larger implications that affect how security is *thought* and *done* more broadly and point to the ability of the Alliance to (re)produce and cement specific meanings of (energy) security through discourses and practices of international security. Behind all NATO's programmes there is the expectation that partners will accept, emulate and adapt to the organization's guidelines and techniques. The introduction of the Individual Partnership Action Plan (IPAP) to deepen the cooperation with the PfP allies follows this direction. The IPAP, which was joined by Azerbaijan in 2005, required partners to set up a system of reforms in the security and defence sector, and provided them with NATO's support to define and implement them through joint and highly coordinated efforts. The creation of energy security programmes has given to the Alliance multiple instruments to define the geographical, temporal and institutional space of energy security, regulate its governance, organize international and intersectoral relations by networking actors, as well as diffuse existing mechanisms and adopt new ones. The following sections examine NATO's discourse and practices of energy securitization in Azerbaijan.

NATO's security discourse: energy as a global concern

NATO is an international military organization, originally founded in 1949 to guarantee the security of its European and North American members through political and military tools and collective defence. Even though the Alliance is not an energy institution, it has taken a serious interest in and commitment to the security of energy. NATO first mentioned energy security in its 1999 Strategic Concept (NATO 1999): Article 24 warned against the dangers caused by 'the disruption of the flow of vital resources'. This first image of energy as a flow is paramount, not only because it has become a sticky way of thinking about energy, but also because it contains the very core of energy as a global concern: it is a thick image that puts emphasis on the most corporeal aspect of energy, not only as natural resources but as a stream of materiality in constant movement through space. This generates a material interconnectedness that transcends state borders and that NATO, which is not an energy organization, argues affects 'the international security environment and can have far-reaching security implications for some Allies'

(NATO website). It is this way of conceptualizing energy materiality that justifies the call for international interventions in energy security.

These interventions reflect NATO's wider character and modus operandi: the Alliance is a military institution, which maintains a conventional approach to security based on the use of force and principally operates through military tools. In Article 45 of the 2006 Riga Declaration (NATO 2006), NATO resorted to the same image of 'the disruption of the flow of vital resources' to arrange 'coordinated, international effort to assess risks to energy infrastructures and to promote energy infrastructure security'. The use of 'disruption' and 'infrastructure' pinpoints once again the physicality of energy security threats. In the following official statement, NATO's discourse began outlining energy security as an international and global practice. Article 48 of the 2008 Bucharest Declaration (NATO 2008) linked energy security to multiple types of security practices, all of which implied and increased multilateral interventions and international cooperation. In particular, the Declaration aimed at establishing 'information and intelligence fusion and sharing; advancing international and regional cooperation; supporting consequence management; and supporting the protection of critical energy infrastructure'.

In 2010 the Alliance published its new Strategic Concept (NATO 2010), an influential document that outlined the roadmap for the following decade. The Concept planned an enduring commitment to energy security that started with the establishment of an institutional architecture to centralize decision making and increase coordination. It launched the creation of the Energy Security Section within the newly created Emerging Challenges Unit to reflect contemporary concerns about non-state violence and less conventional forms of conflict and insecurity. The Concept also refined NATO's commitment to global energy security and highlighted the need to 'develop the capacity to contribute to energy security, including protection of critical energy infrastructure and transit areas and lines'. Given that the 2010 Strategic Concept was set to last ten years, NATO's attention to the material, the priority of physical security and the emphasis on energy as a mobile and *transitional* space have become the enduring imperative pillars of energy security. Article 45 of the 2012 Chicago Declaration (NATO 2012) insisted on fostering international capacity through consultations and invites NATO to enlarge its approach to non-member states through 'outreach activities' to be established 'with partners on case-by-case bases'. The 2016 Warsaw Summit Communiqué (NATO 2016) upheld the role of the Alliance as an expert adviser in energy security to operate alongside members' and partners' national governments, which are recognized to maintain the prime security responsibility in the field.

NATO is set 'to develop capacity to support national authorities in protecting critical energy infrastructure, as well as enhancing their resilience against energy supply disruptions that could affect national and collective defence' (NATO 2016). The same principles are reiterated in the Brussels Summit Declaration (NATO 2018), which further specified NATO's energy security activities in developing strategic awareness, intelligence sharing, and close collaboration with energy organizations like the International Energy Agency and the International Renewable Energy Agency. In the latest documents, energy security emerges as a multifaceted concern, which retains its highly material character but manifests also through a dangerous political culture: on the one side, attention is drawn to energy infrastructure, its interconnectivity and the need to physically secure energy routes against potential attacks, including 'malicious hybrid and cyber activity'; on the other, energy is seen as a political weapon to exert 'political and economic pressure' through 'political or coercive manipulation'.

Outlining the trajectory of its approach to energy security serves to embed NATO's specific construction of energy security in Azerbaijan in the social, cultural and political context in which it has developed. As Hansen explains (2013, p 7), texts often 'build their arguments and authority through references to other texts: by making direct quotes or by adopting key concepts and catchphrases'. The analysis of three NATO–Azerbaijan Reviews of the IPAP reveals a way of thinking of and doing energy security that is analogous to NATO's broader energy security discourse. The IPAP Reviews offer a picture of energy security interventions: they map out and provide data on NATO–Azerbaijan activities, identify joint strategic goals and methods, inform on the organization of security actors, and provide rich information on what and how energy is secured. Proving Hansen's point, these links to the Alliance's older Declarations and Concepts offer a venue to anchor energy security in Azerbaijan to a discourse that has already achieved a degree of legitimation and authoritativeness. Although imbued with NATO's discourse of global energy security, these three texts do not merely mimic NATO's previous provisions but reinsert their rendering of energy security in the context of the NATO–Azerbaijan wider relationship. As a result, NATO's construction of energy in Azerbaijan signals the specificities of the context, including the social, cultural and political relations in which it develops. As Hansen (2013) points out, the new texts 'never reproduce the originals in a manner which is fully identical but weave them into the present context and argument'. In the particular case of the NATO–Azerbaijan Reviews of the IPAPs, the energy security discourse influences and is influenced by specific constructions of NATO's and Azerbaijan's identity, as well as by certain imaginaries of the global order and its security in which the NATO–Azerbaijan relationship develops. In this respect, the analysis of NATO's discourse confirms the argument brought forward by the previous chapters: energy security relies upon representations of identity; in particular, specific problematizations of energy security (re)produce and fabricate a sense of self and its relations to the other. Looking at NATO, however, complements the understanding of the nexus between energy securitization and identity by locating the construction of certain subjectivities in relation to the construction of a distinctive social order. In the case of NATO, energy securitization is the affirmation and diffusion of a strategy of doing energy security embedded in militarism and underpinned by specific cognitive structures and values that find their explanation in the Alliance's effort to build, secure and enhance the liberal order.

In the three IPAP Reviews, energy security remains a broad policy principle, which prioritizes the physical aspects of the oil and gas industry, mainly energy facilities and especially the transport infrastructure, and pays attention to the transnational, global character of energy, particularly its materiality, symbolized by the interconnectedness of the market and the energy network and the flow of energy across borders. Its emphasis on the physicality of energy is translated in the prominence of physical protection, which ends up favouring the military dimension of security, especially as military cooperation and interoperability. The three Reviews of the IPAPs make constant reference to the criticality of energy security as the security of 'vital energy sources' and 'vitally important facilities' and insist on the urgency of addressing, through military and defence measures, the multiple security risks, challenges, threats and vulnerabilities connected to the sector. The three texts identify a wide range of security threats – from interstate conflicts to territorial disputes, terrorism, cyber-attacks and piracy – and a broad set of solutions that point to different strategies and operations, including maritime security, counterterrorism, cyber defence, border security and civil protection. NATO builds an idea of energy security that embraces its wider discourse of global security as a landscape in transformation. This recognized heterogeneity of threats and responses is constructed as the result of the peculiar hybrid ontology of energy security: described as 'non-traditional' and 'cross-cutting', energy emerges as a one-of-a-kind problem that old security tools and strategies are inappropriate and unsuited to address. Together with its criticality and vulnerability, NATO's discourse signals the novelty of energy security: the label 'emerging challenge', which recurs throughout the texts, points to the unprecedented and increasingly prominent nature of energy security and captures the ever evolving, unexpected and unpredictable character of contemporary security. Because they are 'emerging', these challenges remain fundamentally unknown. They hardly find a clear space in the traditional categorizations of security to the extent that it becomes difficult to limit their existence and distinguish between the moment of security and that of insecurity. Energy securities are therefore framed as permanent and omnipresent. Their ongoing potentiality evokes a logic of perpetual risk, whereby decisions must be taken in a context of uncertainty, doubt, ignorance, fear and anxiety. NATO's discourse imagines a new security environment, marked by a higher degree of unpredictability, ambiguity and mobility. The use of the term 'challenge' increases the ontological hybridity given to energy security as a space between the actuality of threats, understood as identifiable causes of insecurity, and the potentiality of risks, intended as the multiple possibilities of harm.

Merging threats with risks favours a spatial and temporal expansion of security: the cognitive assumptions behind 'emerging challenges' are conducive to preventive and pre-emptive security practices that aim at managing the ubiquitous potentiality of these risks, together with defeating identifiable threats, anytime and anywhere. While traditional threats stem from rival states, emerging challenges like energy security are located in and flow through global networks and systems. Framed as an emerging challenge, energy security calls for a new set of responses: securitization emerges in the constant call for exceptional and out-of-box solutions. The peculiarity of the threat makes energy securitization appear necessary and adequate: NATO's discourse normalizes the proactive and widespread presence of the military, the actual and potential use of force, the manifold and constant training and drills, the constant search for better practices, and the ambition to control and even prevent the threats. The emphasis on the global character of energy security threats elevates the scale of the danger and asks for a new vision of how to manage it. The global ontology of energy security implies a new form of polity and governance based on international solutions. As such, energy securitization legitimizes NATO's interventions, the creation and sustained proliferation of its energy security programmes, and the enlargement of its institutional architecture through the formation of ad hoc energy security-oriented units.

Through the analysis of NATO's discourse of energy security in Azerbaijan, it emerges that the rhetorical shift towards energy security as a global threat transforms the space of authority: the discourse has the power to determine who holds authority and how they should exert it; in doing so, it gives a certain order to power relations. In particular, it captures the intersection between the local and global dimensions of energy security, by inserting local practices in global circuits of expertise and knowledge and by translating global know-how in localized actions.

The ontological diversity of the energy security challenges allows who can intervene in the energy field and how to be reconceptualized. The unconventional character of the energy security threat legitimizes unconventional responses from unconventional actors. In other words, NATO's energy security discourse recognizes and creates a space for alternative authority that falls outside the traditional monopoly of force held by the state. There is obviously a concrete reality behind the expansion of governance: the interconnectedness of energy security, which bypasses borders, has led to a proliferation of security professionals, including non-state actors and non-regular security forces, which have an interest in securing energy. NATO legitimizes the space it has created for itself by exalting this material aspect of energy – as flowing, transnational, crossing and global – and using it to normalize its intervention. The global nature assigned to energy security enables NATO's presence and interventions beyond the territorial confines set by its membership. It also justifies the Alliance's revision of its role as a global security provider, including through its partnerships with non-members. NATO's discourse constructs not only a strategy of doing, but also a strategy of being, whereby practices and actions embody and maintain a certain idea of the self and the other (Ciuta 2007; Flockhart 2012, 2016). As explained earlier, NATO's energy security discourse buttresses a cognitive structure that, by claiming a global scope and acquiring a pedagogical function, is adopted and becomes normalized beyond the transatlantic region. In the construction of energy security problems and solutions, the discourse reasserts and projects how NATO sees itself and the other in the international system. The 'emerging' character of energy security has provided the Alliance with a platform to reinvent its mandate and affirm the necessity of its existence in the post-Cold War era and against those who predict its disappearance (Lepgold 1998; Walt 1998; Forster and Wallace 2001): in reclaiming its space, the Alliance argues that 'the new security realities of the twenty-first century demand a significant response from NATO' (Monaghan 2014). Energy security has legitimized the creation and expansion of NATO's institutional architecture through new units, new programmes and new statutory frameworks. Through the establishment and spread of these practices among and beyond its membership, NATO has carved out a reputation for itself as a global expert. By virtue of this acquired epistemic authority, the Alliance has established its values and norms as the only pathway to security and has proved its continuing relevance as a reactive force in a changing security landscape.

Together with the 'emerging challenge' narrative, NATO's energy security discourse accommodates also a more traditional account of security that reawakens Cold War mentalities and identifies Russia as the major source of threat. This narrative acquired a special force in the aftermath of the Ukraine crisis in 2010, which was seen by the Alliance as a turning point in Euro-Atlantic security. Granting the Alliance's energy security was seen as an essential part of a larger strategy to counter Russia's power: 'energy security and economic stability limit Russian freedom of action more so than any sort of direct military to military balance' (Monaghan 2014). The crisis simultaneously 'creates new security realities for the twenty-first century and demands a significant response from NATO' (Monaghan 2014), while also 'recast[ing] the role [the Alliance] envisaged in 1949' (NATO 2014). If the novel character of energy security has enabled the

Alliance to claim its relevance in the face of the uncertainty of the modern era, the attachment of energy security to a long-established narrative of NATO–Russia animosity serves as a reassuring device, whose legitimizing force lies in the familiarity of these beliefs. The connection between traditional threats and emerging challenges has practical implications: it reinforces the legitimacy of a continued effort to expand security, boosting old measures and adding new tools.

Within this narrative, the identity of the 'other', in this case Azerbaijan, is also constructed. The texts refer to Azerbaijan as a loyal security partner, a reliable energy supplier, and an alternative to Russia's energy exports. The old belief of the world as divided into two competing blocs emerges in the imaginary of Azerbaijan as a 'bridge' between the two worlds of the west and the east. Given its historical geopolitical culture, the Alliance has traditionally constructed and othered geographical subjectivities depending on the perceived distance from or proximity to its western-ness. The very idea of its system of collective security is based on the construction of a collective self, based on geographical belonging and ideological closeness. NATO's energy security discourse creates a sense of both physical and cultural nearness between the Alliance and Azerbaijan. The documents have multiple references to geography and insist on describing the country as an in-between territory, connecting Europe and Asia, and therefore geographically contiguous to the transatlantic region. The country's cultural and political alignment principally results from its adherence and contribution to the liberal market: Azerbaijan is repeatedly described as an important contributor to the global and European energy market. Its proximity to NATO is also narrated as an original feature of the country's state building trajectory: the IPAP Reviews note that Azerbaijan's cooperation and partnership with NATO is practically the same age as the very independence and sovereignty of Azerbaijan. In the same spirit, the NATO–Azerbaijan relationship is said to be founded on the country's integration in the Euro-Atlantic structures and security cooperation, which finds correspondence through practices, especially the pursuit of military interoperability. Fostering interoperability implies that NATO brings forth a set of prescriptions that allow members' and partners' forces to align and act coherently, effectively and efficiently together. Azerbaijan is, therefore, socialized into western-defined norms of security via interoperability, best practices, training and joint drills. In defining the making of energy security, these norms also determine and regulate the relationship between the branches of the states involved in the design and realization of energy security policies.

The discourse also assigns specific roles to Azerbaijan and NATO. Azerbaijan's geographical location is used to justify the Alliance's presence in a region that is considered strategically important and exceptionally vulnerable. In this narrative, Azerbaijan's energy infrastructure materializes as of interest for members' security and as a global, European and transatlantic responsibility in need of external protection. This request for external protection comes to identify NATO as the natural guarantor of energy security. The legitimacy given to its intervention serves to validate the liberal, western order out of which the Alliance was born and in which it operates. The creation of NATO in 1949 responded to the desire to reduce the risk of interstate war through international regulation, institutions and cooperation: the establishment of new norms of international security went hand in hand with the construction of a wider system based on economic openness, free trade, multilateral institutions and interdependency. The transatlantic community – as the embodiment of the west – built a sense of self around a shared set of liberal norms, which are contained in the idea of security that is at the heart of NATO. The defence of the liberal order is the defence of the west; hence, the western, liberal order becomes the defining feature of global security, which, in spite of its global aspirations, remains anchored to a specific, geographically located and circumscribed order. The existence and survival of the western liberal order become the only *real* conditions for global security. In the 20th century, the foundation of the transatlantic security community came to symbolize the importance of shared liberal values as an identity and ontological affirmation, which set the west as the cradle of the best possible global order, in opposition to the communist east. The construction of the self and the other passes through the fabrication of a specific and normative imaginary of order. In the case of NATO and its security discourse, the liberal order emerges as a universal ordering principle based on international law and multilateral institutions and centred on the promotion of democracy, the rule of law, human rights and the market economy. At the heart of the liberal order lies a distinctive conception of the economy as a founding political act: its economic interdependence, based on free trade, that grants order and stability. This idea necessitates a particular view of security as the protection of the free globalized market. In NATO's energy security discourse, energy security as the protection of the liberal model emerges in the emphasis given to the 'global energy market' and the celebration of a successful Azerbaijan–Europe energy trade. Phrases like global markets, international trade, international corridors, and global network fuse security with liberal economics: free trade is presented not only as a successful economic model, but also as a defining feature of order, as opposed to the undesirable condition of disorder, and as a synonym of stability and security. The liberal order is both the condition for and the end point of global security. This discourse is also reinforced by the explicit identification of those behaviours that defy free trade, such as Russia's nationalist energy politics, as threatening to security. In this sense, not adhering to liberal values emerges as a form of insecurity. According to NATO's security discourse, energy security incorporates the core liberal belief whereby economic interconnectedness and trade are a source of peace and security among nations and, as such, commerce and economic growth can flourish only in a secure environment.

While there is a clear line between the self and the other, the western order is, as Coker (2009) notes, inclusive: it claims its universal character, has global ambitions and aims at expanding towards and integrating the non-west. Lehti et al (2020, p 18) stress that while 'liberal and the West are separate ideas ... they are often discursively conjoined'. That NATO's energy security discourse keeps its focus on the security of the west while speaking of 'international' and 'global' energy security as part of the liberal order the Alliance aims to protect, is indicative of the inferred juxtaposition of 'western' and 'liberal'. Pairing the west with the liberal order, while still recognizing the global character of that order, provides western actors and institutions with a source of legitimization that grants them superiority and leadership over the non-west. Acting as a global ordering principle, the liberal order imposes a global hierarchy, whereby the west acts as a self-appointed mastermind. Energy securitization, in this context, renders the western approach to energy security the only solution to the problem and requires the other to conform to its model and tailor its practices to fit NATO's.

The other, like Azerbaijan, are construed as in relation to the western liberal order. This process is mutually performative and relational to the extent that also western identity and the liberal order are not inherent and fixed, but learnt and exportable: it is by the acceptance of certain forms of governance and economics that a subject becomes a part of the liberal system. NATO's securitizing efforts would not be successful without the acceptance of its discourse and the adoption of its practices by the domestic stakeholders. In NATO's discourse it is largely stressed that Azerbaijan liberalized its energy industry, opened its oil and gas sector to western companies, partnered with NATO immediately after its independence from the USSR, and supported the west in the War on Terror. In NATO's discourse, Azerbaijan exemplifies the victory of the liberal world in the ex-Soviet space.

This particular account of energy security in Azerbaijan is not contested domestically, but rather embraced and reinforced. Within the diversity and complexity of the assemblage, the global and international elements have the ability to affirm themselves over the national and the local, while still requiring the engagement, support and coalition of the domestic actors. The country finds in NATO's discourse an alignment with certain imaginaries, values and expectations that are part of its national discourse, especially with regard to a dominant idea of modernity tied to the west, its lifestyle and its socio-economic model based on market capitalism. While modernity is a complex concept, and reflecting on its genealogy goes beyond the scope of this study, the most common – albeit problematic – view situates the term in relation to European and North American societies, specifically the industrial and democratic revolutions of the 19th century that established the 'Western liberal model': scholars have noted that modernity celebrates western civilization (Mignolo 2011), specifically its emphasis on technology and its capitalist economic model, able to 'replicate its resources indefinitely' (Armstrong 2002).

The appeal of western liberal modernity has found a space also in Azerbaijan's national security discourse: as Chapter 3 has shown, the country believes that economic, social and technological progress belong in its participation in western (neo)liberal institutions and the free market. As Chapter 3 pointed out, Azerbaijan's process of nation building, including the construction of its identity and polity, in the early years of its independence has passed through its attempts to be included and recognized by the others. The 'international' has affected the formation of Azerbaijan's sense of self, by informing its values. norms and practices, by fostering the desire to belong and be recognized, as well as by integrating it into institutional and political structures. Azerbaijan prides itself on its role as reliable energy supplier and security partner. These beliefs have supported Azerbaijan's political efforts to cement its relationship and cooperation with the west and its institutions, including NATO. While Baku does not openly declare an interest in acquiring the status of member, it sees the organization as the best equipped, most successful and most technologically advanced security institution. During the interviews, NATO's representatives described Azerbaijan's policymakers and intellectuals as eager to boost and deepen the partnership with the Alliance; according to them, there was hope, among the Azeri political entourage, for a more direct involvement of NATO in the physical security of the national energy network. Interviews in Azerbaijan confirmed this sentiment: the political elite showed a clear willingness to establish some sort of external guarantee for its energy infrastructure, which would include NATO's 'boots on the ground'. Azeri literature uses the North Atlantic Treaty to equate energy security with an instance of collective defence, requesting the presence of the Alliance military forces around critical energy assets. According to local scholars, the exceptionality of energy security can justify the expansion of the Alliance's founding principle to partners: they argue that the current system of partnerships, which is based mostly on consultation, is not sufficient to neutralize energy security threats and suggests a form of collective defence comparable to Article 5 to address the problem. At a joint conference on NATO's role in ensuring energy security in the Caspian Basin and protecting important energy infrastructure, Azeri participants insisted on the Alliance's promise to protect their country's energy infrastructure. This idea has created expectations in Azerbaijan's government regarding the possibility of deploying NATO's personnel on its territory and using energy security as a pretext to achieve wider national security interests. In particular, mirroring the national security discourse (see Chapter 3), this narrative seeks to conflate the insecurity of energy infrastructure with the threats of Armenian secessionists in Karabakh to finally obtain western support with the hope that a closer cooperation with NATO can give it leverage against its regional enemy. Official declarations from Azerbaijan's President Ilham Aliyev support this stance, claiming that a solution to the Karabakh conflict is possible only with the inclusion of the Alliance. In turn, NATO's energy security discourse makes no reference to Armenia and Karabakh. Albeit often left undiscussed and salient, this issue of contestation shows the tension between actors' interests, expectations and objectives. Interviewees at NATO expressed concern over Azerbaijan's 'real' intentions. It emerged that the conflict represents a major obstacle for Azerbaijan–NATO energy security cooperation. In particular, the west has not developed a sense of proximity to or responsibility in the conflict for multiple reasons. The general distrust towards Azerbaijan's leadership has hindered the rhetorical power of the country's narrative of the war and has affected the willingness of western states to provide support to the regime. A widespread geopolitical culture also limits the internationalization of this conflict, which occurs in a space that tends to be othered as a Russian concern.

According to NATO's Head of the Energy Security Section, Michael Rühle, as Azerbaijan sees energy security as 'a free ride for NATO protection in the region', it transforms energy security as a 'political and psychological means' to boast about its privileged tie with NATO and its protection net. Azerbaijan's approach to energy security is represented as emotional and irrational – 'a voodoo, pure faith'; its detachment from its materiality – according to Rühle, 'it is about psychology, rather than energy' – strips away any claim of objectivity and legitimacy from Azerbaijan's discourse. This contrasts with the depiction of NATO's approach, especially the apparent neutrality that official texts give to NATO's energy security interventions in Azerbaijan. The three IPAP Reviews use dull language: they avoid rhetoric, favour broad terminologies, and report facts and numbers. Their attention to energy materiality translates into an emphasis of its peculiar mobile, flowing, vast and varied character; these are conceived as necessary and given traits of energy and its security. In this sense, securitizing energy emerges in NATO's discourse as a neutral, technical decision, a rational calculus, rather than a political choice. These official documents represent energy security as a product of technical and rational considerations; they seek to depoliticize energy security, denying the political roots and dynamics that sustain its construction. The inherent political nature of NATO's discourse is, however, unquestionable: it emerges not only in its ability to securitize energy – and securitization is a political act – but also in its effort to allocate and affirm authority, govern energy security problems and organize responses.

NATO's energy security practices: interoperability, standardization and pedagogy

As the first military organization to include energy security in its portfolio, NATO has gained a prominent role in securing energy worldwide, even in territories that lie beyond the borders of its membership. The PfP framework and the IPAP have offered a platform to develop and implement energy security initiatives with partner states. In Azerbaijan, for instance, energy security has become a major driver, target and focus of cooperation with NATO. Energy has allowed the Alliance to strengthen its ties and presence in the country, also in line with – or as a response to – western states' and companies' considerable interests in Azerbaijan's oil and gas, especially following the liberalization of the country's energy market. The aim of this section is to analyse NATO's energy security practices in Azerbaijan and reflect on the expert role that the Alliance has taken up. Through training, capacity building and best practices, NATO's energy security programmes have become exportable anchoring practices, which states like Azerbaijan adhere and adapt to. There is a pedagogical intent that underpins NATO's intervention in energy security in Azerbaijan; analysing it helps locate and problematize the formation of epistemic authority that acts both locally and globally, while revealing how knowledge and authority flow from security practices between organizations and across borders. To understand energy securitization, it is important to approach energy security not only as a distinctive way of thinking and doing security, but also as an expression of power and its configuration: the success and dissemination of NATO's energy security practices as *the best* way of securing energy not only prove the enduring relevance and prominence of the Alliance, but are also effective tools to impose and (re)produce a specific political model of governance. Discourse analysis has revealed that energy security contains specific ideas of order that centre around liberal norms and values; this positions the Alliance as the legitimate and most suited guarantor of the security of that system. NATO's interventions in energy security in Azerbaijan go in this direction: they imply integration into NATO's arrangements as a token of the global order and shape an unprecedented framework and network that enable the Alliance's sustained involvement in energy worldwide. The western, liberal order is considered the best and only option for global security. This idea, which flows beyond the physical and institutional space of the Alliance, has spread a desire for emulation and integration. Scholars have shown that the power of the liberal order is not coercive but lies in its appeal, intended as the extent of its acceptance and the desire to be a part of it (Cox 1983; Hopf 2013; Schmidt 2018). The hegemonic force of the liberal order implies not only material, economic and military supremacy, but also the 'social and cultural dominance of [its] ideas and constitutive normative principles' (Lehti et al 2020, p 18). Its ideational order is (re)produced and legitimized through everyday practices that build consensus and transform a distinctive way of *doing* politics into the norm. NATO's interventions in energy security in Azerbaijan are based on a (sometimes tacit, other times more explicit) consensus on the Alliance's expertise, authority and legitimacy. Consensus is generated from establishing and spreading axiomatic principles, seemingly self-evident practices, and universalized modi operandi *globally*. These contain the liberal ethos and norms of the Alliance and, therefore, legitimize and normalize the everyday (re)building of the liberal order. NATO–Azerbaijan energy security cooperation happens under those instruments – namely the PfP, the Euro-Atlantic Partnership Council (EAPC) and the IPAP – that were designed and established to build consensus around the Alliance, including among non-member countries. Consensus and harmony were achieved by creating partnerships that would include third states into NATO's structure and practices, apart from its collective defence. In 1992 the creation of the North Atlantic Cooperation Council (NACC) paved the way for the development of the Azerbaijan–NATO relationship: the consultative forum, formed with other former Soviet republics and joined by Azerbaijan in 1992, offered a platform for political discussion through joint summits and ministerial and operational committees. Transformed into the EAPC in 1997, the Council has kept working as 'a ready-made framework for consulting on political-military issues' (Wallander 2000, p 722). Within the PfP and the IPAP, Azerbaijan has been able to define specific areas of practical engagement and bilateral cooperation: these two assets set out tangible objectives and priorities and intervene to build capabilities, information-sharing and interoperability among military forces. Wallander (p 731) notes that NATO's mechanisms for cooperation with non-members are built on 'NATO practices and procedures developed during the Cold War, including such mundane details as how to conduct training exercises and NATO's encompassing principles of transparency, integration, supranational defense, and civilian control'. Harmonization with the Alliance's structures and practices emerges as a guiding principle of NATO–Azerbaijan energy security cooperation. The Alliance has special training programmes across all ranks, sets the criteria to structure military staffs and troops, and contributes to defining military strategic policies. NATO was directly involved in writing Azerbaijan's National Security Concept, the Military Doctrine and the Maritime Security Strategy. NATO–Azerbaijan energy security practices centre around capacity building, joint training and education activities. NATO's Energy Security Division (ESD), which is the main body in charge of energy security within the organization and retains a political role, is a marginal actor in energy security cooperation with Azerbaijan: it principally lies with the country to raise awareness and promote cooperation, insisting on the need to protect the flow of supplies and the infrastructure. However, the ESD is still a relevant piece in the securitization of energy: the Division is an important political actor, whose responsibilities centre around political dialogue, diplomacy and mediation; as such, it has the ability to create, consolidate and spread NATO's values and norms. Political cooperation on energy security has developed also through the NATO Parliamentary Assembly, of which Azerbaijan became an associate member in 2002. The country's participation implies contributing to the Plenary Sessions of the Assembly and its deliberations; joining intergovernmental meetings, consultancies and visits; and taking part in the Parliamentary Transatlantic Forums and Rose-Roth seminars. Across these events and activities, energy security is a recurring theme. Principally, energy security is dealt with under the rubric of geopolitics and situated within Azerbaijan's regional security. These events usually discuss the challenges and opportunities of energy exports for the Caspian and Caucasus regions, while always maintaining as central the idea of a mutually beneficial cooperation between Azerbaijan and the transatlantic region. Together with political discussions, NATO's interventions in energy security possess a clear military character. In fact, most energy security practices are established within and coordinated through NATO's military bodies and the programmes that have clear practical and operational goals. The PfP and the EAPC have specific chapters on energy security and critical energy infrastructure protection. Under the remit of the Partnership and the Council, NATO organizes multiple activities and events to develop know-how and share its expertise on the protection of energy assets. As a partner, Azerbaijan participates in and hosts more than 100 learning initiatives on energy security every year. It is estimated that around 1,000 military and security professionals from Azerbaijan attend these events annually. The nature of these initiatives varies deeply – they range from academic conferences to professional training and military drills; the areas of capacity building cover tactical and operational planning and logistics, the definition of strategies and policies, and military education, including drills, exercises and learning curricula. The importance of NATO acting like a hub of practitioners and setting not only the strategic and operational side of energy security practices, but also their social dimension can be understood through the idea of 'community of practice'. Adler (2008) explains that communities of practice are groups of practitioners who work together to learn and apply a common practice; they embody 'not only the conscious and discursive dimensions and the actual doing of social change, but also the social space where structure and agency overlap and where knowledge, power, and community intersect' (p 199). While defining what energy security is, NATO also creates a collective purpose and an idea of community. Frequent meetings and joint activities provide a space for socialization, which builds relationships and networks, fosters a sense of belonging, establishes shared norms, encourages conformation and conformity, and develops a common culture. Drills and educational activities that establish best practices, procedures and guidelines, not only determine the modus operandi of energy security practices, but also instil a shared basis of understanding of threats and a respect for global norms.

Multiple educational activities and training have seen the co-participation of NATO's and Azerbaijan's forces to secure energy. These include live drills both offshore and onshore to conduct patrolling, organize checkpoints or respond to potential attacks, as well as command-post exercises and computer-assisted simulations. Most energy security practices focus on infrastructure protection, often within the framework of counterterrorism: in NATO–Azerbaijan cooperative efforts, there are important overlaps between counterterrorism and the protection of energy infrastructure. For instance, as part of the EACP, NATO launched the Partnership Action Plan against Terrorism (PAP-T), a multilateral and intergovernmental forum that established working groups to study, discuss and define solutions to multiple threats and risks connected to terrorism, including energy security and critical energy infrastructure protection. The PAP-T groups conduct risk analysis, strategic assessments, consultations, and tactical and operational planning between the Alliance and non-member countries.

Since 2008, Azerbaijan has chaired the Working Group on the protection of critical energy infrastructure, which aims at developing a common understanding of the threats and the risks to energy infrastructure, while developing best practices and shared strategies and operations in counterterrorism in the energy sector. Other joint educational activities have been launched under the NATO SPS Programme, which was instituted to promote practical cooperation between members and partners on scientific and technological innovation through knowledge exchange. Within this programme, NATO trains partner countries on the use of tools and mechanisms that prevent and increase the resilience of energy systems. Whereas the SPS Programme draws on scientific, technological and engineering research, it still retains a military focus and pays most attention to physical security, resilience and defence from potential attacks against oil and gas pipelines. For instance, in 2013, under the SPS Programme, NATO and Azerbaijan held a conference in Baku, which brought together military and security experts to address energy security within strategies of cyber defence and counterterrorism.

The NATO Energy Security Centre of Excellence (ENSECCOE) offers another institutional framework for establishing and sharing expertise in energy security with NATO members and partners. While the ENSECCOE is an external agency, it is coordinated by the HQ of the Allied Command Transformation, NATO's main military structure. The centre works to prevent and mitigate the potential effects of energy scarcity worldwide, favouring viewing security in military terms. NATO and Azerbaijan discussed the creation of a Partnership Training and Education Centre on Energy Security based in Baku that would mimic the ENSECCOE and would provide 'qualitative training and education in line with the interoperability objectives and priorities in energy security' (NATO 2014). Although there is a lot of enthusiasm in Azerbaijan among government officials and the media, NATO's representatives are more sceptical about the effective possibility of establishing a joint centre in the country. So far, the centre has never been set up; interviews point to multiple challenges that prevent its establishment. Azerbaijan seems unwilling to accept NATO's binding conditions that determine the creation of its Centres of Excellence. These include the mandatory participation of all NATO's partners, including Armenia; the presence of the Internet across the country and without censorship; and more governmental transparency and the promotion of civil participation in decision making. This suggests that there is harmony only on certain aspects of the liberal order: while there is an alignment on the view of energy as an expression of military security and the market economy, emancipatory political liberal values are ostracized. As such, it seems implausible that the centre will ever become a reality.

In the meantime, Azerbaijan has established a summer school in Baku, called NISA (NATO International School of Azerbaijan). The extent of NATO's involvement in the school is unclear, as well as the school's affiliation to the Alliance. Nonetheless, NATO officers and experts participated in the courses to lecture young Azeri practitioners on issues related to energy security. The curriculum includes energy and border security, critical energy infrastructure protection, maritime energy security and cyber energy security. The Ministry of Defence promotes NISA as a unique learning opportunity for national forces, especially to gain combat capability and achieve coordination and interoperability with NATO's members. Since the early 2000s, Azerbaijan's Higher Military Academy, the War College of the Armed Forces and the Education and Training Centre of the Armed Forces have adopted NATO's criteria and guidelines for the military education system. Every year, these schools offer training to senior security and military professionals, including ad hoc courses on energy security and energy infrastructure protection. Under NATO's mandate, US military personnel were deployed to shape the curriculum of Azerbaijan's military institutes and enhanced their IT systems. In 2019, for example, Azerbaijan's army personnel participated in tactical and computer-assisted military exercises that targeted energy infrastructure security in the Caspian region. These educational activities aim at preparing Azerbaijan's military forces and bases for NATO exercises and achieving operational interoperability, which remains a leading principle of NATO–Azerbaijan cooperation. Interoperability implies the modernization of Azerbaijan's security and military forces, structures and strategies. For

NATO, a major objective of its cooperation with non-member countries is to develop the capabilities and assets that third countries need to operate alongside Allied nations. NATO–Azerbaijan energy security cooperation shares this goal: NATO and Azerbaijan have been working to upgrade the country's army's logistics support and system, modernize and replace its military equipment, and renovate its communication system. In the past decade, most modernization effort has focused on developing capability in emerging technology. NATO has substantially invested in disruptive technologies based on the use of command and control, big data, artificial intelligence, autonomous systems and hypersonic vehicles.

Compared to western countries, Azerbaijan's technological capability is considered to be inadequate. In the energy sector, the Alliance and Azerbaijan share concern over the country's lack of technological assets, especially offshore. Azerbaijan suffers from limited capability in Maritime Domain Awareness (MDA), especially compared to its Caspian neighbours. To counter its lack of technology, Azerbaijan has physically deployed a large number of vessels to identify what happens within its waters and close to its energy fields. In the 2010s Azerbaijan owned only limited shore-based radar, which covered no more than 30 per cent of its maritime section and functioned only within 25 miles of visibility from the coast, meaning it could not reach the oilfields that lie between 75 and 100 miles from its shores. The Alliance, especially US forces under NATO's remit, helped Azerbaijan upgrade its MDA to comply with NATO's standards: in 2013 the US EUCOM provided control and communications equipment and installed an interoperable command system, including sensors and communication networks for Azerbaijan's navy and air force. They established a joint command-and-control centre for the navy and the coastguard and installed a long-range, round-the-clock radar capability for coastal surveillance in the city of Baku. The coastal surveillance system was then complemented with land-based sensors and cameras, additional radar on Chilov Island approximately 30 miles from the Azeri coast, and a new maritime surveillance system to provide real-time, over-the-horizon surveillance of large sea areas. Given the extensive presence of military and security personnel, there is clear evidence that the digital culture has not replaced the more traditional, 'off the grid' and tangible modus operandi. Conversely, the emphasis and centrality given to technology and automation point as much to a material need for energy securitization as to a certain ideational vision, which belongs in the idea of modernity previously discussed. In particular, it amplifies the faith, which belongs in western liberal modernity, in science and technology as tools that can potentially neutralize what threatens human life and make absolute security a possibility. The desire to control and ideally annihilate insecurity reorients the focus of energy security practices towards risks and probabilities: this means increasing the use of tools to prevent and manage risks, enlarging their geographical and institutional space, and extending their duration time wise. These practices are making energy security about the management of risks rather than of threat; they are oriented towards future scenarios and prevention. Technology, in this sense, emerges as a new provider of energy security, which affects the tangible, material, contours of energy securitization.

As anticipated, technological devices and automation also speak to the social configurations that compose the assemblage as a cultural process. There is a clear reputational ambition and a distinctive view of progress and modernity that pushes Azerbaijan to acquire and update its MDA, IT systems, and disruptive and surveillance technologies to comply with international standards. Supporting a partner country transitioning towards the automation of security provisions is not only NATO's way of providing out-of-the-box solutions to an emerging challenge, but also a mode of accruing its credibility as the global expert, guarantor and supplier of security. In so doing, the Alliance is promoting a specific way of doing energy security, as well as a distinctive form – which is the *right* form – of being modern, advanced and avant-garde. As previously mentioned, the marriage between security and modernity is reflected also in the way contemporary societies reorient their security towards risk. This is expressed in the work of famous sociologists such as Giddens and Beck, who have used the term 'risk society' to identify an increasing preoccupation with the future (Giddens 1990) and 'a systematic way of dealing with hazards and insecurities induced and introduced by modernization itself' (Beck 1992, p 21). Modernity, as an embodiment of the western liberal order, renders NATO's energy practices a widely accepted global benchmark, especially for those countries, like Azerbaijan, that aspire to be *modern*.

The political dimension of energy securitization is clear. It emerges, for example, through the tension that exists within the assemblage. Between the national and the international there are multiple forms of disagreement as to what energy ought to be secured and how. There is, for instance, a discrepancy between NATO's declared intention of not militarizing energy in Azerbaijan and its committed effort – welcomed by the domestic elite – to improve, enhance and broaden the provision of military security in and around energy sites. Similarly, there is not always correspondence between the geopolitical imaginaries of NATO and Azerbaijan, especially the sentiments towards Armenia, Russia or Iran. These contrasts and divisions tend to be reassembled through attempts at depoliticization. Energy security is treated as a technical and neutral problem; its reference object and its threats are often left undefined and inexplicit. NATO's responsibilities, duties and interventions in energy security largely remain imprecise, giving the Alliance more flexibility and options to cooperate with Azerbaijan and overcome potential political impasses and conflict. The multilateral character of the Alliance also obscures its role in initiating and articulating specific policies and practices. Labelling energy security as 'global' effectively hides the localized interests that sustain it, allowing for its consolidation and diffusion. While leaving the areas of tension open and ignored, energy securitization operates by reinforcing the points of convergence between Azerbaijan and NATO, which in neither case defies the status quo: energy security practices rely on the state's existing security structures, confirm the Alliance as the main international security actor and global interlocutor, and finally insert both the global and the local in a liberal circuit which finds consensus on both sides.

Moreover, NATO's pedagogical efforts, its harmonizing intents and its benchmarking practices point out specific characteristics of the (neo)liberal order that amplify its market-driven nature and try to hide their political character. Building on the work of Fougner (2008, p 308), best practices can be seen as attempts to depoliticize practices and political actors, by constituting 'states as technocratic agencies' and 'competitive entities driven not by internal socio-political processes, but rather by external or global standards of conduct'.

This chapter has positioned the assemblage as the most appropriate metaphor to account for the heterogeneity of energy securitization, beyond traditional binaries. In particular, it has shown that energy securitization is not defined by the borders of the state. In its actually existing dimension, the 'national' does not exhaust the ideational and material space of energy securitization but assembles with a tendency to understand and govern security threats at the global scale. To understand energy securitization as an assemblage that (dis)entangles the national and the global points to increasingly common political processes, whereby 'localised problems began to acquire increasing international significance' (Fussey 2013, p 353). This changes not only the nature and scale of the threat – namely its ontology – but also the political vision that sustains the energy security project. The reimagination of energy security as a global concern requires moving beyond the idea that securitization stems exclusively from national and nationalist mentalities and practices. Failing to recognize the role of non-national actors in energy securitization confines securitization to an oversimplified and abstract space, marked by false spatial dichotomies. As explained in Chapter 2, the division between national/international, global/local, internal/external and domestic/foreign is not only erroneous, but also neglects the complexity and relationality of the social space of energy securitization and prevents a serious engagement with the cultural, social and political nature of energy security. The following chapter focuses on another neglected dimension of securitization, namely the role of private companies as securitizing actors, to overcome the theoretical and empirical fallacies hidden by an idea of securitization along public-private binaries.

6

Energy Securitization and the Private Sector: The Case of BP

When Heydar Aliyev signed the Contract of the Century with a consortium of multinational corporations in 1994, he opened up Azerbaijan's oil and gas sector to foreign investors. While the government decided not to privatize the industry and retain control over its assets and wealth, they also realized that the prospect of profits and new business projects required substantial investments. Aliyev saw external financial intervention as the main hope for the country's economic recovery and decided to make the industry reliant on external financing. Seeing no incentive to limit foreign participation, Aliyev sought to create the most favourable investment environment by eliminating any entry barrier to foreign private companies and inviting energy multinationals to take a direct role in managing and developing the country's natural resources. Aliyev's decision stands out when compared to the choices made by the leaders of Azerbaijan's neighbouring countries: in the early years after the dissolution of the USSR, among the newly born countries there was still much reticence towards international actors, to the extent that Turkmenistan and Uzbekistan opted to keep full state ownership of their energy industry and rejected the possibility of foreign investments, while the Russian Federation decided to privatize the industry domestically, opening the sector only to Russian capitalists (Luong and Weinthal 2001). Kazakhstan emerges as a peculiar and exceptional case: while in the first years of its independence (1991), the government opted for liberalizing the sector and opening the oil and gas industry to foreign investors, since the mid 2000s it has reversed its policy and opted for a progressive nationalization of its energy assets (see Orazgaliyev 2019).

Today, Azerbaijan's energy industry is fully integrated into the global energy market and completely dependent on foreign investments. This is not an exceptional case but reflects larger trends within the energy sector. Overall, the energy industry – especially oil and gas – is considered by many as the most capitalized and globalized sector on the planet (Boal et al 2005; Di Muzio 2016). It is understood as emblematic of the globalized neoliberal, capitalist economy: it abides by capitalist rules, and capitalism cannot survive without energy production and consumption. Oil, in particular, emerges as the most influential commodity: with a market value of trillions of dollars, it provides liquidity to markets, while generating the capital that is then used to finance the capital-intensive extractive industry. Scholars point to the commodification and monetization of energy resources; the centrality of oil and gas to most – if not all – contemporary socio-economic and industrial process as indicative of 'a global petro-market civilisation' (Di Muzio 2016), the transformation of oil into 'a key item of market currency' (Boal et al 2005). I have already argued against empty, metonymical understandings of energy and oversimplified views of the energy–security nexus (see Chapter 1), in favour of an attention to actually existing energy securitization. However, energy securitization cannot be fully grasped without an appreciation of the intersection between security and the neoliberal, capital-oriented order, especially considering the role of Azerbaijan's oil and gas industry in the global market. This pragmatically translates into an analysis that looks at the private sector as a fundamental piece of the energy security assemblage.

In this chapter, I aim to expose the privatized dimension of energy securitization. This analysis situates energy security in discourses and practices of security that are defined ontologically and politically by private property. In particular, this chapter looks at the case of the British energy company BP with the aim of reflecting on its peculiar role in securitizing energy in Azerbaijan. By doing so, I continue the exploration of the often overlooked dimensions and transversal elements of energy securitization by focusing on the private sector as a securitizing agent. While this analysis inevitably engages with and contributes to the rich literature that has explored and questioned the proliferation of private security and military companies since the mid 20th century and their impact on international politics and security (Avant 2005; Neocleous 2008; Abrahamsen and Williams 2011; Dunigan and Peterson 2015), its case study is singular and distinct: rather than examining a security and military firm, this book looks at an energy company that takes on responsibility and authority for security operations.

It remains to clarify what I intend by the terms neoliberalism and neoliberal order. The other case studies have already indicated that energy securitization in Azerbaijan interlaces security with a specific economic model, based on the (neo)liberal principles of interdependence and free trade. Both Azerbaijan and NATO securitize energy security through specific construction of the market as a source of peace and security and as an object that deserves protection. Bilateral partnerships and western multilateralism find their reason in the global interconnectedness of the energy markets and make security about the protection of trade, including the protection of the physical structures that enable commerce. So far, this book has shown that energy securitization connects security with distinctive economic norms, values, imaginaries and also biases that are typical of the western liberal order in which energy security operates. The 'liberal order' has previously been framed as the specific post-war order established by western democracies, with its ideologies, norms and values that are centred on western cooperation and multilateralism. This chapter focuses on the case of BP to unpack the relationship between securitization and neoliberalism, here intended as 'a particular regime of liberalism' (Phelan and Dawes 2018). David Harvey (2005, p 19), a leading Marxist scholar, understands neoliberalism as a system that 're-establish[es] the conditions for capital accumulation and restore[s] the power of economic elites', specifically by maximizing market transactions and bringing the social into the domain of the market. Of course, neoliberalism – like liberalism – is a complex and contested term and should not be approached as a single, unitary project; however, as Madeleine Reeves (2015) puts it, 'the devaluing of [neoliberalism as] a descriptive currency' – that is to acknowledge its essentially contested essence – does not deny the existence of 'a complex set of intersecting material, political and economic processes … that are both systematically interlinked and present in ever more domains of social and public life'. Therefore, it is possible to detect in neoliberalism certain specific rationalities and practices. Specifically it points to an entrepreneurial twist of the more general liberal project: neoliberalism emphasizes entrepreneurial values, self-care and personal responsibility; it exalts the primacy of capital; it values practices that are oriented towards the maximization of profits; it foments privatization and public-private partnerships; it transforms public goods into marketable commodities; and it tends to – ontologically and politically – see actors as consumers. Recognizing the bundle between neoliberalism and securitization enables a reflection that does not stop at security and recognizes its mutually constitutive and performative relationship with the economic order in which it operates.

This chapter is organized as follows. The first section provides a historical overview of the role of private energy companies, especially the British BP, in the development of Azerbaijan's energy industry, with the aim to introduce the deep connection and shared interests that characterize public-private relationships in the country. The second and third sections present the empirical findings of my research on BP's security discourse and practices. To conclude, this chapter uses a case study to reflect upon the assembly between securitization and neoliberalism and its theoretical and empirical implications.

Based on the empirical analysis, which combines discourse analysis, mapping and semi-structured interviews, the following sections bring forward four main arguments. First, this research signals the assembly of the private with the public sector, the constant mediation between the state and private companies in the definition of energy security practices, and the skein of authority and expertise that their assembly forms. This chapter reveals that also BP acts as a securitizing actor of energy in Azerbaijan: its discourse and practices position energy security as the primary condition for the company to exist, while attaching it to defence and enforcement. In the analysis, it emerges, once again, that the way security is problematized lacks emancipatory potential and persistently refers to defence and enforcement. However, the case of BP also points to something unique, something that has timidly come to the surface in the other two case studies but here becomes a predominant factor, namely the encroachment of neoliberal rationalities and techniques in securitization. This analysis shows that in BP's discourse and practices, energy securitization and neoliberalism interlace in a particular way, whereby security enlarges private profits and the neoliberal propensity towards the maximization of profits reinforces security as securitization. This transforms how energy security is thought and done.

In its second argument, this chapter contends that energy securitization ends up embodying and diffusing the neoliberal principles of autonomy, efficiency and privatization, creating a legitimate space for energy companies and private security contractors to provide security services that break the state's monopoly over force. In particular, energy securitization in Azerbaijan has allowed BP to enlarge its corporate structure and create an ad hoc security department, expand its business portfolio, increase its resources, expand its remits, spread its network, deepen its ties with the state, boost its role and power in the country, and establish itself as a source of expertise and a legitimate administrator of force.

As a third point, this case study highlights that, although neoliberalism is usually associated with limiting state control while promoting and instituting the market as the main governing principle, it does not do so by neutralizing the state; conversely, this reconfiguration of power and authority, which is enabled and consolidated by and through security, brings benefits to both the state and the private sector.

Through the analysis of BP, this chapter advances a fourth argument: by maintaining and feeding the desire for security, energy and security companies comply with and consolidate a way of doing security that is typical of the state of Azerbaijan; this normalizes and reasserts security as securitization by fomenting militarization and policing. As such, securitization and neoliberalism are not only co-constituted, but also mutually reinforced. What emerges out of their assembly is illustrative of the illiberal nature that underlines both energy securitization and neoliberalism and that is exacerbated in their conjunction.

The peculiar liberalization of Azerbaijan's oil and gas industry

After independence, in the dawn of its transition out of Soviet communism, Azerbaijan did not immediately move towards integration into the world economy. In 1991, early attempts at price liberalization and privatization led to GDP shrinking and hyperinflation rates, making new governments cautious about drastic changes. When Elchibey took power in 1992, the liberalization of the economy was not the priority. Elchibey's party, the APF, was fervently nationalist, possessed a heavily protectionist approach to the economy, and showed ambivalence towards international institutions like the IMF and the World Bank. Yet, the country could no longer boast the advantages and safety of being part of an integrated economic bloc and had to confront the reality of operating in an increasingly global and competitive market. The problem of what economic model the new republic had to adopt to become competitive and survive was, therefore, central to the new republic and had to be addressed while building the state. To the new government, it soon appeared evident that oil could be the potential answer to the country's economic volatility; it could grant access to the global market and help Azerbaijan outlive the political chaos of the first years of its transition. While Elchibey was eager to open up the oil industry – which the government saw as the only hope for the country's economic relief and growth – to western companies and investment, he was not motivated by either a faith in the free market or by honest enthusiasm towards neoliberal values and aspirations. In other words, Elchibey was not interested in integrating Azerbaijan's economy into neoliberalism. Instead, developing partnerships with western energy companies was part of Elchibey's government's vision to affirm the country's national sovereignty and newly found independence, especially against Russia and its political influence. According to Elchibey and his political entourage, the USSR's policy towards Azerbaijan's oil had imposed a colonial model on the industry, whereby Russia could retain control over the country's resources and revenues without developing or investing in its indigenous capabilities. Elchibey intended to render the oil and gas sector autonomous from Soviet structures and systems; this move represented both a symbolic and a tangible sign of the country's re-established autonomy and self-determination: trade agreements would give access to new markets, and novel infrastructure would create alternative transport networks. It was with this spirit that Elchibey accepted the requests of the UK government and the British oil company BP to meet and discuss the possibility of British investments in Azerbaijan's oil sector. During a ceremony with then Prime Minister Thatcher, Elchibey signed a preliminary agreement with BP to allow the company to start exploration at the Chiraq and Shah Deniz fields near the capital city of Baku. A few months later, in September 1993, a political coup interrupted Elchibey's government and his policy efforts. Nonetheless, the overthrow did not stop the economic transition and the opening up of Azerbaijan's energy industry. With the arrival of Heydar Aliyev, Azerbaijan's partnerships with foreign energy companies deepened. Unlike his predecessor, Aliyev – a former high-ranking Soviet official – discerned oil development from nationalist principles and prioritized foreign capital and the integration of Azerbaijan into the global market economy over anti-Russian sentiments. His pragmatic focus on profits resulted in an appeasing and pragmatic attitude towards Russia: Aliyev recognized that Moscow had the ability to obstruct Azerbaijan's oil deals and operations and, as a consequence, he decided to adopt a balancing foreign policy aimed at finding a compromise with its neighbour. Despite his conciliatory attitude towards Russia, Heydar Aliyev kept looking to the west as his primary interlocutor and prioritized cooperation with western states, western organizations and western companies further. Unlike Elchibey's government, Aliyev was not suspicious of the global economic and financial institutional architecture. The first years of Heydar Aliyev's regime were marked by serious economic reforms in line with the stabilization programme agreed with the IMF. These restructurings, embedded in neoliberal theories and principles, centred around the oil industry as a catalyst for and insurer of growth and wealth through integration in the global market. In its assessment, the IMF (1993) considered Azerbaijan unable to develop the potential of its energy industry or manage its existing access through its indigenous capability, largely due to the country's lack of advanced technology and investments. The reforms pushed for the liberalization of trade and prices, the abolition of subsidies and the simultaneous introduction of foreign loans and stocks, and the reorganization of the economy around the export-oriented and capital-intensive oil sector. According to economists, neoliberal programmes aimed to reorganize the economy in such a way that the market would allocate resources and the state would be financially solvent (Przeworski 1991). Islam (1993) identified four key drivers of the neoliberal transition, the so-called interlocking wheels of market-oriented reforms, which included macroeconomic stabilization, liberalization, privatization and institutional reforms. These changes not only brought inflows of money through funds and investments, but also shifted the country's political focus, driver and referent object away from domestic social welfare and towards integration into the global economy as a priority and a founding political act.

In Azerbaijan, the structural economic adjustments that marked the transition out of Soviet socialism sought to bring a deep transformation and restructuring of the state governance too. Based on the neoliberal principles of efficiency, cost-effectiveness and simplification, the reforms aimed at creating space for the private sector at the expense of the state's bureaucracy. Nonetheless, in the country, as in other former Soviet Union states, integration into the global market did not bring a full liberalization of the economy but coexisted with the centralized ownership and management of key economic assets. In the case of the energy industry, for example, the domestic sector has remained under government control and vertically integrated: SOCAR, Azerenergy and Azerigas have remained under state ownership. This is, at least partially, a result of a chaotic process of privatization (Flegel 2016), but more importantly they are a legacy of Azerbaijan's Soviet past. Scholars of post-socialism (Ganev 2005; Collier 2011; Reeves 2014; Leykin 2019) have demonstrated that the transition towards neoliberalism and the consolidation of the neoliberal project in the former communist republics did not result in a departure from the Soviet heritage. Rather than one of the two poles of a binary, neoliberalism has fused its logics with Soviet forms of knowledge in ways that challenge the conceptual validity of the traditional and essentialized dichotomies of public versus private value; social versus post-social; the state versus the market; solidarity versus individualism (Collier 2011). This thesis espouses what geographers Brenner and Theodore (2002, p 349) have identified as the broader 'contextual embeddedness of neoliberal restructuring projects'. They correctly argue that neoliberal projects 'have been produced within national, regional, and local contexts defined by the legacies of inherited institutional frameworks, policy regimes, regulatory practices, and political struggles' (p 349). In her study on women and entrepreneurship in post-Soviet Azerbaijan, Farideh Heyat (2002) notes that following the country's independence, most private companies were still controlled by former Communist Party leaders and Aliyev's extended family, claiming that this pattern was 'not so different from that of the late Soviet period' (p 20). Marina Ottaway (2013) explains that despite his programme of neoliberal reforms, Heydar Aliyev's efforts to maintain control over most assets replicated a well-established model of unchallenged control and institutionalized corruption. These arguments resonate with the research behind this book and reinforce my previous reflections on the pervasiveness of Soviet ideas, imaginaries and practices of power, which found a home in the hyper-personified and authoritarian regime of the Aliyev family (Chapter 3). The authoritarian character of Heydar and Ilham Aliyev's regimes has, in fact, an important impact in maintaining forms of economic monopolization: it has prevented the diffusion of authority and power and enhanced the consolidation and fixation of elitist poles. As Chapter 4 has shown, in post-Soviet Azerbaijan power has remained clustered around established close-knit clans. Access to the wealthiest sectors such as oil has mostly stayed in the hands of leading members of the government and the security elite, despite the opening up of the sector. In the country there is an overlap between the state and private businesses to the extent that distinguishing between state and private interests is not always possible. The integration into the global market coexists with a domestic business environment marked by patronage and rentierism. In the country political power grants access to wealth, and access to wealth is often restricted to those who exert political power. The country's private companies are either directly owned or influenced by members of the government. Nonetheless, the World Bank describes the country as a 'top global reformer', which has managed to grant an optimal environment to foreign investments by protecting private interests and property. The coexistence of neoliberal rationalities with Azerbaijan's cultural, historical and political idiosyncrasies points to the tensions and struggles that constitute the assemblage of energy securitization. These blur the lines of division, which traditionally distinguish between the local and the global, and the private and the public. In particular, energy securitization renders visible the constant (dis)assembly between persistent local(ized) forms of governance and global(ized), neoliberal and largely western structures and rationalities. At the same time, it also illustrates the encroachment of the private sector into the public sphere. In these bundles, securitization and neoliberalism mutually reinforce their respective logics. It is this mutual benefit that creates a sense of coherence in the assembly of heterogeneous elements and diverse projects – the security and the economic, the local and the global, the private and the public. In particular, what emerges out of their assembly is indicative of the illiberal nature that undergirds both energy securitization and neoliberalism.

This seems to contrast with the idea of neoliberalism as an evolution of the liberal project. However, by recognizing the contingencies, peculiarities and even incoherence of neoliberalism, scholars have dismissed the conventional stereotyped idea of an alleged inevitable link between (neo)liberalism and democracy. Studies have highlighted how neoliberal economic principles can coexist with illiberal practices: while the detachment of neoliberal economies from liberal values and policies represents well the case of Azerbaijan, a 'neoliberalism without liberals', as Matza illustrates, is also indicative of the wider 'flexible promiscuity, discursive power, and political life of neoliberal techniques' (2009, pp 493–4). Other scholars have explored security as a strategy for expanding capital (Neocleous 2008), enabling accumulation and dispossession (Massé and Lunstrum 2016), bolstering corporatism and capitalism (Taylor 2009), and reproducing and multiplying the social, economic and even physical, geographical divisions that have emerged out of neoliberal globalization (Davis 1998, 2006; Sloterdijk 2009; Graham 2010). This is an important point that is confirmed by this analysis: energy securitization in Azerbaijan embodies neoliberal rationalities and techniques that inhibit transparency, accountability and oversight and exacerbate the illiberal character of security. It initially emerges in three evident ways. First, the role of private companies in securing energy feeds the desire for and fixation on security as military and policing. Second, ownership defines authority and transforms energy security from a good that should benefit the collective to a private property and commodity that serves the interest of a private. Third, ownership and autonomy legitimize private actors as security providers, subjected to independent regulations and largely exempted from public scrutiny.

Security as autonomy, efficiency and self-responsibility

As the previous section explained, BP was the first oil company that the Azeri leadership approached in its first years of independence and transition out of the Soviet Union. BP started operating in Azerbaijan in 1994, when the Contract of the Century entered into effect. Since then, the company has turned into the foreign leader of Azerbaijan's oil sector, becoming the largest investor and the prime shareholder in the AIOC. This implies the company owns the major share of the energy infrastructure that the AIOC commissions and builds. As a consequence, following the Contract of the Century, BP has taken the lead in the development of the country's oil and gas industry. Although other PSAs were signed with other companies, the most substantial contribution to the country's oil and gas production rate came almost entirely from BP's managed assets. The company operates Azerbaijan's main producing field, that is the Azeri-Chirag-Gunashli complex, as well as the Shah Deniz natural gas and condensate fields. It also owns the largest shares of the Sangachal Terminal, one of the world's biggest processing terminals, the BTC pipeline and the South Caucasus Pipeline, of which it is also the main operator. BP is responsible for the long-term planning and day-to-day operations in the country's main oil and gas sites and largest offshore facilities, and it manages the regional pipelines in all transit states.

Throughout its long presence operating in Azerbaijan, BP has developed a clear strategy and vision of security and has established institutions and practices accordingly. These are founded on and expressed by BP in numerous documents, in which a specific energy security discourse emerges. The analysis of this discourse indicates what the company views as the energy security referent, what threats it fears, and whom it considers to be the legitimate agent of security. To identify and examine BP's energy security discourse, I considered a large quantity of BP's official documents, including all the Sustainability Reviews published between 2003 and 2016. Every year, BP Azerbaijan – the company's branch in the country – releases a corporate report, the so-called Sustainability Review, which outlines the activities and results of the division, offers a rich amount of data and statistics, and comments on the company's performance. The analysis of the Reviews has been complemented with the study of the 'BP-Azerbaijan Protocol on the implementation of security and human rights principle in the provision of security', which is a legal contract signed by the company and the government in 2007 to regulate defence and enforcement operations on energy sites and define their legal boundaries. This study has also integrated the analysis of the Voluntary Principles, a blueprint produced in 2000 between the extractive industries and civil society organizations and NGOs backed by the US and UK government to establish a set of principles that determine how companies should conduct their security operations while respecting human rights.

These documents point to a process of energy securitization, which constructs energy as a critical security concern – the company's 'top priority' – and attaches it to the conventional logic of security, aimed at a mix of defence and enforcement. The documents introduce a distinction between safety and security, but this is not truly embraced in its discourse, which remains centred on security. In the reports, safety is defined as the absence of accident and harm to people; the company's commitment to safety responds to its efforts to avoid unnecessary risks in the workplace, guarantee safe, reliable and compliant operations, and address numerous risks, such as fire, chemical dangers or heat stress. Security is not defined as clearly as safety but is always associated with military and paramilitary practices. All Sustainability Reviews contain specific chapters on security which inform on defence and enforcement operations and explicitly warn against the risks of terrorism and armed attacks. The distinction between security and safety does not weaken the securitized dimension of BP's discourse; in turn, safety is absorbed by security, it is itself treated as a primary security issue which, added to traditional security threats, gives a picture of multiple and variegated risks. Safety as a part of security increases the perception of danger and the call for security solutions that remain in the military and paramilitary spheres.

The identification of energy security threats is not a central question in the documents; the main focus of the security sections remains on the military and paramilitary operations of energy security, BP's investments in the provision of security, and the assessment of BP's security tools and measures. While the previous two case studies – namely, Azerbaijan's national security discourse and NATO's global security discourse – have paid considerable attention to what and who threaten energy security, BP's documents provide only marginal analysis of energy security threats but offer a detailed overview of the security providers. Thus, it emerges that BP's discourse principally aims at addressing the question of authority. For BP, energy securitization is less concerned with the process of threat construction and more oriented towards the question of threat management, especially who holds legitimate authority in the field. BP's discourse revolves around the question of legitimacy, agency and authority. All documents contain a large number of details about who provides energy security. Along national security actors, labelled as 'public' or 'governmental' security, BP also recognizes and claims a space for non-state actors and private entities, which work to ensure 'operator security'. In doing so, BP's discourse sets the private sector as a legitimate security provider and, therefore, implies that the company and its contractors can rightfully use or threaten to use force to secure energy. The point of BP's discourse is to affirm the existence, relevance and rightfulness of private security actors as legitimate sources of security, as well as of authority. This is a crucial point as the creation of a political authority is inherently tied not only to who uses force but also to who has the ability to decide about the use of force.

While the following section shows that the creation of legitimate authority is mirrored by a wide range of security activities, the status of experts given to private actors, and their participation in multilateral, institutional platforms, here I want to reflect on the cardinal rationalities that emerge in BP's discourse. The assemblage remains once again a pertinent and evocative metaphor to encompass the multiplicity and diversity of energy securitization. In fact, BP's discourse makes evident that, while security is central in its construction of legitimate authority, it is not the only element. Energy securitization assembles a diversified array of values, imaginaries, norms and logics that are not exhausted by security itself. In particular, as energy security threats are subjected to commercial evaluations, neoliberal rationalities and techniques are central to BP's securitizing efforts and have clear implications for the definition of energy security practices, their objectives, their tools and their evaluation criteria. Whereas these cannot necessarily be explained in terms of security, they do affect how security and securitization work. In particular, three distinctive features, which can be identified in BP's discourse, are deeply tied to neoliberal rationalities and techniques. First, there is a shift in the conceptualization of energy: BP's discourse moves energy away from the idea of energy as a public good and establishes it as a commodity and an object of private property. Second, BP's discourse introduces a different set of values, ascribable to a neoliberal, entrepreneurial culture, which centres around autonomy and efficiency. Third, BP sets private companies as the legitimate, capable and optimal providers of security. These three points are analysed here.

In BP's discourse, the legitimacy of the company's use of force resides in its ownership of energy assets. The referents of energy security are the infrastructure, the facilities, the physical assets and the capital that the company owns and manages. There is clear reference to the onshore and offshore facilities, the oil and gas pipelines, the platforms and the terminals that are BP's responsibility, as well as the offices and buildings it owns partially or totally. The spatiality of security is, therefore, defined by the contours of property, on which lies the foundation of the company's authority and of its security mandate. This also has ontological implications for energy security itself: as energy is defined by ownership, it emerges as a private – rather than a public – good. Whereas public goods are collectively accessible and are by definition non-excludable and non-rivalrous, private commodities are inherently excludable and exclusionary: they are at and for the service of the owners. As a consequence, the right to security is held and defined by who owns the property.

Moreover, the emphasis on ownership prioritizes a look at the most material, tangible aspects of the security referent: energy security threats are foremost a danger to the physical existence of the company. This is in contrast with the previous two cases, whose claims of authority and the boundaries of security were defined by the menace posed by energy insecurity not just to their bare, material existence, but also to their identity and sense of self. Both Azerbaijan and NATO attach the idea of security as survival to the protection of ideational, political, cultural and moral symbols that are critical not only for the construction of their identity, but also for the building of the nation and of the western, liberal order, respectively. In the case of BP, the emphasis on the physical aspects of energy anchors security to the most tangible elements that materially enable both the survival of the company, as well as the survival and security of the free market, intended here not just as an order of values and norms, but also as the material exchange of commodities and a space marked by private property. As such, the ideational factors that uphold energy securitization are only marginally tied to the construction of the threat, and they tend to emerge more vividly in the definition of how to manage insecurity. According to BP, security is essentially about 'good business'. BP's discourse embraces an entrepreneurial, corporate and business-oriented culture that focuses on the ability and responsibility of an individual or an institution to provide security. BP's discourse is rich in references to security as 'everyone's responsibility', 'collective responsibility', 'operating responsibly' and the 'task of every employee'. These terms connect security to individual behaviours but also resort to the idea of security as 'the sense of security'. In doing so, they evoke corporate values to claim an ethical commitment to good practice, while transforming security – as safety, well-being, survival – into a business strategy. The emphasis on individuality encourages a different ethos, centred on the responsibility of the singular and grounded in a 'do-it-yourself' culture that flourishes in an environment marked by private property rights, free markets and free trade. Energy securitization resonates with the neoliberal rationalities that attempt to order societies through market logics based on the responsibilization of the individual, rather than the state. This depoliticizes the social and structural roots of social problems and renders security a service rather than a collective right.

The emphasis on autonomy and self-responsibility should not be reconnected exclusively to the act of a singular person, but to the company itself: as a matter of fact, a corporation – like BP – is legally defined as a singular entity that possesses all the rights of a person. It is in this spirit that BP's discourse should be approached. This opens up the earlier-mentioned question of authority. Framing security as a matter of individual responsibility allocates legitimate authority to private actors and becomes crucial to justify and normalize the increasing presence, independence and power of private entities in the provision of security. Moreover, neoliberal, entrepreneurial values are also expressed in how BP's discourse defends the autonomy of the company and the private security contractors in securing energy assets, as well as their efficiency in conducting their operations. Autonomy and efficiency belong in the typical neoliberal imaginary of the invisible hand of the market; more precisely, the two principles drive the widespread ideal of the private sector as the optimal service provider, which acts exclusively according to a rational cost-benefit calculus. The efficiency of the private sector is constructed in opposition to the inefficiency of the public, which becomes a metaphor for incompetence, inactivity and impotence. BP's discourse emphasizes that the security services offered by the company and its contractors contribute, support and complement the work of the state personnel. In the fieldwork, it has emerged that relationships between private security agents and state security professionals are characterized by mutual mistrust; the company tends to underline that the private sector is traditionally a much more efficient, effective and capable actor. Some interviewees mentioned that the state often obstructs energy security practices. The state's lengthy bureaucratic processes are perceived to inhibit private companies and their ability to respond more quickly to potential threats. Similarly, comments were shared with regard to the state's security agents operating outside BP's perimeter, who were described as frequently unprepared and unprofessional. That BP is taking up the expert status signals a change in the way security is governed, which is not exempted from resistance and struggle, including attempts to challenge the quality of state authority: some interviewees highlighted that BP has been employing more and more private contractors over the years, who are often unskilled and unequipped. These testimonies cite examples of severe operational mistakes, lack of compliance with basic security guidelines, and overall unprofessional behaviours, including failures in conducting simple tasks like closing fences properly.

By embedding the principles of autonomy and efficiency in security, BP transforms its provision into a service and reinforces the idea that private actors have a role and a responsibility in meeting its demand. When energy security is framed through a supply–demand relation, the main focus remains the management of the threat, rather than the threat itself; this buttresses the company's legitimacy and authority in providing security services. The validation of BP's role in supplying security has allowed the company to develop a considerable portfolio of security services, establish an ad hoc department with armed personnel, and hire private security contractors. In the case of BP, energy securitization needs to be seen in relation to the company's objective of protecting and maximizing its profits: the provision of new security services has enlarged its business portfolio, raised profits, increased resources, expanded its remits, spread its network, and boosted its role and power in the country.

The autonomy of the sector, which is a pillar of BP's rationalities, is mirrored in its practice, as I discuss later. Here, it is important to note that autonomy affects accountability and transparency. Chapter 7 exposes the infamous record of wrongdoing, abuse and violence behind energy security practices: BP was found guilty of irresponsible and illicit land grabbing; on several occasions, its security personnel has violated civil and human rights, abused their authority and misused force; on its sites, labour strikes and protests were silenced; episodes of worker discrimination were documented. To respond to increasing criticism against its security operations, BP has made the protection of human rights a cardinal principle of its activities and has included it in its energy security discourse. Yet, this is merely a rhetorical shift, rather than a substantial change in the conceptualization of energy security. More precisely, the inclusion of human rights has come to reinforce BP's securitizing tendency, instead of evoking more emancipatory practices. Although in BP's discourse security has come to include human rights and civil liberties, it remains associated with military and paramilitary activities; there is a limited account of what the nexus between security and human rights might entail, against very detailed descriptions of defence and enforcement efforts. Associating the defence of human rights with security as force denies the possibility of security outside securitization. The human rights discourse remains marginal and does not affect the ontology of security but needs to be read in the light of BP's business logic and interests. To begin with, a commitment to human rights increases reputation and minimizes the risk of prosecution. As a discourse, it gives a further chance to the company to establish itself as a legitimate – if not *the* legitimate – security actor. The documents resort to the Voluntary Principles (VP) as the foundation of BP's commitment to the defence of human and civil rights. As such, the VP endorse de facto the authority of the company in the provision of security alongside the state: by regulating firms' behaviours and operations, the VP recognize that extracting companies hold a responsibility as well as a right in conducting security operations. Their status is equalized to the state's. Finally, the marginality and weakness of the human rights narrative finds confirmation in the non-binding nature of the Principles and its dissonance with Azerbaijan's illiberal context. The application of the VP is vitiated a priori: while it calls for the protection of civil and labour rights, including the freedom of labour association, it neglects the reality of Azerbaijan's political and legal context. Chapter 7 explains that trade unions and labour organizations are strictly limited and controlled by state forces and BP has done very little to grant the respect of human rights on and around its energy fields. The following section outlines BP's energy security practices and reinforces their illiberal character.

BP: an energy company that provides security

When the Contract of the Century was signed, the mandate to secure the energy assets was clearly put under the responsibility of the Azerbaijan government. Similarly, transit countries were considered to be in charge of the security of the pipelines and were expected to protect the corridors through their national forces. However, BP has progressively made a space for itself in the provision of security, declaring on multiple occasions that it would work closely with relevant state authorities to take all necessary measures for the protection of its personnel, operations and assets. As explained earlier, BP feels it has a duty but also a right in protecting everything it owns and manages. Thus, the energy company has its own security department, which is equipped with armed personnel, light weaponry, surveillance technology, patrol boats and other security devices.

Similar to the case of NATO, which is a security organization that took up an interest in energy and has made energy a security concern, BP is an energy company that has transformed security into an organic component of its energy business, mandate, portfolio and corporate structure. As I explain later, the role of the private sector in securing energy increases the hybrid character of energy security in multiple ways, especially by blurring the lines between military and security, between private and public, and between security and insecurity. It also points to the diffuse use of force and the presence of private interests that taint security and defy the illusion of security as a public good.

The security department was established by the BP Azerbaijan quarter from the early days of its operations in the late 1990s. In the country, BP security personnel are armed, and their tasks revolve around patrolling onshore and offshore energy assets, guarding the facilities, controlling access to BP's buildings, and checking on workers' and visitors' credentials. Over the years, BP has expanded its security workforce by outsourcing some of its security activities to external providers. BP regularly hires private security contractors (PSCs), whose responsibilities largely overlap with those of its own security department, as well as the diverse national security forces that operate in the energy fields. Relying on PSCs is a common practice for BP worldwide – from Colombia to Iraq – and it is also widespread across the region, where PSCs are often involved in the protection of energy infrastructure, from pipelines to pump stations and worker accommodation camps.

Private contractors are allowed to carry sidearms and conduct security activities within the perimeter of BP-owned and -managed facilities. Energy security practices confirm what the discourse analysis has anticipated: BP has become a source of authority in the provision of energy security. Its recognized expertise has enabled the energy company to participate in and influence the formation of energy security practices in the country. BP has established and taken the lead of the Interagency Security Committee, a platform designed to facilitate cooperation through information-sharing and joint training between the private and the public security forces that operate on energy sites. This aims to favour dialogue between BP security personnel and BP-hired security contractors and the public security officials, the regional advisers and the municipal authorities involved in energy security operations.

The role acquired by private actors has important implications for how energy security is *done*, blurring and hybridizing the traditional contours of its practices and creating room for paradoxes and contradictions. It enables the coexistence of security as a public good provided by the state and for the state with security as a service managed by and for the market. This creates confusion and ambiguity.

A first grey area emerges in the definition of the security mandates of the private actors. Their work mainly focuses on physical security but it is unclear whether they are military or non-military organizations; their nature remains hybrid. Some local contractors that work for BP, such as Titan D, Group 1 Security and AZCAN Defence Solutions, boast that their professionals are all militarily trained or former military professionals. Moreover, by Azerbaijan law (Decree of the Cabinet of Ministers No 32 of 7 February 2008), all PSCs must complete mandatory military service and are required to attend a special training or preparatory course, organized by state education centres, to obtain their licence. In the early 2000s, one of the most famous private military companies, namely Blackwater, was contracted specifically to help Azerbaijan secure its oil and gas assets or in the words of Blackwater's founder, Erik Prince, their mission was 'to protect the West's new profitable oil and gas exploitation in a region historically dominated by Russia and Iran' (Scahill 2008). In 2004 Blackwater was awarded a USD 2.5 million contract by the US government to provide military training to Azerbaijan's local forces. While it is hard to determine whether the military company is still active in Azerbaijan, its involvement confirms the constant overlaps between military and civil security, private and public, national and international that have characterized the progressive securitization of energy. Blurred divisions do not come without contestation or contradiction. Despite the emphasis on military education, Azerbaijan's law on non-state (private) security activities prohibits private entities from engaging in any military activity and allows them to carry only security services. While it is unclear where to draw the line between military and non-military security, private contractors are entitled to certain enforcement duties: they are allowed to inspect civilians, detain any person who has committed a crime, and 'keep, carry and use special means within the boundaries of the protected facilities'.

Other borderline zones emerge. Legislation on private security regulates not only PSCs, but also the security departments of any legal entity, like BP. Under Azerbaijan's law, certain places that are considered primary national security interests, including oil and gas export infrastructure, can be protected only by state security services. However, the same law recognizes that the security department of a legal entity can provide for the protection of the facilities belonging to the legal entity. Thus, ownership becomes key to determine BP's authority and rights in securing *its* assets. Ownership also determines the specificities of the contracts that regulate the work of private security professionals. As the contracts are stipulated between two private parts, it is the company that sets the contractors' responsibilities, duties and day-to-day tasks in line with its corporate guidelines and code of conduct. Compared to state agents, who can be prosecuted in national or international courts, holding BP and its security contractors accountable for their actions is difficult (see Chapter 7), leaving a responsibility vacuum. In fact, even 'the state in which a company uses or provides security services has its headquarters, would not appear to bear direct responsibility for such violations, unless directly involved' (Martin 2007, p 103).

The wide-ranging authority given to private entities normalizes the inclusion of logics and techniques that belong in the strictest sense to the private sector and have performative implications for energy security. For instance, while the protection of its corporate interests pushes energy companies like BP to invest in the protection of their own facilities, the demand for energy security enlarges its power and resources. To PSCs, insecurity represents a lucrative business. Paradoxically, energy security threats secure their business: if threats and risks remain, so does the demand for the related services. This gets translated into temporary security solutions. There is therefore less incentive to solve the security problem for good. In Azerbaijan, PSCs provide mostly short-term security solutions, which aim at reducing the immediate risks, such as guarding and patrolling, rather than holistic, long-term responses to deal with the root causes of the threat.

Neoliberal rationalities do not supplant the logic of security but coexist with it and serve to allocate political legitimacy to private entities, while still retaining a securitized view of energy security. It is in the assembly of neoliberal rationalities and the logic of security that energy securitization occurs. As previously noted, the rise of private authority belongs in the new configuration of the public and private divide and transforms how security, and power more broadly, are exercised. It remains open to question whether this configuration is really novel though. The rise of private security actors, including the emergence of non-security firms that supply those services, has been understood as a rearrangement of power away from the state. Yet, the state and the private sector depend on one another, especially in managing the energy sector, and therefore their assembly is a fundamental piece of energy securitization. In the energy business, neither governments nor multinational corporations can do without one another to access resources, develop capabilities, manage capital and operate within existing legal frameworks.

In Azerbaijan, the state law enables private security actors, both PSCs and any other legal entities, to use extraordinary security means – including particular weapons – in special cases, defined by 'extreme necessity' and depending on the nature of the offence, the level of the threat, and, more interestingly, the identity of the perpetrator. This exposes the weaknesses behind BP's discourse on the nexus between security and human rights. This research has found that while PSCs are constantly trained, education activities on human rights are almost non-existent. Moreover, rather than recalling international legal frameworks, BP establishes its own standards of human rights as a stand-alone framework and practice. This also signals that private entities set their responsibilities, the actions to comply with them, and the criteria to evaluate their performances, while the rest of the world has to accept them.

Not only are human rights principles – as contained in the VP –non-binding, but also, they do not take into consideration Azerbaijan's restrictive laws. For example, while the VPs recognize the importance of workers' rights, including freedom of association, trade unions and labour organizations are strictly limited and controlled. Labour is still regulated by a law that was created in 1999 and foresaw narrow liberties for any form of unionism. Security operations on BP energy sites are monitored and assessed by an external mediator, which, in the case of BP Azerbaijan, is a private entity, a European law firm. Their job is to evaluate whether the company complies with the VP and respects human and civil rights in its security activities. Nonetheless, the voluntary and self-imposed nature of the standards limit the relevance of the report, and the private nature of the mediator – which is commissioned by BP itself – raises questions as to the transparency and efficacy of the report. In fact, as Chapter 7 explores, security operations on energy are connected to multiple forms of insecurity, which are exacerbated by the already fragile context of Azerbaijan.

Furthermore, that BP security operations are monitored and evaluated by a third private party instils in security practices a widespread approach of dealing with social problems that is typical of neoliberalism and assesses and values practices through a set of 'private sector technologies of performance such as benchmarking, best practice schemes, codes of conduct, performance indicators and auditing' (Leander and Van Munster 2007, p 209). This has two important implications. First, it seeks to depoliticize security and make it a technocratic and standardized practice, while still accepting and normalizing its military core. By setting efficiency and efficacy as the drivers of the energy security practices, BP denies their political nature.

The spread of (para)military techniques, the extensive presence of weapons, access to the use of force, and the illiberal nature of enforcement activities that are deliberately discriminatory are not questioned per se. The necessity for security practices stands out against the deliberate, volitionary and self-imposed nature of human and civil rights, embedded in 'the entrepreneurial ethic of self-responsibility' (Best 2007, p 102). The case of Azerbaijan, however, differs from previous studies on the impact of neoliberalism in non-western, non-liberal contexts. In particular, some scholars highlight how neoliberal rationalities and techniques succeed outside advanced liberal societies because of the weaknesses of the state: Joseph (2009, p 418) records that 'the proliferation of private security companies in Africa occurs … because of the failings of public provision of security'; Abrahamsen and Williams (2006, p 15) clarify that in Kenya the state exercises very limited control over PSCs: 'there is no specific legislation or regulation pertaining to private security companies, and no oversight or monitoring of their practices, services, and training. No special license is needed to open a security company.' Conversely, in Azerbaijan, energy securitization points to an overcrowded security field, where private security professionals work alongside a wide network of state security actors; rather than filling a void, the private sector further expands the space of security. There is an overlap rather than a replacement. While the autonomy and flexibility given to the private sector, including by the state's loose legislative boundaries, affects and distorts the role of the state as the main security provider, it does not empty it of its powers. The encroachment of neoliberal rationalities in the security governance exacerbates a way of doing security, which already belongs to the state and whose primary mechanisms and techniques are (para)military and enforcement measures. The assemblage of energy securitization, in this sense, does not break with Azerbaijan's normal politics; on the contrary it contributes to its illiberal character, producing and aggravating forms of insecurity, violence and oppression.

Rather than undermining the core of securitization, neoliberalism integrates a distinct set of values, norms and forms of doing energy security, embedded in an entrepreneurial and business-oriented culture, which can serve also to expand the reach of security practices. For instance, the prominence of efficiency, which has previously been identified as a pillar of BP's discourse, is mirrored in energy security practices, particularly the increasing reliance on technology and surveillance. BP owns a computerized control system that monitors the processing and storage areas of its compounds. CCTV cameras and scanners are in place to monitor all vehicles entering BP's facilities; aerial radar surveillance systems and drones are used to monitor the security of energy sites from the air. Pipelines, pump stations and rigs have damage control technology installed, which is able to identify when and where there is a breakdown. Facilities and integrity flagship technologies are designed to mitigate and manage security and safety risks by predicting the rate of potential cracks, conducting non-intrusive inspections, quantifying risks and potentially repairing the assets. While the use of technology has been transferred also to the public sector, education and training on installation, maintenance, administration and use have mainly been provided by private firms.

Technology and automation embody the neoliberal logics of modernity, efficiency and effectiveness and, as such, create an expectation of success, which in the security domain refers to the prospect of absolute security. As Bauman (2000) explains, modern security devices aim at making security immediate and constant. Technology instils a sense of necessity in security practices, which is based on the idea that there is a deterministic causality between specific practices and the expected security outcomes. It also assumes that risks and threats can be everywhere and at all times, regardless of any contextual idiosyncrasy, further expanding the temporal and spatial terrain of security.

Energy securitization and neoliberalism

As discussed earlier, most literature understands energy securitization as a subset of national security, reducing the complexity of the process to a theoretical and empirical monolith. The previous chapters have already challenged the idea of national security as the only paradigm that drives energy securitization by putting forward the notion of the assemblage as a pertinent metaphor to account for the diversity and complexity of social phenomena and to explore securitization as an actually existing process, embedded in its idiosyncratic context. While Chapter 5 starts from the national–international binary to deconstruct old assumptions, the following sections question and problematize the private–public divide that has undergirded the traditional approach to security. In particular, International Relations and Security Studies have long placed security in the realm of the state and therefore outside and completely detached from the private sector. This idea rests upon a modern understanding of the state as originally formulated by Weber. His definition of the state, which has driven political theory and IR for more than a century, refers to it as a sovereign entity 'that claims the monopoly of the legitimate use of violence within a given territory' (Webber 1994, p 396). The state's exclusive right to use force has traditionally become the ontological foundation of its sovereignty and has functioned as a determining factor in the definition of interstate relations and, by extension, of the international system. This has long precluded the analysis of private organization as key actors in the international system. Yet, growing awareness of the 'multi-layered and multi-played patterns of global governance' (Homkes 2011, p 21) emphasizes the multiple overlaps between the private and the public sectors, including rising processes of privatization in the management of public concerns. Security is no exception. The rise of private security companies indicates that the state's monopoly over force is an abstraction. Against Weber's theorizing, scholars have noted that this is not a novel phenomenon: history offers a wide variety of examples of various forms of mercenarism and privatization of security (Lanning 2007; Dunigan and Petersohn 2015).

The fragmentation of the monopoly over security affects securitization – as both a political process and an analytical framework – too. Politically, the presence of private actors in the provision and management of security has implications over how security should be governed, by whom, for whom and by what means. Rita Abrahamsen and Michael Williams (2006) note that 'the rise of private authority ... involves substantial transformations in the form and exercise of public as well as private power'. It is in the relationship between the state and the non-state that – as Miller and Rose (2008, p 177) write – we can see 'what funds, forces, persons, knowledge or legitimacy are utilized; and by means of what devices and techniques are these different tactics made operable'. While this inevitably affects the state and its power, it does not necessarily do so by shrinking it; conversely, the privatization of security can reinforce state power by spreading and, hence, validating its modus operandi, its structures, its practices and its values, as well as its security logics. Scholars (Jackson 2013; Neocleous 2008, 2018) observe the complicity between the state and the capital – also in the form of the dominance of private property and private organizations – and the ways in which 'the political and the corporate power are fundamentally entangled' (Di Muzio 2016). In this entanglement between the public and the private, security plays a fundamental role of connection and assembly, emerging as a central tool for accessing and managing capital. This is particularly true in the energy sector, especially in the case of Azerbaijan: while broadly speaking, the state and energy companies tend to depend on each other to manage and develop resources, capabilities and capital within clear legal frameworks, in the country under examination, the line between energy and security as public goods and as private commodities is completely blurred. For instance, the growing role of BP in securing energy in Azerbaijan contributes to legitimizing forms of authority, modus operandi and logics energy security that belong in the state of Azerbaijan. In the first instance, the British company is one of the world's seven oil and gas supermajors;

thus, its long-standing relationship with Heydar and Ilham Aliyev is a source of prestige and authority for the government itself and establishes the family regime as a reliable partner of the west. Furthermore, in Azerbaijan, where politics and business are fused together, the rise of the private sector as a security provider grants the maintenance and consolidation of those poles that already have power and capital. In the country energy securitization, in this sense, relies on and, as such, consolidates a system based on the overlap between who holds the capital and who holds authority. Additionally, BP collaborates with state security agencies in Azerbaijan by instituting multilateral platforms, sharing protocols, establishing best practices and conducting joint training. This has expanded security capabilities, technical know-how and the reputational power of those state agencies that are involved in the country's energy security and belong in the country's elitist clans. Moreover, BP has normalized and even tried to depoliticize militarization and policing in energy sites. The company champions the construction of energy as a traditional security concern; its security practices, based on the deployment of a large number of security professionals and the widespread use of weapons and security technologies, mirror the state's and are sometimes even designed or conducted together with state officials and representatives to foster public-private partnerships and collaboration. At the same time, energy securitization has enabled BP to enlarge its responsibilities, institutional organization, services, resources and authority. In other words, energy securitization in Azerbaijan points to a convergence of interests between the state and the private sector.

While force has, therefore, never been truly monopolized by the state, the privatization of security emerges in a rather unique way in this contemporary historical moment marked by the hype of security and the thriving consolidation of the neoliberal order. When looking at the relationship between security and neoliberalism, some scholars have argued that securitization is replacing neoliberalism (Goldstein 2012; Amar 2013). This confirms the analytical and political force of security but dismisses its embeddedness in larger social and economic dynamics. The current centrality, omnipresence and stickiness of security – which has colonialized political debates, academic theorizing and public opinion worldwide, 'spreading wider, straining outward, a little further, and a little further yet' (Alderman 2017) – tend to obfuscate the intersections and embeddedness of inclusion with and in alternative socio-economic processes, such as neoliberalism. Against the idea that security and securitization are substituting neoliberalism, this chapter contributes to recognizing the multiple ways in which energy securitization and neoliberalism – both their rationalities and techniques – are mutually constitutive. As Neocleous (2018, p 134) correctly argues, 'the explosion and expansion of security in the last two decades might just as properly be connected to the attempt to engrain neoliberalism' in our societies. Thus, energy securitization cannot be understood outside the relationship between security and neoliberalism because understanding how energy security has been formed, shaped and used cannot prescind from the order in which it was generated and which it is expected to secure. In Azerbaijan, the clientelistic nature of the political regime reinforces the multiple overlaps between management of the public goods and private interests. In particular, the neoliberal reforms that have been introduced by Azerbaijan since its independence to join the institutions of global governance and integrate its economy in the global market have exacerbated the centralization of power around the elites. As scholars have noted, in Azerbaijan the energy corporations that operate in the market economy have little interest in pushing for government reforms or liberalization as this would destabilize their relationship with the country's leadership regime by pushing for domestic reforms (Hoff and Stiglitz 2004; Borzel and Risse 2020).

7

Energy (In)Securitization: Abusive Security Practices and Poor Energy Choices

Since its independence, Azerbaijan – the Land of Fire – has seen its oil and gas industry as a quintessential component of its identity and the engine that could first lead to and then consolidate the country's economic success and international reputation. Energy is intrinsically linked as much to nation building as to state building. It has ideationally and materially defined the country's historical trajectory. The centrality of energy has positioned it at the heart of Azerbaijan's national security. The previous chapters have also shown that the security of Azerbaijan's energy has received priority status also internationally, becoming a matter of global security or being embedded in the agenda of states, private companies and regional organizations that have a direct interest in the protection of the industry. These multiple processes of energy securitization have normalized a force-oriented approach to energy security, which enables the deployment of military and security professionals across large parts of Azerbaijan's territory. At the same time, the exclusive focus on oil and gas has constrained our energy imagination to distinct forms of energy production and consumption, as well as to specific economic models. Energy securitization encircles and inhibits the possibility for energy and security outside these established categories. The analysis of energy securitization in Azerbaijan shows that the rhetorical emphasis given to energy security as existentially critical and the routinized character of its practices have trivialized any possible alternative, while making invisible the effects that energy securitization has beyond the egoistic interests of those actors that benefit from that process. This chapter focuses on the multiple forms of insecurity created by the securitization of energy in Azerbaijan to unpack and problematize the implications of its practices. The first section outlines manifold instances where energy security practices have led to abuse, violence and harassment. More specifically, it exposes everyday abusive behaviours by security professionals and the use of force to surveil workers and to repress different energy-related protests, such as marches and rallies against energy projects and energy shortages and blackouts, as well as in defence of energy workers' rights. This analysis also explains how energy securitization has affected Azerbaijan's communities, altering their demographic composition, amplifying socio-economic divides and contributing to gender violence, the spread of diseases and illegal trafficking. Finally, it also reveals how energy securitization is tied to and facilitates land grabbing and expropriation. In other words, energy securitization emerges as a top-down process, which centralizes power around existing power poles, facilitates militarization and disempowers the majority of the population.

The second section of this chapter focuses on the effects of energy securitization on energy policies and highlights that, despite the criticality attached to energy, especially oil and gas, Azerbaijan's energy system is oriented towards export and dependent on oil and gas. This affects domestic consumption and results in poor access and availability, high prices, low sustainability of the energy and economic system, pollution and environmental degradation. This research also exposes a systemic lack of investment in the energy infrastructure, which is largely outdated. In its third section, this chapter problematizes the effects of an overcrowded security terrain, marked by the significant duplication of efforts among forces. This causes inefficiency, fragmentation and a profound lack of coordination among security agencies. Finally, this analysis concludes with an analysis of the loopholes and weaknesses created by the wide range of security practices and the vast crowd of security professionals; in particular, it reveals that energy security practices suffer from duplication of efforts, fragmentation and inefficiency.

The previous chapters have exposed the fallacies of binary thinking and sought to overcome the dichotomy between national and international, public and private, local and global; this section invites us to rethink security beyond its opposition to insecurity. It therefore questions whether energy securitization and its search for absolute security can, in turn, produce insecurity. This points to the Janus-faced relation between security and insecurity and shows the multiple ways in which the processes of securitization are inherently processes of *in*securitization, whereby the fabrication of security can lead to forms of 'institutionally authorised vulnerability' (Rampton and Charalambous 2020, p 77).

The previous chapters have already exposed the revanchist, illiberal and elitist nature of energy securitization, which in Azerbaijan materializes energy security as a means for reinforcing patronage and enhancing power centralization. By looking at the ways in which energy securitization decreases accountability and transparency, jeopardizes public participation, endangers human and civil rights and, finally, produces insecurity, this chapter refocuses the analysis on another aspect of security as an everyday practice. While the previous sections have looked at the everyday through the ordinary lens of everyday practice, this chapter considers the everyday as the experience of ordinary people. In this context, the everyday is used as a synonym for the 'non-elite, referring to people, groups, and environments where access to powerful and prestigious symbolic, cultural, and material resources is (more) limited' (Rampton and Charalambous 2020, p 77). The everyday, as critical IR has shown, has the ability to potentially disrupt 'official accounts [of security] and repoliticise the technocratic foundations of national security policies' (Vaughan-Williams and Stevens 2016, p 42).

(In)security practices: force, abuse and violence

Energy securitization is first and foremost a process of construction, based on the identification and management of energy security threats. Not only does energy securitization define what needs protection and what does not, but also it designates what (or who) is a source of danger, what (or who) becomes an object of fear, and what (or who) must, therefore, be subjected to forms of control and coercion.

The previous chapters have identified the referent objects of energy securitization, noting that, despite the diversity of foci among actors, they cohere around the protection of energy objects and infrastructure. Threats and risks are numerous and have multiple causes; the level of unpredictability is so high that virtually anything and anyone could be a source of danger.

This chapter shows that the legitimation of the use of force, the expansion of the security mandates, and the enlargement of the security field, all enacted by energy securitization, have given the security professionals a power that is often abused. Their fight against terrorists, rebels, criminals and spies is used to justify the policing and prosecution of other targets: citizens, farmers, landowners, foreigners, energy workers and entire local communities, who are considered and treated as potential threats to energy security and are often subjected to multiple forms of brutality, harassment and violence. The salience given to security hides the insecurity that its practices generate. As energy securitization creates a hierarchy of priorities within the political agenda, alternative security needs are dismissed or sacrificed in the name of higher energy security priorities. In Azerbaijan, this has marginalized and made invisible the forms of insecurity caused by energy security practices on several levels. Energy securitization feeds the structural obstacles that marginalize how ordinary people experience (in)security in the country: it multiplies fear, justifies state violence and oppression, deprives local communities of their resources, and downgrades the everyday experience as a trivial, unimportant side-effect of more important security concerns. The following sections document the other side of energy securitization, by focusing on insecuritization. They centre on three main areas of insecurity: first, the abuse of force and the forms of harassment and violence associated with energy security practices; second, the rise of socio-economic inequalities; and third, the practices of land grabbing and expropriation tied to energy securitization.

Abuse, harassment and violence

A first form of insecurity emerges from the many reports of the abusive behaviours of the security professionals that work in and around energy sites. These security concerns have long preoccupied local communities living near energy sites. During the fieldwork, it emerged that patrolling activities are frequently abusive, involving the unjustified use of force, intimidation and coercion to scare citizens living close to those sites. Interviewees remark that the SSPS and local police officers deployed in the villages near the energy fields often bully the local communities. Interviews affirmed that security agents threaten, terrorize and beat local citizens even without apparent reasons. Similar concerns were raised with regard to private security guards in areas close to the BTC, in the region around the city of Ganja. Their constant presence on the territory has been used to restrict, even pre-emptively, people's mobility in multiple areas, as well as to gather intelligence through peer-to-peer surveillance. Local testimonies explained that security and military personnel impedes residents' access to vital resources, including potable water springs, whenever they are deemed to be too close to the protected site. Testimonies of violence and abuse by the security forces that operate around energy sites have been known for years. During the construction of the BTC, international organizations and NGOs that monitored human rights recorded multiple incidents. The OSCE (2012) confirmed that local communities continued to experience 'intimidation and harassment by the police and authorities' even after the pipeline was built. Fear is a common emotion among local citizens. They are sometimes reluctant to share their disappointment and anger about these forms of abuse because they are afraid that the government might retaliate against them. It is known that the government uses surveillance to monitor citizens' activity, especially political engagement, and to access personal information and private communications to intimidate, deter and retaliate against possible dissidents (Pearce and Kendzior 2012). Any unauthorized and unjustified presence in the rural areas around the oil and gas pipelines is subjected to the watchful eye of the security forces. For foreigners – like myself – approaching the energy sites proved to be complex, not feasible and dangerous.

Energy security has provided a pretext to increase forms of control and surveillance on and beyond the energy sites to secure all those spaces that are considered to be *critically* important and/or *critically* vulnerable. Forms of everyday intimidation and abuse include targeted repression and the use of heavy-handed responses to suffocate any forms of social dissent within local communities; energy sites are not an exception. A second recorded form of insecurity has emerged in relation to the use of force against energy-related protests. Azerbaijan has seen multiple forms of rebellion against maxi energy projects and pipelines, especially in opposition to the BTC pipeline. Before and after its construction, large protests against the pipeline erupted across the country, including in the capital city of Baku. The government has principally responded violently to these forms of dissent, deploying baton-wielding riot police to beat and flog protesters. Other protests have occurred in relation to poor energy services and recurrent shortages and blackouts; these have been silenced with extraordinary force. For instance, in 2017, police brutality traumatized the local population living in the village of Nardaran, in the Absheron peninsula. Although the peninsula hosts the richest oil and gas onshore reserved in the country, access to electricity and gas in the region is poor. Tired of lacking basic services, local citizens protested against the umpteenth electricity shortage. Their protest was blocked with the deployment of force and the protesters were violently beaten.

Energy workers' marches and rallies are also subjected to repression, and energy workers have become a popular target of police brutality and intimidation. On energy sites, working conditions are dire, marked by poor safety standards, inadequate safety training and lack of proper insurance. Energy workers' attempts to strike and protest are usually suffocated by security forces; many leaders and organizers have been imprisoned. A restrictive reading of existing laws on unionism denies the right and freedom of assembly to energy workers. There are a few unions but they are subjected to government control. The former Union of Oil Workers, which was the only autonomous trade union in the country, was dissolved in 1997 when the leadership replaced it with the Union of Oil and Gas Industry Workers, which was placed under the government's control. In this overall context of intimidation and suppression, the diffuse presence of security professionals on the energy sites acts as a deterrent to discourage any form of dissent and effort to unionize. This situation is unlikely to improve in the short term: in 2017 Baku quit the Extractive Industries Transparency Initiative (EITI), which was established to protect civil society freedoms and human rights in the extractive sector. The EITI provided for recurring missions of control, where external, international observers visited oil, gas and mining projects to evaluate working conditions. As Azerbaijan has withdrawn from the EITI, today there are fewer incentives to protect workers' rights. On energy plants, private and public security agents, including from the secret services, conduct murky activities of due diligence and spy on energy workers to counter what they define as the risk of infiltrators. This led in the past to the removal of dozens of employees from their workplace, although it is unclear what they were accused of. Official documents reveal that these secretive operations tend to target workers that belong to ethnic minorities or religious groups as they are considered to represent a higher security threat to energy security, and consequently to national security. Biased policing on energy sites mirrors larger trends of policing activity in the country: abuse and harassment by police officers and security agents tend to target minorities, especially Lezgis, Avars and north Azerbaijani highlanders, who are subjected to more police abuse and humiliation than 'westernised' Azerbaijanis (see Souleimanov and Ehrmann 2013). This is also confirmed by the Law on Private Security, which legitimizes use of extraordinary force by security contractors based on the identity of who is committing the crime.

The dissolution of the trade union needs to be understood not only within the authoritarian environment of Aliyev's regime and his moves to control civil society, but also within the process of neoliberal reforms that Azerbaijan has adopted under the aegis of the IMF since the late 1990s. Liberalization halted subsidies and shrank the welfare net established during Soviet times, limiting not only the symbolic and leverage power traditionally held by the workers, but also their wealth, resources and access to social services. Moreover, the transition of Azerbaijan into an oil and gas-based economy has disempowered workers because economic growth became attached to financial and resource capital, rather than the human workforce, and shifted the focus of industrial policies towards corporate profits. To reinforce this point, it is worth noting that over the years, incidents on oil and gas platforms, both onshore and offshore, have resulted in workers' deaths and injuries that have not been satisfactorily compensated, either financially or with structural investments to improve safety at work. The following section provides further details on how energy securitization neglects the socio-economic costs paid by energy workers, as well as the wider local communities.

The social costs of energy securitization: rising inequality

While the representations of energy security in Azerbaijan evoke ideas of national unity, the practices reveal very different security outcomes. The presence of security and military personnel has become so widespread that it has altered the demographic composition of the villages. As energy security has become an everyday practice, security and military professionals have moved permanently into the villages near the most important energy sites. For example, Sangachal town, which hosts the Sangachal terminal, one of the largest oil and gas facilities in the world, was once a small fishing village. Data estimate that in 2013 military personnel already represented the 15 per cent of the local population.

The fast and uncontrolled growth of the industry has also had a major impact on exacerbating the socio-economic divide within Azerbaijan's society. This inequality also reflects a racialized bias, which can be traced back to a widespread xenophilic culture, and the legitimacy given, also nationally (see Chapter 3), to the dominance of foreign interests over the interests of local ordinary citizens. Energy money has favoured foreigners over nationals, Bakunians over villagers, the elites over the larger population. According to a report published by BP in 2013, the company was aware of the inequalities that energy projects would create within local communities, especially those living near pipelines and energy sites. The creation and expansion of energy infrastructure created new jobs for locals; however, these were only temporary and would not last after the construction ended, putting large segments of the population in a condition of precarity and unemployment. Those jobs have also been a further divisive factor within local communities: as BP workers receive much higher salaries compared to local wages, local communities experienced a higher degree of internal rivalry and resentment. At the same time, it has emerged that foreign employees – especially western expatriates working temporally for BP in the country – are typically paid more than locals.

Salary gaps and income instability have increased resentment and animosity also among workers. Some local workers also noted that local personnel work longer hours, often outside their regular shifts and without extra benefits, such as housing and healthcare. Moreover, important parts of the new oil extraction processes were either outsourced or performed by teams of professionals imported from various countries (interviews in Baku, 2005). Azerbaijan's workers lost the important degree of control they had exercised over production in the Soviet structure.

Although the energy security discourse insists on the economic advantage of energy projects and investments, Azerbaijan's rural communities and part of the urban population have remained poor. The unimaginable wealth brought by the national energy industry has not benefited the majority of Azerbaijanis. Baku's luxury and opulence, granted by oil money, conceal the reality that lies behind the 'Belt of Happiness' (as eloquently defined by Azerbaijani investigative journalist Khadija Ismayilova), a concrete wall that runs across the capital to seclude its poorest neighbourhoods. Azerbaijan's immense oil and gas revenues have fed Azerbaijan's economic boom; yet, this has interested mostly the city centre of Baku, which has become a rich, cosmopolitan business hub. There is no evidence of luxury shops, modern skyscrapers and fancy cars outside downtown Baku; the outskirts of the city offer landscapes that recall Soviet imaginaries, while in the small rural villages outside the highways, time has stopped at the beginning of the 20th century. In Azerbaijan there is a direct material correlation between energy and the lack of wealth distribution, which further constrains socio-economic development. This pertains to the geographical concentration of the resources around Baku: oil and gas fields, as well as the energy production and development sites are located near the capital city. This material proximity has allowed Baku and its ruling elites to centralize economic resources, as well as political power and decision making, and bypass the mediation with regional authorities. Outside Baku, large sectors of the population have not been touched by oil wealth, especially in the countryside. Some of Azerbaijan's large energy infrastructure that connects the oil-rich areas to remote parts of the country lies in those regions that were already vulnerable to socio-economic instability and that have long shown the country's highest rates of poverty and social insecurity. For example, the Sangachal terminal stands near a former rural area that could not adapt to the quick rates of the region's industrialization. Those households and communities that did not manage to contribute or take part in the industrialization process, for instance by finding employment at the plants, or could not relocate easily after expropriation, ended up in a situation of extreme vulnerability, including homelessness and displacement. This has contributed to the formation of the Umid refugee camp and the Sahil settlement, which lie in the areas adjacent to the terminal.

Azeri economist Gubad Ibadoghlu (2019) raises the question: 'what have the citizens of the country gained from the 100 billion USD of oil revenue the government has received from the ACG oil reservoir alone?' According to his study, Azerbaijan lacks basic public services, from education to health, and suffers from high unemployment rates, which have forced Azerbaijanis to migrate. Against the national discourse, the relationship between the development of oil and gas and the creation of wealth, labour and growth is not straightforward: the industry is capital but not labour intensive and contributes to only 1 per cent of total employment. In Azerbaijan, despite the economic growth generated by the energy windfall since the mid 2000s, corruption and weak governance have hindered socio-economic development. The transformation of energy from public good to commodity and the overlap between the state interest and the private interests of the elite have prevented the distribution of wealth. Social welfare is a relatively low priority for government spending and easy access to oil rents has reduced interest in tax collection, allowing the state to maintain public services and social welfare protections at the minimum.

Bankwatch (2005, 2006, 2012), a network of NGOs operating in central and eastern Europe, also noted that the development of the BTC pipeline exacerbated multiple forms of gender inequality and worsened socio-economic conditions: in particular, their study highlights that the BTC project has not granted or improved women's access to natural resources; it has not brought any substantial improvement to the country's wider infrastructure; it has not contributed to employment; it has not created permanent income;

and finally, it has not improved the decision-making processes. Moreover, around those energy sites under construction or enlargement, prostitution, human trafficking, and drug smuggling and trafficking tend to rise. For instance, BP relies on a large foreign workforce, whose temporary presence in the rural Azeri villages has proved to be disruptive and damaging and closely linked to an upsurge in illegal behaviours. Rising trends in the levels of prostitution and HIV have been recorded in the three adjacent regions along the BTC trajectory, Shamkir, Tovuz and Aghstafa. According to the head of the police of an affected region, the increased narcotics trade and AIDS spread is directly connected with increased prostitution due to the pipeline's construction.

Land expropriation and grabbing

Most apprehension and anger concerns BP's practices of land expropriation, including the modalities through which the company exerts its *rights*. In the early 2000s, at the dawn of the BTC project and the expansion of the national energy industry, a more extensive interpretation of the Land Use legislation was introduced. This has established that oil and gas pipes, high voltage electric lines and hydro facilities are part of the national security interest; hence the state can legitimately seize private property if the seizure is in the interest of the country. This is obviously largely defined and has a wide margin for interpretation. As a consequence, expropriation has become common in those areas close to the oil and gas fields or in the rural regions crossed by the pipelines. Many landowners have permanently lost access to their land and compensations have been imposed at prices below market rates. Land ownership, from expropriation to acquisition, has moved from being an issue of contractual law to becoming a security matter, managed by security guards and enforcement agents. To inform owners about upcoming expropriation procedures, in the Shamkir district BP's employees from the Land Acquisition Team are always accompanied by security contractors or police agents, formally to prevent or address any *undesirable incident*. The presence of security professionals has a clear deterrent intent, which relies on the widespread fear and distrust among Azerbaijanis of security personnel, and aims to discourage local citizens from fighting for their rights. In the early stages of the BTC pipeline, the landowners and the local communities around the BTC areas had no access to information regarding the construction sites. National legislation has made it hard for citizens to make BP and security agents accountable for their actions. The complaint system does not oblige the company to respond to citizens' grievances; litigation is limited to lengthy and often inconclusive discussions between the two sides and the mediators. In the Shamkir region, the controversy between some landowners and BP in relation to the construction and expansion of the

South Caucasus Pipeline has lasted almost a decade. The local citizens have criticized BP's lack transparency when illustrating landowners' options in the face of expropriation and have denounced its non-compliance with the compensation agreements signed following the construction of two oil and gas pipelines that crossed cultivated land in a village of the Shamkir district. In particular, these villagers accused BP of not having paid land compensation, in its entirety or parts of it. Land expropriation, especially when it is not correctly compensated, has corollary costs and creates significant loss of profits for landowners, who are usually farmers that use the land for their own sustenance. Even when contested, land expropriation forces farmers to halt cultivation for long periods. Most of them complain that they were not able to resume or relocate their work during the whole litigation process. Land expropriation has an enormous impact on local communities: it affects access to food, housing, work and sources of sustenance and violates multiple rights, including the rights to property, development and self-determination. Moreover, the lack of transparency that characterizes these processes favours widespread corruption and condones illicit behaviours.

As previously mentioned, in Azerbaijan, oil and gas-related expropriation caused internal displacement of thousands of citizens; those who lost their houses lived in tents and refugee camp for years, waiting to being relocated. Even when the land is not expropriated, the construction, maintenance or expansion of maxi energy projects, such as transnational pipelines, are invasive for the local communities and often harm the land, the quality of the soil and cultivation, and damage private and public infrastructure, from roads to buildings and private houses. These remain damaged for years; when rarely repaired or restored, works come from the private initiatives of the citizens, neighbours or owners themselves. However, this has widened social differences. In fact, the ability to fix damage depends on the households' income. It has been noted that reparation works happen infrequently in rural villages, where the local population has modest or low economic capabilities.

In the mid 2010s, BP set up a Social Investments Team to improve its relationships with and impact on local communities by investing in educational and development projects. This was backed by local and international civil society organizations. Within the country, Azerbaijanis call out the company and urge measures to increase transparency and accountability. There is a widespread perception that the violation of human rights and civil liberties is left unpunished by the government, BP and the international community. Attitudes to the international community vary deeply among the population and are often contradictory. The desire to belong in or be accepted by the west is largely affected by the disappointing lack of interest of western states in the *occupation* of Karabakh. The sentiment of disillusion seems to prevail. Discontent has also emerged in relation to the poor impact of energy wealth on the wider Azeri population, as well as to the negative implications linked to the construction of energy facilities. This dissatisfaction contributes to a general frustration at a corrupt political elite and the country's bad governance but is also addressed to BP, which is considered responsible for overall indifference to and complicity with illicit behaviours.

Energy securitization and Azerbaijan's energy policies

In July 2018 Baku and 40 other districts experienced a severe blackout, the worst since Azerbaijan's independence from the Soviet Union. It was an exceptionally hot summer, with temperatures over 40 degrees; the use of air conditioning peaked, causing an electric overload that damaged an electric plant, the Mingachevir thermal power plant, situated almost 300 kilometres from the capital city of Baku. The Mingachevir thermal power plant is an old oil facility that has been in operation since 1955 but still serves a large part of the territory. That summer, the rise in consumption rates overburdened the plant, which broke down, sparking a fire that caused the collapse of a considerable portion of the national electricity grid. Citizens across the country were left in the dark for days; in some cases, access to potable water was interrupted because the blackout left water treatment plants without electricity, leaving hundreds of households without basic services. The incident in Mingachevir halted hospital activities, interrupted services on the Baku subway, and it also stopped oil and gas drilling. The day before the blackout – the local media note with some irony – BP had announced that gas from the Shah Deniz II field to Europe had begun flowing to enhance European energy security.

The previous chapters have focused on what energy securitization *does*; this section highlights what energy securitization *does not do*. In particular, it focuses on energy trends and policies and shows that energy securitization in Azerbaijan does not grant or achieve domestic energy security: the country's energy system lacks access, availability, affordability and sustainability; a large part of the energy infrastructure is outdated; and energy wealth is not reinvested in the industry but redirected mainly towards the military sector.

Energy securitization and the domestic energy market

The previous chapters have shown that Azerbaijan, NATO and BP provide a similar account of the country as a reliable energy supplier. All discourses celebrate Azerbaijan's prosperity in energy resources, the stability of its market, the industrial potential of its new fields, and its excellent business environment. The country's energy system is not only oriented towards exports but also dependent: the oil and gas industry relies almost exclusively on foreign investment, as much as the national economy does on export revenues. Production and exploration agreements set exports as the legal precondition for the funds. Despite energy security featuring as an issue of national security, as previous chapters have shown, it is oriented towards the outside. However, the exclusive attention to exports has overshadowed internal problems. There are several loopholes in Azerbaijan's energy system: the country suffers from a lack of diversification of energy sources, a perished energy infrastructure network, and a dysfunctional and unbalanced energy system that devotes most production to exports. By embracing the traditional supply-oriented approach to energy security and a neoliberal emphasis on profits, Azerbaijan has undermined domestic services. While Azerbaijan's reserves are indeed proliferous, economic and political choices have neglected domestic access, availability, affordability and sustainability.

First, the country's energy production does not meet its internal demand. As the country sells most of its energy, it is not able to cover its own electricity needs. Azerbaijan could be self-sufficient: the national electricity production is around 25 billion kWh against consumption rates of around 18 billion kWh; yet energy exports amount to 26.5 billion kWh. To address the deficit, Azerbaijan imports electricity from neighbouring states, specifically Russia, Iran, Turkmenistan and more recently also Georgia. Imports are crucial for Azerbaijan's national energy consumption and in many parts of the territory, such as the Nakhichevan exclave, are the sole source of electricity.

Moreover, energy services in the country are of poor quality. During the interviews, most Azeri energy experts agreed that the country's electricity power system does not take into consideration the country's *energy security* and is not built around domestic needs but exports. As a consequence, Azerbaijan suffers from unreliable and inadequate power supply and frequent electricity shortages. One of Azerbaijan's major energy problems comes from poor availability and access; the country's energy system is, in fact, unreliable. Urban areas, including the capital city of Baku itself, suffer persistent blackouts due to electrical overloads. Outside the city of Baku, in many secondary towns and rural districts, the distribution network is at the end of its life and frequently experiences power outages. Rural areas are subjected to frequent disruption in the provision of electricity, gas and heat and are particularly vulnerable to energy poverty, which refers to those households that have no access to adequate energy services.

The focus of Azerbaijan's energy policies on international trade affects not only the access and availability to gas and electricity, but also their affordability. Because most energy goes to exports, electricity and gas are very expensive for the country's living standards. In order to increase production capacity, meet the demand for electricity and ensure the sustainability of power supply, a price adjustment in 2017 raised the price of natural gas, and consequently that of electricity. This rise is assumed to have tripled prices for households and wholesale customers. Although the electricity tariffs in Azerbaijan are much lower than in other countries, interviewees stressed that the prices are very high for the average Azeri population, especially given the worsening conditions of the national economy. The burden of electricity prices on households and consumers was particularly felt following the 2015 depression and consequent devaluation of the national currency. Moreover, as both electricity and natural gas are calculated in per capita terms, family size becomes a factor of vulnerability in terms of energy security. The new tariff affects mostly those parts of the country that suffer from multiple energy insecurities, from unreliable access to energy to unsustainable consumption. For instance, in the Absheron peninsula – the richest district in terms of oil and gas resources, yet one of the energy poorest – households' electricity bills have gone up by 57 per cent: because the region is not supplied with natural gas, imported electricity is used intensively, including for heating, making consumption rates higher than average. Data reveal that while households represent the second-largest portion of gas consumption (exports being the first), it is losses that hold the third place. While energy security practices address energy losses, they do not focus on their main roots – namely consumption patterns – but emphasize the less pressing issue of theft prevention. Energy experts recognize that inefficiency in power and heating has not been adequately addressed. Although Azerbaijan has supported international efforts to enhance energy efficiency, participating in multilateral programmes and international agreements – such as the Energy Charter Treaty and the Protocol on Energy Efficiency and Related Environmental Aspects – governmental interventions have been considered to be inconsistent and superficial. Overall, the lack of attention to sustainability contributes to deepening wider indifference to the environment.

Environmental degradation

The environmental dimension of energy security also offers an interesting source of debate. Chapter 3 shows that energy is also tied to environmental protection; however, the national security discourse inserts the environment within a nationalist narrative motivated by anti-Armenia sentiments, which gives limited scope to environmental policies. Over the years, little has been done to reorient energy security towards green options. The OECD (2019) notes that Azerbaijan still lacks a coherent political strategy to target environmental protection. The energy industry is one of the major polluters in the country: oil spills have contaminated surface water and groundwater and remain a constant environmental risk; hydrocarbons represent the largest contributor to the country's CO_2 emissions; at the national level, oil and gas waste is inadequately managed and processed. The pollution caused by the energy industry has had major implications for Azerbaijan's environment, affecting the quality of the air and the land, as well as the people's health in local communities across the country, particularly in those regions where the oil production is intense, as in the Absheron peninsula. Previous research calculated that oil development contaminated 30 per cent of the country's coast and 50 per cent of its rivers, with the Azeri-Chirag-Guneshli field discharging 100,000 tons of oil into the Caspian Sea every year. Emissions linked to oil production represent 90 per cent of the noxious pollutants found in the country's air.

Policy responses have been modest. Unlike security technology (see Chapter 6), experts note a lack of investment in those technologies that could detect and address the impact of oil and gas production on the environment. For instance, Azerbaijan's air quality monitoring network is an underdeveloped and obsolete system, which was inherited from Soviet times. Investing in alternative, clean forms of energy could address most of these issues: low-carbon energy sources could provide accessible, affordable, sustainable and healthier substitutes for hydrocarbons. In particular, Azerbaijan has significant potential for solar and wind power; yet this remains widely unexploited. Some lonely wind turbines and a few solar panels can be seen sporadically across Azerbaijan's territory. At the time of writing, Azerbaijan has made only a few investments in wind and solar: renewables represent a risible contribution to the country's energy mix, providing for only 0.2 per cent of Azerbaijan's energy production. When in the field, I met energy experts and stakeholders, who argued that Azerbaijan's government is reluctant to develop renewable energy projects. While Azerbaijan could potentially become an important producer of renewable energy, the government has shown no interest in moving towards alternative forms of energy. According to my interviews, the government sees the transition towards renewable energy as a potential threat to the national oil and gas industry, which remains the main source of national wealth. In 2019 the dissolution of the State Agency for Alternative and Renewable Energy Sources, established only in 2009, confirmed the government's unwillingness to transition towards green energy. In other words, the lack of energy diversification, which is affecting the country in multiple ways, is not attributed to material or systemic challenges but mainly to a lack of political intention. According to energy experts, the government fears that renewables could become a direct economic competitor of the oil and gas industry and, as such, undermine the multiple private interests that lie behind it. In fact, since there is not enough indigenous capital to develop a competitive solar and wind industry, the creation of a low-carbon sector would depend, once again, on foreign investors. However, unlike oil and gas, which are owned by the state, renewables could not be placed under the direct control of the government. The development of renewables would, therefore, create an independent business sector, which could directly affect the interests of the local oligarchs and magnates, as well as those of the ruling family. Resistance towards the creation of green energy businesses reflects a wider trend in the country's industrial environment: despite the national and international recognition of Azerbaijan as an excellent business partner, outside the oil and gas sectors the government has not shown any willingness to favour private investments. Unlike oil and gas, the state intends to retain its strict control over other industrial sectors (Flegel 2016).

Poor investment in the energy industry

The effects of energy securitization can be seen in how energy wealth is allocated. For instance, this research reveals that while the energy industry suffers from poor investment, oil and gas revenues have boosted the security sector. Although the energy industry accounts for the largest contribution to the state budget, only a minor part of its revenues is reinvested in the sector. In particular, the utility sector receives only 2.4 per cent of oil and gas proceeds against the 9.7 per cent of the defence sector. Government interventions are often inadequate, weakening rather than strengthening the oil and gas industry. In 2017 the Ministry of Transport, which had oversight of energy transport, merged with the Ministry of Communication and High Technologies; this move reduced de facto the institutional and financial resources allocated to the energy distribution network. The severe lack of public investment mirrors a general neglect of the oil and gas infrastructure: in Azerbaijan, over 20 per cent of all energy equipment and over half of its network facilities are beyond their useful life. As the previous sections have explained, ageing infrastructure affects the reliability and efficiency of the power network, causing power shortages and failures. In the second half of the 2010s, the government injected some money to renovate the facility with the aim to increase the quantity of the electricity delivered by the existing assets; yet experts agreed that the move was insufficient given the chronic deficit of power lines and power stations in the country.

Conversely, steady investments in the defence sector made Azerbaijan's military capability one of the largest in the Caucasus (Global Fire Power 2018). Energy revenues have largely been used to modernize the national army and military equipment. Historically, there has been a strict correlation between Azerbaijan's oil boom and its military build-up. The steady cash inflow brought by the boom in oil production between 2005 and 2014 facilitated the country's extraordinary military expenditure, which went from USD 309 million to USD 1.5 billion in 2017, reaching a peak of USD 1.9 billion in 2015, when Azerbaijan became one of the ten countries with the highest levels of militarization in the world (Sipri 2017). From 2000 to 2016 the Azerbaijan military budget oscillated between 2.5 per cent and 5.6 per cent of its GDP; this is spectacularly high if compared to other states' budgets during the same period, including those of the UK (between 1.8 and 2 per cent), the US (between 3 per cent and 4.6 per cent), Russia (between 3.5 per cent and 5.3 per cent) and Turkey (between 1.7 per cent and 3.6 per cent) (World Bank 2017). In 2016, the drop in oil prices slowed down the country's military expenditure, but only partially as investments in the sector remained high: in 2016, the money flow amounted to almost USD 1.4 billion and USD 1.5 in 2017 (Sipri 2018). If the military build-up has proved to be resilient to the economic recession, the energy industry has not: the decline in income has resulted in a harsh downscaling of investment, which has in turn hindered the energy industry, particularly the gas sector where development works have slowed down significantly (Pirani 2016).

Moreover, investments in the oil and gas sector often lack transparency and accountability: as corruption is endemic in Azerbaijan's energy industry, investments are motivated by the possibility of personal gain, rather than by targeted strategic development plans and are subjected to politically motivated scrutiny. While there have been some efforts to fight it through the launch of anti-corruption policies, Azerbaijan still ranks 126th out of 180 countries in the Transparency Initiatives Corruption Index (2019). In their study, Tanja Börzel and Yasemin Pamuk explain that the 'Azeri government has been quite selective in implementing and enforcing anti-corruption measures in such a way as to consolidate their power by disciplining political rivals and centralising control over the corruption system' (2011, p 89). Although in the country the oil and gas sector is one of the greatest sources of corruption, given the selective nature of anti-corruption policies, the situation is unlikely to change. Energy agreements are negotiated with ample discretion of the ruling elite, which, without a check and balance system to watch over the government, determines the terms of the contracts without transparency, accountability and mediation with other political actors.

This analysis confirms what the previous chapters have argued: while energy securitization has brought the proliferation of foreign actors in the oil and gas sector, it has not undermined Azerbaijan's state machine. The variety of interests and objectives that lie behind different processes of energy securitization does not break with Azerbaijan's ordinary politics. While the previous chapters have pointed to the leverage that NATO and BP have over the leadership, including their influence on the processes of nation- and state building, this has not hindered the state at home. The regime maintains its grip over society, which energy securitization has helped reinforce.

Energy securitization and chaotic security practices

A few final considerations on the insecurities concealed by energy securitization are concerned with the security practices themselves, specifically how they are conducted. The previous chapters have shown that energy securitization does not emerge as a coherent set of practices, but rather as a varied and far-reaching combination of actors, organization, activities and technologies. The number of military personnel and security professionals from local, international and private organizations is extremely high. This heterogeneity, as well as fragmentation, has several implications.

First, the heterogeneity of the security practices translates into broadness. This is inherently tied to the material characteristics of energy, specifically the physical vastness of the energy networks, its gigantic infrastructure and its numerous facilities spread across the country. The previous chapters have shown that no line can easily be drawn to define the territorial, temporal and even professional boundaries of energy security practices. For instance, the geographical areas that are deemed critical for energy security have become wider and are not defined by the strict proximity to key facilities. This research has shown that energy security has gone through considerable expansion since the end of the 1990s: military and security professionals have enlarged their remits, spread their geographical scope, and become a permanent presence in all those sites that are considered to be critical for energy security not just at the local level but at the global level too. Moreover, given that some assets are built underground, it is not always possible to circumscribe the security areas. The rising role of technology has also contributed to making control and policing an uninterrupted practice. The empirical analysis has also revealed that security agencies have progressively expanded their mandates, acquiring more responsibilities, financial resources and military capability.

While the spatiality of energy enlarges the space of security, it also poses enormous pragmatic challenges, especially in terms of operational efficiency and clarity. Most security professionals are not bound by clearly defined mandates. As the security professionals that operate in the energy fields come from distinct social universes – from the national defence and enforcement sector to international security organizations and private companies – the space of energy security is transformed, disaggregated: practices conducted *in* Azerbaijan are often designed and approved outside the country, in the offices of multinational companies and the headquarters of international organizations in western Europe. The social diversity of actors also implies different sources of ownership, authority and legitimacy. Each agency has its own legislative corpus, its chain of command, its overall objectives, its regulatory mandate and its modus operandi, which are all guided by specific, sectorial interests.

One of the most pressing issues that emerges out of this study is the significant duplication of effort among forces. This points to a high level of inefficiency and fragmentation and a profound lack of coordination among security agencies. It has emerged that the problem is not only inter-sectorial but also intra-sectorial. For example, the duplication of effort within the public sector is critical: the three branches of Azerbaijan's armed forces and the enforcement and paramilitary agencies all conduct the same activities, such as patrolling, guarding, controlling, defending and providing surveillance. Concerns were also raised over the severe lack of clarity regarding how overlapping and intersecting practices are managed. A disordered regulatory framework has created and progressively harshened the level of competition between private and public security professionals. Despite the presence of interagency networks to facilitate interoperability and cooperation, it is unclear how different security agencies manage their information-sharing activities. The chapters of this book have revealed the inconsistencies, opposed interests and contradicting practices that coexist, often thanks to intentional silences, ambiguity and neglect.

Energy securitization creates a space where fragmented and disentangled practices assemble and disassemble, overlap and conflict with each other, and, very often, duplicate efforts and resources. In spite of the wide range of practices and the large crowd of security professionals, interviews question the efficacy of the system.

Blast walls and fences might protect from intruders but may be useless in the face of mortars or grenade attacks. In 2007, when there was high alert on energy security, Bill Schrader, then president of BP in Azerbaijan, warned that breaking BP's security system was relatively easy, 'all it would take is one guy with a mortar or six guys in a boat' (US Embassy 2008).

8

Conclusion

This book has explored the particular visions of order, the forms of authority and the patterns of social organization around which the problematization of energy as a security concern coheres. To do so, it has used discourse analysis to examine the discursive construction of energy as an existential security issue and conducted a critical mapping of the national, international and private actors involved in the labour of performing energy security in Azerbaijan. Unlike most studies of energy securitization, this book has not limited its inquiry to a state-based conceptualization of the analytical space. Conversely, it has been mindful of the constant intersections amidst local, national, global and private forms of authority. In fact, this research has focused on three case studies as representative of three distinct social selves involved in the securitization of energy in Azerbaijan: the state security actors, which stand for the national social universe; NATO for the international; and the British energy company BP for the private. This book has focused on four main issues. First, it has paid attention to the fixation on energy security practices that imply the actual or potential use of force, explaining how and why they have been normalized and taken for granted. In this regard, this book has exposed the similarities of discourses and practices amidst the different actors under scrutiny. Empirical evidence has shown that the construction and management of energy security threats in Azerbaijan portrays an idea of security that is fundamentally aggressive. This aggressivity presupposes protection and controllability, materializes through a combination of practices of coercion and control, and embeds the logic of security into the technical, economic and material domains of the oil and gas industry.

However, it has become evident that energy securitization is not simply about defining threats to specific energy objects but refers to a much more complex sociotechnical process. Thus, this research has also looked for the diversities that define the actually existing character of energy securitization. Securing energy emerges as a cultural and political practice, indicative of specific beliefs, judgements and imaginaries that determine the identification of energy security threats and solutions. Energy security practices can be taught, passed on and spread across territories. This analysis has explained that the diversity of perceptions and interests results in competition and mediation that allow knowledge about energy security to flow between actors and sectors; certain practices are spread, taught, imposed and absorbed. The ways elements assemble and disassemble are political and reflective of power relations.

This book's second focal point has been analysing the co-constitutive and relational character of energy securitization and the actors' identity and material expression of their power. Energy securitization in Azerbaijan helps reinforce existing political and social hierarchies at both the domestic and the global dimensions. In the empirical analysis, it has emerged that, in Azerbaijan, energy securitization cannot be understood as separate from the process of nation- and state building that Azerbaijan has experienced since its transition out of the Soviet Union. This is partly because the country's independence happened almost simultaneously with the development of the industry. In addition, the progressive securitization of energy has intersected with the political processes that have come to define power and allocate authority in the country, while also forming a sense of self that could legitimate the newly established regime of the Aliyevs. Hence, the formation of energy security embodies values, expectations, imaginaries and even assertions of what Azerbaijan ought to be while also containing the expression of the clan and elite groups that managed to physically impose themselves in the local political arena. In the idea of energy securitization as part of the national security project lies a variety of interests and institutions that constantly mediate between diverging stakes and priorities. At the same time, comprehension of energy securitization cannot be enclosed in the national and local environment but needs to be seen in conjunction with larger processes of internationalization and globalization that pertain to the (neo)liberal order building. Energy security practices contain the seeds of foreign and global agency and the ability to influence and even determine local practices. The centrality of external, foreign actors and the importance of international and intersectoral cooperation is indicative of the global changes in security governance. In particular, it points to the rise of private security professionals, the consolidation of NATO as a global (rather than regional) actor and expert, and the transformation of corporations and multinationals into legitimate authorities with security mandates, as well as the salience of homogenizing security globally by establishing and spreading global standards and best practices.

Third, this research has emerged from the realization that the literature on energy securitization pays little attention to the relationships and dynamics between state and non-state, particularly between public and private actors, when executing energy security tasks. Transnational perspectives should be incorporated to explore and understand how global hegemonic structures define the relationship beyond national borders. Scholars from multiple disciplines have explained that globalization, colonization and western imperialism ask us to rethink existing ideas about the geographies of security.

This study has shown how practices assemble and disassemble beyond the national boundaries and imply a constant negotiation between different sources of authority. International and private interventions insert local practices amidst global and globalized circuits of expertise and knowledge and translate global know-how into localized actions. This has led me to conclude that energy securitization in Azerbaijan is explicitly about building and consolidating a neoliberal order through making energy more interdependent, interconnected and profitable. The analysis of energy security practices illustrates that Azerbaijan is socialized into western-defined norms of security via interoperability, best practices, training and joint drilling. International standards, justified by the need for efficiency, efficacy and autonomy, cannot be fully grasped without a reflection on the intersection between securitization and neoliberalism. Since the Cold War and especially after the dissolution of the Soviet Union, NATO pushed for multilateral cooperation and the protection of the market by retaining a focus on state relations and as means to *impose* the western liberal order as the only pathway towards peace. While International Relations and Security Studies have long argued that liberal security norms focus on liberal peace and democracy, they have missed the chance to understand the close ties between security and the protection of private economic interests within the neoliberal order. Today, it is also global corporations that push for processes of standardization: energy securitization is also about the protection of the global energy market and shared global norms that are aligned with neoliberal principles and grant the maximization of the capital. In Azerbaijan, energy securitization hinges on security to enlarge private profits and on the neoliberal propensity towards the maximization of profits to reinforce security as securitization. While previous studies have shown how the lines between security sectors are blurring – for example between military, police, intelligence, and custom and border controls – this book has exposed that even the divisions between a security and a non-security sector like the oil and gas industry are less clear.

Moreover, the standardization of practices via best cases, intersectoral cooperation or interoperability rests on the false assumption that energy security practices are technocratic and depoliticized and, as such, can and should be spread across territories to achieve the most efficient and effective outcome in as many places as possible. Standardization crowds out alternative options, investing unconventional solutions with a political aura that depicts them as inefficient, incompetent and partisan. Energy securitization in Azerbaijan has standardized a force-oriented approach to energy security and normalized the presence of national, foreign and private military and security professionals across large part of the country's territory. Simultaneously, the emphasis on the security of oil and gas has constrained the imagination for alternative forms of energy production and consumption, as well as economic models. Energy securitization limits our ability to think about and do energy security outside securitization.

As a fourth point, this book has reflected on the implications of energy securitization in Azerbaijan. My primary intent has been to problematize the merger of energy with security. This research has moved from a concern with the implications of energy securitization and the visceral and paradoxical relationship between security and insecurity. The analysis of energy security practices in Azerbaijan shares similar conclusions of other works on broader security practices. However, unlike the energy security field, which has not engaged much with the problem of praxis, the literature of security practices in other fields and terrain (for example, the border, the airport and the environment, among others) is abundant. Security practices tend to be moved by an obsession with the identification and measurement of the threat, the discovery and decontextualized replication of best practices, the desire for control, and the firm belief in achieving total security. Yet, these connotations of security practices have several detrimental and even paradoxical implications. For instance, the fixation on security hides the multiple forms of insecurity that it generates. It is easy to remain hung up on security: if security is understood as a life-or-death situation, there is not – there cannot be – anything outside of it, anything more pressing, anything above it. Thus, security becomes omnipresent and sticky: it pervades our thinking, practices and relations; it determines our space in the world and our behaviours; it shapes our life in the everyday, defining what we are allowed to do; and finally, it materializes as a larger design that regulates local, national and global politics. I have been particularly interested in exposing how the particular rendering of energy security as a conventional security threat expands the military and enforcement, defence and policing, and coercion and control towards uncharted territory. Like many other colleagues, I have resorted to the concept of securitization to indicate the growing colonization of security of multiple areas of society and life. Security emerges as a project of control that aims at making the future secure and manageable. Schuilenburg (2017) talks of securitization as a virus that invades several aspects of life. This book has shown that energy securitization in Azerbaijan fuels a system of fear, violence, oppression and control by expanding the proactive, constant and diffuse involvement of security and military professionals in and beyond the country's energy sector. The role of international and foreign actors in securitizing energy in the country empowers the domestic political and economic elites, conferring legitimacy on the leadership, contributing to a strong authoritarian state machine, and further centralizing force, economic assets, and authority around well-established poles.

Theorizing energy securitization

Based on the empirical findings, a number of concluding remarks can be drawn. Energy security is not based on purely material and technical evaluations and is not simply a matter of ensuring a certain number of material supplies. The empirical analysis has made clear that energy security discourses intertwine with energy security practices and energy materiality; similarly, exceptional narratives coexist with and may succeed in routinizing everyday practices. Energy securitization in Azerbaijan assembles internal security with external security, military with civil, defence with enforcement, coercion with control; it relies on surveillance and policing technologies as much as on maritime defence and counterterrorism; it intertwines the national and the international, as well as the public and the private domains; it builds ties among different security actors and institutions that belong in different social universes; it merges security logic and neoliberal rationales, as well as security techniques and neoliberal modi operandi; it intersects energy security with local dynamics, power structures and histories while also encircling into patterns of international cooperation and corporate strategy. This book has found that the geographical, institutional and social terrain of energy securitization in Azerbaijan is disaggregated.

In this regard, this research has argued for the importance of a theoretical approach that can account for the ontological heterogeneity and complexity of energy securitization. The 'assemblage' has provided an optimal tool to embrace the diversity of the process and to visualize the relationality that underpins it. Not only does the assemblage recognize the manifold social universes of the practitioners involved and the multiple practice intersections between actors, but it also identifies its space as made of constant interactions, namely the overlaps, as well as disconnections, among numerous elements. It is important to highlight that energy securitization interacts and intertwines with other assemblages of security that are already in place. While previous studies of energy securitization (Adamides 2020) have recognized the limitations of securitization theory, especially in light of the peculiarity of energy, they have opted to expand the framework of the School of Copenhagen by creating a new sector that specifically targets energy. In their eyes, energy cannot be fully grasped by the previously identified sectors, namely the military, political, societal, economic and environmental sectors, and needs an independent label. In other words, they try to level out the diversity and heterogeneity that ontologically define energy security, instead of recognizing and foregrounding them. The assemblage has also enabled account to be taken of both the material and the ideational dimensions of energy securitization. In this work, I have been especially mindful of the co-constituted character of the relationship between energy and security. This has pushed me to take energy materiality seriously and extend the latitude of my research beyond the conventional division between material and ideational factors. Overcoming the division between the material and the ideational has allowed me to see with much more clarity how energy materiality affects securitization, by enacting and constraining what can be said and done to secure it. Attention to energy materiality has exposed the vastness, mobility and complexity of the physical space where energy and security conjoin, pointing to the fallacies of binary thinking.

The assemblage has helped expose the misconceptions of a space defined by the dichotomies between national and international, public and private, local and global, which have traditionally influenced International Relations and Security Studies, including the securitization scholarship. Those conceptual binaries obscure our understanding of security by oversimplifying and flattening its complexity. This is an important point as it suggests that energy securitization cannot be separated from other social realities, but is embedded in and dependent on them.

Contribution and ways forward

As I come to the end of my book, I want to outline the contribution of this study and identify potential routes for future research. As previously explained, this book has offered a different way of theorizing energy securitization. Questioning who securitizes energy in Azerbaijan and how has provided an innovative conception of energy securitization as a socio-technical practice, accounting for ideational and material factors.

One of the most substantial contributions of this study lies in its empirical extent and output. This book has produced original knowledge on the case study of energy securitization in Azerbaijan, opening a window on the hardly accessible and often overlooked context of the country. The focus on Azerbaijan contributes to a growing effort to open up the fields of International Relations and Security Studies and escape the epistemological trap of western centrism. By engaging with domestic, foreign and private stakeholders, it has escaped the idea of securitization as a purely national phenomenon. Similarly, this study has avoided the limitations of discursive ontology through a more inclusive look at practices. In doing so, this book has delineated a comprehensive account of relevant security actors and performances.

The processes of energy securitization under examination have occurred in Azerbaijan since its independence, hence over a time period of three decades. In this timeframe, there has been a consolidation of and boost in energy securitization: the number of professionals has been growing, the territories under control have expanded, the tools and technologies have become more incisive, widespread and advanced. The call for security interventions in the energy field have become not only more common, but also more acceptable and hence *normal*. Unlike other studies of energy securitization, this book has recognized the importance of the everyday and the routinized character of its practices instead of exalting the exceptionalism of its rhetoric. In doing so, it builds on the previous work of International Political Sociology and understands the everyday as a socio-cognitive orientation that exposes how securitized practices permeate everyday life. Although securitization embraces a logic of urgency and exceptionalism, its everyday reiteration operates in the intersection between the ordinary exception and the exceptional ordinary. As Rampton and Charalambous (2020) explain, the everyday can signify 'non-exceptional' and/or 'non-elite'. This book has addressed both aspects. Its interest in the everyday contains two etha: one that draws attention to the banal aspects of security, which, given their banality, have often been taken for granted; and another one that is concerned with the implications that security, as the maximum expression of high politics, has on the life of ordinary people. This book has shown that energy securitization has affected local communities on multiple levels, altering their demographic composition, amplifying socio-economic divides and contributing to gender violence, the spread of diseases and illegal trafficking. In other words, the process of energy securitization in the country has emerged as a top-down process, which has further centralized power around existing power poles. In this sense, energy securitization is, essentially, a process of insecuritization.

I have made clear in the Introduction that this book does not have a normative intent and does not prescribe a single path towards political change. Nonetheless, this research has been motivated by a defined political sensitivity and a strong concern with security and its contemporary practices. The analysis of energy securitization in Azerbaijan confirms that today's politics seems to pay attention to issues only when they are framed as security problems. At the same time, it uses security to consolidate existing expressions of power, even when detrimental to democracy, freedom and civil liberties. Security is moved by an ambition of control that is not only an illusion but also a dystopian one. I agree with those scholars that urge us to find new ways of thinking and doing politics beyond security. As Neocleous (2008) says, 'what this might mean, precisely, must be open to debate'. Recent research invites us to accept insecurity as organic to the human condition and challenges the centrality of human beings; it is acknowledging that human beings are 'ethically bound to the social, ecological and cosmic systems' (Burke 2014) that enables their life and therefore should be recognized as holders of rights, dignity and survival. In this spirit, some scholars have outlined a normative agenda that pursues planet politics 'as an alternative thought and process: a politics to nurture worlds for all humans and species co-living in the biosphere action' (Burke et al 2016).

Important work on energy security and energy securitization that embraces environmental sensitivity has been published in recent years, calling for ethical energy justice. Challenging energy security implies reflecting on what energy system we should adopt or transition to. The case of Azerbaijan has shown that in securitization, alternative accounts of energy security are not only overshadowed, but also downgraded and penalized. Energy securitization in the country has neglected the widespread vulnerabilities that are caused by the current energy system, including poor access to and availability of gas and electricity, high energy prices, low sustainability of the energy and economic system, land and water pollution, and environmental degradation. The transition towards green energy is seen as a threat rather than an opportunity. Azerbaijan's energy system lacks an emancipatory, user- and community-oriented approach to energy and security. An important area that can be further explored is how to reconcile energy transition and mitigation with workers' security against labour precarity.

Hopefully, this book will inspire future research to think about novel theoretical ways to approach energy securitization, including approaches that see traditional security as the starting point but not the end.

References

Abrahamsen, R. and Williams, M.C. (2010). *Security beyond the state: Private security in international politics*. Cambridge University Press.

Abrahamsen, R. and Williams, M.C. (2011). Security privatization and global security assemblages. *The Brown Journal of World Affairs*, *18*(1), 171–80.

Abrahamsen, R. and Williams, M. (2016). Tracing global assemblages, bringing Bourdieu to the field. In *Reassembling international theory* (pp 25–31). Palgrave Pivot.

Adamides, C. (2020). Energy securitization in a protracted conflict environment. In *Securitization and desecuritization processes in protracted conflicts* (pp 165–79). Palgrave Pivot.

Adler, E. (2008). The spread of security communities: Communities of practice, self-restraint, and NATO's post—Cold War transformation. *European Journal of International Relations*, *14*(2), 195–230.

Adler, E. and Pouliot, V. (eds.) (2011). *International practices* (Vol. 119). Cambridge University Press.

Alderman, N. (2017). *The power*. Hachette UK.

Aliyev, H. (2014). Civil society in the South Caucasus: Kinship networks as obstacles to civil participation. *Southeast European and Black Sea Studies*, *14*(2), 263–82.

Aliyev, H. (2015). Examining the use of informal networks by NGOs in Azerbaijan and Georgia. *Journal of Civil Society*, *11*(3), 317–32.

Altstadt, A.L. (2017). *Frustrated democracy in post-soviet Azerbaijan*. Columbia University Press.

Amar, P. (2013). *The security archipelago: Human-security states, sexuality politics, and the end of neoliberalism*. Duke University Press.

Aradau, C. (2004). Security and the democratic scene. *Journal of International Relations and Development*, 7(4), 388–413.

Armstrong, K. (2002). *Islam: A short history*. Modern Library.

Avant, D. (2005). Private security companies. *New Political Economy*, *10*(1), 121–31.

Babajew, A. (2009). Politische Transformation im postsojwetischen Aserbaidschan. Dissertation. Universität Mannheim, Mannheim. Fakultät für Sozialwissenschaften. Available at https://ub-madoc.bib.uni-mannheim.de/2925/1/Dissertation_Babajew.pdf

Baghdasaryan, G. (2013). 'Working the Enemy's Mill' – putting the brake on internal development in Nagorny Karabakh: A media study of the image of the 'enemy'. In *Myths and conflicts in the South Caucasus. Instrumentalisation of conflict in political discourse* (2) (pp 92–108) 2 volumes. International Alert.

Balzacq, T., Basaran, T., Bigo, D., Guittet, E.P. and Olsson, C. (2010). Security practices. In *Oxford research encyclopedia of international studies* (pp 1–30). Blackwell.

Bankwatch (2005). BTC Pipeline – An IFI Recipe for Increasing Poverty. Available at https://bankwatch.org/publication/btc-pipeline-an-ifi-recipe-for-increasing-poverty

Bankwatch (2006). Boom Time Blues: Big oil's gender impacts in Azerbaijan, Georgia, and Sakhalin. Available at https://bankwatch.org/publication/boom-time-blues-big-oils-gender-impacts-in-azerbaijan-georgia-and-sakhalin

Bankwatch (2012). The Oil Road – How a done deal continues to unravel. Available at https://bankwatch.org/publication/the-oil-road-how-a-done-deal-continues-to-unravel

Barnett, M. and Duvall, R. (2005). Power in international politics. *International Organization, 59*(1), 39–75.

Barry, A. (2013). *Material politics: Disputes along the pipeline.* John Wiley & Sons.

Bauman, Z. (2000). Time and space reunited. *Time & Society*, *9*(2–3), 171–85.

Bayulgen, O. (2010). *Foreign investment and political regimes: The oil sector in Azerbaijan, Russia, and Norway.* Cambridge University Press.

Beck, U. (1992). From industrial society to the risk society: Questions of survival, social structure and ecological enlightenment. *Theory, Culture & Society*, *9*(1), 97–123.

Bertelsmann Stiftung, BTI (2012). *Transformation index BTI 2012: Political management in international comparison.* Bertelsmann Stiftung.

Bertelsmann Stiftung, BTI (2016). *Azerbaijan country report.* Bertelsmann Stiftung.

Best, J. (2007). Why the economy is often the exception to politics as usual. *Theory, Culture & Society*, *24*(4), 87–109.

Bigo, D. (2000). When two become one: Internal and external securitisations in Europe. In *International relations theory and the politics of European integration: Power, security and community* (pp 171–205). Psychology Press.

Bigo, D. (2002). Security and immigration: Toward a critique of the governmentality of unease. *Alternatives*, *27*(1_suppl), 63–92.

Bigo, D. (2005). Global (in)security: The field of the professionals of unease management and the ban-opticon. *Traces: A Multilingual Series of Cultural Theory*, *4*, 34–87.

Bigo, D. (2006). When two become one: Internal and external securitisations in Europe. In *International relations theory and the politics of European integration* (pp 171–204). Routledge.

Bigo, D. (2007). Internal and external aspects of security. *European Security*, *15*(4), 385–404.

Blum, D. (2018). Contested national identities and weak state structures in Eurasia. In *Limiting institutions?* Manchester University Press.

Boal, I.A., Clark, T.J., Matthews, J. and Watts, M. (2005). *Afflicted powers: Capital and spectacle in a new age of war*. Verso.

Bolukbasi, S. (2011). *Azerbaijan. A political history*. I.B. Tauris.

Börzel, T. and Pamuk, Y. (2011). *Europeanization subverted. The European Union's promotion of good governance and the fight against corruption in the Southern Caucasus* (Working Paper, KFG The Transformative Power of Europe No. 26). Freie Universität Berlin.

Borzel, T.A. and Risse, T. (eds.) (2020). *From Europeanisation to diffusion*. Routledge.

Brenner, N. and Theodore, N. (2002). Cities and the geographies of 'actually existing neoliberalism'. *Antipode*, *34*(3), 349–79.

Burke, A. (2002). Aporias of security. *Alternatives*, *27*(1), 1–27.

Burke, A. (2014). (We Have Always Been) Posthuman. *Installing Order.* 19 December. Available at https://installingorder.org/2014/12/19/31-we-have-always-beenposthuman-post-3-of-3/

Burke, A., Fishel, S., Mitchell, A., Dalby, S. and Levine, D.J. (2016). Planet politics: A manifesto from the end of IR. *Millennium*, *44*(3), 499–523.

Butler, J. (1993). *Bodies that matter: On the discursive limits of sex*. Routledge.

Buzan, B., Wæver, O. and De Wilde, J. (1998). *Security: A new framework for analysis*. Lynne Rienner Publishers.

Chayes, S. (2016). *The structure of corruption in Azerbaijan*. Carnegie Endowment.

Chehabi, H.E. and Linz, J.J. (eds.) (1998). *Sultanistic regimes*. JHU Press.

Chester, L. (2010). Conceptualising energy security and making explicit its polysemic nature. *Energy Policy*, *38*(2), 887–95.

Christou, O. and Adamides, C. (2013). Energy securitization and desecuritization in the New Middle East. *Security Dialogue*, *44*(5–6), 507–22.

Ciarreta, A. and Nasirov, S. (2012). Development trends in the Azerbaijan oil and gas sector: Achievements and challenges. *Energy Policy*, *40*, 282–92.

Ciută, F. (2007). Narratives of security: Strategy and identity in the European context. In *Discursive constructions of identity in European politics* (pp 190–207). Palgrave Macmillan.

Ciută, F. (2010). Conceptual notes on energy security: Total or banal security? *Security Dialogue*, *41*(2), 123–44.

Coker, C. (2009). *Rebooting the West: Can the Western alliance still engage in war?* Routledge.

Collier, S.J. (2011). *Post-Soviet social: Neoliberalism, social modernity, biopolitics.* Princeton University Press.

Collins, K. (2004). The logic of clan politics: Evidence from the central Asian trajectories. *World Politics*, 2, 224–61.

Cornell, S.E. (2015). *Azerbaijan since independence*. Routledge.

Côté, A. (2016). Agents without agency: Assessing the role of the audience in securitization theory. *Security Dialogue*, *47*(6), 541–58.

Cox, R.W. (1983). Social forces, states and world orders: Beyond international relations theory. *Millennium*, *10*(2), 126–55.

Dalby, S. (2013). The geopolitics of climate change. *Political Geography*, *37*, 38–47.

Dannreuther, R. (2017). *Energy security*. John Wiley & Sons.

Davis, M. (2006). *Planet of slums*. Verso.

Deleuze, G. (1988). *Foucault*. University of Minnesota Press.

Deleuze, G. (1992). What is a dispositif. In *Michel Foucault: Philosopher* (pp 159–68). Harvester Wheatsheaf.

Deleuze, G. and Guattari, F. (1988). *A thousand plateaus: Capitalism and schizophrenia*. Bloomsbury Publishing.

Der Derian, J. and Shapiro, M.J. (eds.) (1989). *International/intertextual relations: Postmodern readings of world politics*. Lexington Books.

Deudney, D. (1990). The case against linking environmental degradation and national security. *Millennium*, *19*(3), 461–76.

Dillon, M. (1996). *Politics of security: Towards a political philosophy of continental thought*. Routledge.

Di Muzio, T. (2016). Energy, capital as power and world order. In *The Palgrave handbook of critical international political economy* (pp 267–87). Palgrave Macmillan.

Dunigan, M. and Petersohn, U. (eds.) (2015). *The markets for force: Privatization of security across world regions*. University of Pennsylvania Press.

Fierke, K.M. and Fierke, K.M. (1998). *Changing games, changing strategies: Critical investigations in security*. Manchester University Press.

Finkel, E. and Brudny, Y.M. (2012). No more colour! Authoritarian regimes and colour revolutions in Eurasia. *Democratization*, *19*(1), 1–14.

Flegel, T. (2015). *Foreign actors' influence on Azerbaijan's energy policy: Decisions under complex uncertainty*. Springer.

Flockhart, T. (2012). Towards a strong NATO narrative: From a 'practice of talking' to a 'practice of doing'. *International Politics*, *49*(1), 78–97.

Flockhart, T. (2016). Understanding NATO through constructivist theorising. In *Theorising NATO: New perspectives on the Atlantic alliance* (pp 140–60). Routledge.

Floyd, R. (2016). Extraordinary or ordinary emergency measures: What, and who, defines the 'success' of securitization? *Cambridge Review of International Affairs*, *29*(2), 677–94.

Forster, A. and Wallace, W. (2001). What is NATO for? *Survival*, *43*(4), 107–22.

Foucault, M. (1980). *Power/knowledge: Selected interviews and other writings, 1972–1977*. Vintage.

Foucault, M. (1981). The order of discourse. In *Untying the text: A poststructuralist reader* (pp 48–78). Routledge.

Foucault, M. (2019). *Power: the essential works of Michel Foucault 1954–1984*. Penguin UK.

Fougner, T. (2008). Neoliberal governance of states: The role of competitiveness indexing and country benchmarking. *Millennium*, *37*(2), 303–26.

Fraenkel, E. and Meierhenrich, J. (2018). *The dual state: a contribution to the theory of dictatorship*. Oxford University Press.

Friedman, T. (2009). The first law of petropolitics. *Foreign Policy* (May/June), *88*(3), 28–36.

Frowd, P.M. (2018). *Security at the borders: Transnational practices and technologies in West Africa*. Cambridge University Press.

Fussey, P. (2013). Contested topologies of UK counterterrorist surveillance: The rise and fall of Project Champion. *Critical Studies on Terrorism*, *6*(3), 351–70.

Ganev, V.I. (2005). The 'triumph of neoliberalism' reconsidered: Critical remarks on ideas-centered analyses of political and economic change in post-communism. *East European Politics and Societies*, *19*(03), 343–78.

Gentile, M. (2013). Meeting the 'organs': The tacit dilemma of field research in authoritarian states. *Area*, *45*(4), 426–32.

Giddens, A. (1990). *The consequences of modernity*. Stanford University Press.

Gilbert, E. (2012). The militarization of climate change. *ACME: An International Journal for Critical Geographies*, *11*(1), 1–14.

Global Fire Power (2018). *World Military Strengths Database*, Global Fire Power.

Global Witness (2013). Azerbaijan anonymous: Azerbaijan's state oil company and why the Extractive Industries Transparency Initiative needs to go further. Available at https://www.globalwitness.org/en/archive/azerbaijan-anonymous/

Göksel, O. (2015). Beyond countering Iran: A political economy of Azerbaijan-Israel relations. *British Journal of Middle Eastern Studies*, *42*(4), 655–75.

Goldstein, D.M. (2012). *Outlawed: Between security and rights in a Bolivian city*. Duke University Press.

Gould, J.A. and Sickner, C. (2008). Making market democracies? The contingent loyalties of post-privatization elites in Azerbaijan, Georgia and Serbia. *Review of International Political Economy*, *15*(5), 740–69.

Graham, S. (2010). *Disrupted cities: When infrastructure fails*. Routledge.

Guliyev, F. (2005). Post-Soviet Azerbaijan: Transition to sultanistic semiauthoritarianism? An attempt at conceptualization. *Demokratizatsiya: The Journal of Post-Soviet Democratization 13*(3), 393–435.

Guliyev, F. (2011). Personal rule, neopatrimonialism, and regime typologies: Integrating Dahlian and Weberian approaches to regime studies. *Democratization*, *18*(3), 575–601.

Guliyev, F. (2012). Political elites in Azerbaijan. Challenges of the Caspian resource boom. In *Domestic Elites and Policy-making* (pp 117–30). Palgrave Macmillan.

Guliyev, F. (2014). The 'Contract of the Century' 20 years after. Available at SSRN: https://ssrn.com/abstract=2498276 or http://dx.doi.org/10.2139/ssrn.2498276

Guliyev, F. (2020). Formal-informal relations in Azerbaijan. Formal and informal political institutions, *Caucasus Analytical Digest*. Research Collection, ETH Zurich.

Gurbanov, S., Nugent, J.B. and Mikayilov, J. (2017). Management of oil revenues: Has that of Azerbaijan been prudent? *Economies*, *5*(2), 19.

Hansen, L. (2013). *Security as practice: Discourse analysis and the Bosnian war*. Routledge.

Harvey, D. (2005). *The new imperialism*. Oxford University Press.

Heradstveit, D. and Strømmen, K.E. (1999). *Nation-building in Azerbaijan: Democratic development and human rights*. Norwegian Institute of International Affairs [Norsk utenrikspolitisk institutt (NUPI)].

Heyat, F. (2002). Women and the culture of entrepreneurship in Soviet and post-Soviet Azerbaijan. In *Markets and moralities: Ethnographies of postsocialism* (pp 19–31). Routledge.

Hoff, K. and Stiglitz, J.E. (2004). The transition process in post-communist societies: Towards a political economy of property rights. In *Toward pro-poor policies: Aid, institutions and globalization* (pp 231–45). World Bank.

Hoffman, D.I. (1999). Oil and development in post-Soviet Azerbaijan. *NBR Analysis*, *10*, 5–28.

Holm, U. (2004). Algeria: Securitization of state/regime, nation and Islam. In *Contemporary security analysis and Copenhagen peace research* (pp 217–28). Routledge.

Homkes, R. (2011). *Analysing the role of public-private partnerships in global governance: Institutional dynamics, variation and effects* Doctoral dissertation, The London School of Economics and Political Science.

Hopf, T. (2013). Common-sense constructivism and hegemony in world politics. *International Organization*, 317–54.

Hug, Adam (ed.) (2012). *Spotlight on Azerbaijan*. Foreign Policy Centre.

Huysmans, J. (1998). Security! What do you mean? From concept to thick signifier. *European Journal of International Relations*, *4*(2), 226–55.

Huysmans, J. (2002). Defining social constructivism in security studies: The normative dilemma of writing security. *Alternatives*, *27*(1_suppl), 41–62.

Huysmans, J. (2006). *The politics of insecurity: Fear, migration and asylum in the EU*. Routledge.

Huysmans, J. (2011). What's in an act? On security speech acts and little security nothings. *Security Dialogue*, *42*(4–5), 371–83.

Huysmans, J. (2014). *Security unbound: Enacting democratic limits*. Routledge.

Ibadoghlu, G. (2019). State oil fund of Azerbaijan: Huge spending and overwhelming poverty. Available at SSRN: 3489617.

IEA. (2017). *Energy security*. Available at https://www.iea.org/topics/energy-security

Innes, A. (2015). *Migration, citizenship and the challenge for security: An ethnographic approach*. Springer.

International Crisis Group (2010). Azerbaijan. Vulnerable Stability. *Europe Report*, 207.

International Monetary Fund (1993). *Annual Report*.

Isbell, P., Gault, J., Ramsay, W.C. and Qabazard, H.M. (2007). Security of supply. In *Oxford energy forum* (No. 71). Oxford Institute for Energy Studies.

Islam, S. (1993). Conclusion: Problems of planning a market economy. In *Making markets: Economic transformation in Eastern Europe and post-Soviet states*. Council on Foreign Relations Press.

Ismayilov, E. (2015). Islam in Azerbaijan: Revival and political involvement. In *Religion, nation and democracy in the South Caucasus*.

Ismayilov, M. and Tkacik, M. (2009). Nation-building and state-building in Azerbaijan: The challenges of education abroad. *Turkish Policy Quarterly*, *8*(4), 89–104.

Jackson, W. (2013). Securitisation as depoliticisation: Depoliticisation as pacification. *Socialist Studies/Études Socialistes*. Available at https://socialiststudies.com/index.php/sss/article/view/23510

Janeliūnas, T. and Tumkevič, A. (2013). Securitization of the energy sectors in Estonia, Lithuania, Poland and Ukraine: Motives and extraordinary measures. *Lithuanian Foreign Policy Review*, *30*, 65–90.

Janenova, S. (2019). The boundaries of research in an authoritarian state. *International Journal of Qualitative Methods, 18*. Available at https://journals.sagepub.com/doi/full/10.1177/1609406919876469

Jasanoff, S. and Kim, S.H. (eds.) (2015). *Dreamscapes of modernity: Sociotechnical imaginaries and the fabrication of power*. University of Chicago Press.

Joseph, J. (2009). Governmentality of what? Populations, states and international organisations. *Global Society, 23*(4), 413–27.

Judge, A. and Maltby, T. (2017). European Energy Union? Caught between securitisation and 'riskification'. *European Journal of International Security, 2*(2), 179–202.

Kalicki, J.H. and Goldwyn, D.L. (eds.) (2013). *Energy and security: Strategies for a world in transition*. JHU Press.

Kamalipour, H. and Peimani, N. (2015). Assemblage thinking and the city: Implications for urban studies. *Current Urban Studies, 3*(4), 402–8.

Kamrava, M. (2001). State-building in Azerbaijan: The search for consolidation. *The Middle East Journal, 55*(2), 216–36.

Koch, N. (2013). Introduction–Field methods in 'closed contexts': Undertaking research in authoritarian states and places. *Area, 45*(4), 390–5.

Kratochvíl, P. and Tichý, L. (2013). Discurso de la UE y Rusia sobre las relaciones energéticas. *Política Energética, 56*, 391–406.

Krause, K. and Williams, M.C. (eds.) (2002). *Critical security studies: Concepts and strategies*. Routledge.

Kustova, I. (2018). Unpacking the nexus between market liberalisation and desecuritisation in energy. In *Energy security in Europe* (pp 203–20). Palgrave Macmillan.

Kuzemko, C. (2013). *The energy security-climate nexus: Institutional change in the UK and beyond*. Springer.

Lake, D.A. (2013). Theory is dead, long live theory: The end of the Great Debates and the rise of eclecticism in International Relations. *European Journal of International Relations, 19*(3), 567–87.

Lanning, C.M.L. (2007). *Mercenaries: Soldiers of fortune, from Ancient Greece to today's private military companies*. Presidio Press.

LaPorte, J. (2016). Semi-presidentialism in Azerbaijan. In *Semi-Presidentialism in the Caucasus and Central Asia* (pp 91–117). Palgrave Macmillan.

Latour, B. (2005). *Reassembling the social: An introduction to actor-network-theory*. Oxford University Press.

Leander, A. and Van Munster, R. (2007). Private security contractors in the debate about Darfur: Reflecting and reinforcing neo-liberal governmentality. *International Relations, 21*(2), 201–16.

Lehti, M. and Pennanen, H.R. (2020). Beyond liberal empire and peace: Declining hegemony of the west? In *Contestations of liberal order* (pp 17–59). Palgrave Macmillan.

Lehti, M., Pennanen, H.R. and Jouhki, J. (eds.) (2020). *Contestations of liberal order: The West in crisis?* Springer.

Lepgold, J. (1998). NATO's post-cold war collective action problem. *International Security, 23*(1), 78–106.

Leung, G.C., Cherp, A., Jewell, J. and Wei, Y.M. (2014). Securitization of energy supply chains in China. *Applied Energy, 123*, 316–26.

Leykin, I. (2019). The history and afterlife of Soviet demography: The socialist roots of post-Soviet neoliberalism. *Slavic Review*, *78*(1), 149–72.

Linz, J.J. (2000). *Totalitarian and authoritarian regimes*. Lynne Rienner Publishers.

Lippert, R. and O'Connor, D. (2003). Security assemblages: Airport security, flexible work, and liberal governance. *Alternatives*, *28*(3), 331–58.

Loughlan, V., Olsson, C. and Schouten, P. (2014). Mapping. In *Critical security methods* (pp 39–72). Routledge.

Luke, A. 2002. Beyond science and ideology critique: Developments in critical discourse analysis. *Annual Review of Applied Linguistics*, *22*, 96–110.

Lunstrum, E. (2014). Green militarization: Anti-poaching efforts and the spatial contours of Kruger National Park. *Annals of the Association of American Geographers*, *104*(4), 816–32.

Luong, P.J. and Weinthal, E. (2001). Prelude to the resource curse: Explaining oil and gas development strategies in the Soviet successor states and beyond. *Comparative Political Studies*, *34*(4), 367–99.

Månsson, A., Johansson, B. and Nilsson, L.J. (2014). Assessing energy security: An overview of commonly used methodologies. *Energy*, *73*, 1–14.

Martin, S. (2007). The United Nations and private security companies: Responsibility in conflict. *Deusto Journal of Human Rights*, *4*, 89–108.

Massé, F. and Lunstrum, E. (2016). Accumulation by securitization: Commercial poaching, neoliberal conservation, and the creation of new wildlife frontiers. *Geoforum*, *69*, 227–37.

Matza, T. (2009). Moscow's echo: Technologies of the self, publics, and politics on the Russian talk show. *Cultural Anthropology*, *24*(3), 489–522.

Mignolo, W. (2011). *The darker side of western modernity: Global futures, decolonial options*. Duke University Press.

Miller, P. and Rose, N. (2008). *Governing the present: Administering economic, social and personal life*. Polity.

Monaghan, A. (2014). The Ukraine crisis and NATO-Russia relations. *NATO Review*, *1*.

Moore, D.C. (2001). Is the post-in postcolonial the post-in post-Soviet? Toward a global postcolonial critique. *Publications of the Modern Language Association of America*, 116(1), 11–28.

Müller-Kraenner, S. (2008). *Energy security: Re-measuring the world*. Earthscan.

Müller, M.O. Stämpfli, A. Dold, U., and Hammer, T. (2011). Energy autarky: A conceptual framework for sustainable regional development. *Energy Policy*, *39*(10), 5800–10.

Mulligan, S. (2011). Energy and human ecology: A critical security approach. *Environmental Politics*, *20*(5), 633–49.

NATO (1999). Strategic Concept, Brussels: NATO.

NATO (2006). Riga Declaration, Brussels: NATO.

NATO (2008). Bucharest Declaration, Brussels: NATO.

NATO (2010). Strategic Concept, Brussels: NATO.

NATO (2012). Chicago Declaration, Brussels: NATO.

NATO (2014). Energy insecurity: What can NATO do? *NATO review*.

NATO (2016). Warsaw Summit Communiqué, Brussels: NATO.

NATO (2018). Brussels Summit Declaration, Brussels: NATO.

Neocleous, M. (2000). Against security. *Radical Philosophy*, *100*, 7–15.

Neocleous, M. (2007). Security, liberty and the myth of balance: Towards a critique of security politics. *Contemporary Political Theory*, *6*(2), 131–49.

Neocleous, M. (2008). *Critique of security*. Edinburgh University Press.

Neocleous, M. (2011). *Inhuman security*. Routledge.

Neocleous, M. (2018). The bleak rituals of progress; Or, if somebody offers you a socially responsible innovation in security, just say no. In *Socially Responsible Innovation in Security* (pp 129–40). Routledge.

Neocleous, M., Rigakos, G. and Wall, T. (2013). On pacification: Introduction to the special issue. *Socialist Studies/Études Socialistes*. Available at https://socialiststudies.com/index.php/sss/article/view/23502

Nietzsche, F. (1968). *Twilight of the Idols; And, The Anti-Christ; Translated, with an Introduction and Commentary, by RJ Hollingdale*. Penguin UK.

Nyman, J. (2014). 'Red storm ahead': Securitisation of energy in US–China relations. *Millennium*, *43*(1), 43–65.

Nyman, J. (2018a). Rethinking energy, climate and security: A critical analysis of energy security in the US. *Journal of International Relations and Development*, *21*(1), 118–45.

Nyman, J. (2018b). *The energy security paradox: Rethinking energy (in) security in the United States and China*. Oxford University Press.

OECD (2019). Sustainable Infrastructure Development for a Low-Carbon Transition in Central Asia and the Caucasus: Mapping of Potentially High-impact Infrastructure Projects and Needs Assessment Strategic Infrastructure Planning for Sustainable Development in Azerbaijan. Available at https://www.oecd.org/officialdocuments/publicdisplaydocumentpdf/?cote=ENV/EPOC/EAP(2019)6&docLanguage=En

O'lear, S. (2007). Azerbaijan's resource wealth: Political legitimacy and public opinion. *Geographical Journal*, *173*(3), 207–23.

Orazgaliyev, S. (2019). *State ownership and nationalization in energy sector: The case of Kazakhstan's oil industry* (No. 1042). ADBI Working Paper Series.

Osborne, P. (ed.) (2013). *A critical sense: Interviews with intellectuals*. Routledge.

OSCE (2012). *After the BTC Pipeline and EITI Validation: Where are Prosperity and Transparency in Azerbaijan?*. Available at https://www.osce.org/files/f/documents/9/e/94979.pdf

Ottaway, M. (2013). *Democracy challenged: The rise of semi-authoritarianism*. Carnegie Endowment.

Pascual, C. and Elkind, J. (eds.) (2010). *Energy security: Economics, politics, strategies, and implications*. Brookings Institution Press.

Pashayev, H.M. (2006). *Racing up hill: Selected papers of Azerbaijan's first ambassador to the United States of America.* Global Scholarly Publications.

Pearce, K.E. and Kendzior, S. (2012). Networked authoritarianism and social media in Azerbaijan. *Journal of Communication*, *62*(2), 283–98.

Pfister, T. (2004). From state to stateness. *Queen's University, Belfast School of Politics and International Studies*, *20*(1), 22.

Phelan, S. and Dawes, S. (2018). Liberalism and neoliberalism. In *Oxford Research encyclopedia of communication*. Available at https://doi.org/10.1093/acrefore/9780190228613.013.176

Phillips, A. (2013). A dangerous synergy: Energy securitization, great power rivalry and strategic stability in the Asian century. *The Pacific Review*, *26*(1), 17–38.

Pirani, S. (2016). Azerbaijan's gas supply squeeze and the consequences for the Southern Corridor. Available at https://doi.org/10.26889/9781784670627

Przeworski, A. (1991). *Democracy and the market: Political and economic reforms in Eastern Europe and Latin America*. Cambridge University Press.

Rampton, B. and Charalambous, C. (2020). Sociolinguistics and everyday (in) securitization. *Journal of Sociolinguistics*, *24*(1), 75–88.

Reeves, M. (2014). *Border work: Spatial lives of the state in rural Central Asia.* Cornell University Press.

Reeves, M. (2015). Afterword: Neoliberal opportunism, *Anthropology Matters.* Available at https://www.anthropologymatters.com/index.php/anth_matters/article/view/416/542

Reyes, A.S. (2006). Protecting the freedom of transit of petroleum: Transnational lawyers making (up) international law in the Caspian. *Berkeley Journal of International Law*, *24*, 842–80.

Ringmar, E. (2002). The recognition game: Soviet Russia against the West. *Cooperation and Conflict*, *37*(2), 115–36.

Risley, S. (2006). The sociology of security: Sociological approaches to contemporary and historical securitization. In *Annual Meeting of the American Sociological Association, Montreal Convention Center, Montreal, Quebec, Canada* (Vol. 5).

Safiguliyev, C., Abbasov, N., Rzazadeh, S. and Huseyn, A. (2008). *The encyclopaedia of the successful land acquisition process of the Baku–Tbilisi–Ceyhan and South Caucasus pipelines projects in Azerbaijan*. BP Exploration (Caspian Sea) Limited.

Sahin, H. (2018). *Host government agreements and the law in the energy sector: The case of Azerbaijan and Turkey*. Routledge.

Salter, M.B. and Mutlu, C.E. (eds.) (2013). *Research methods in critical security studies: An introduction*. Routledge.

Scahill, J. (2008). *Blackwater: The rise of the world's most powerful mercenary army*. Hachette UK.

Schlichte, K. (2005). *The dynamics of states: The formation and crisis of state domination*. Routledge.

Schmidt, B. (2018). *Hegemony: A conceptual and theoretical analysis*. DOC Research Institute.

Schuilenburg, M. (2017). *The securitization of society: Crime, risk, and social order* (Vol. 12). NYU Press.

Shaffer, B. (2006). *Borders and brotherhood and the challenge of the identity of Azerbaijan* (trans. Azar, Y.S.). Ulus Publisher.

Shaw, D.L. (2013). Good governance in the post-Soviet south: Testing theories of the resource curse in Azerbaijan. *Journal of Politics & International Studies, 9*, 520–61.

Shepherd, L.J. (2008). 'To save succeeding generations from the scourge of war': The US, UN and the violence of security. *Review of International Studies*, 93–311.

Souleimanov, E. and Ehrmann, M. (2013). The rise of militant Salafism in Azerbaijan and its regional implications. *Middle East Policy, 20*(3), 111–20.

Sovacool, B.K. and Mukherjee, I. (2011). Conceptualizing and measuring energy security: A synthesized approach. *Energy, 36*(8), 5343–55.

Statistical Committee of the Republic of Azerbaijan. (2017). *Structure of exports by products*. Available at https://www.stat.gov.az/index.php

Stockholm International Peace Research Institute (2017). *Azerbaijan, military expenditure database*. SIPRI.

Taylor, M. (2009). The contradictions and transformations of neoliberalism in Latin America: From structural adjustment to empowering the poor. In *Post-neoliberalism in the Americas*, 21–36. Palgrave Macmillan.

Tokluoglu, C. (2005). Definitions of national identity, nationalism and ethnicity in post-Soviet Azerbaijan in the 1990s. *Ethnic and Racial Studies, 28*(4), 722–58.

Tokluoglu, C. (2012). Perceptions of state and leadership in post-Soviet Azerbaijan (1991–2009). *Middle Eastern Studies, 48*(3), 319–43.

Transparency Initiatives. (2019). *Corruption Index*. Available at https://www.transparency.org/en/cpi/2019/index/aze

Trombetta, M.J. (2008). Environmental security and climate change: Analysing the discourse. *Cambridge Review of International Affairs, 21*(4), 585–602.

US Embassy in Baku (2008). Azerbaijan Faces Challenge of Protecting Critical Energy Infrastructure, Wikileaks Cable: 08BAKU625_a2008, 2 July.

Valentine, S.V. (2011). Emerging symbiosis: Renewable energy and energy security. *Renewable and Sustainable Energy Reviews, 15*(9), 4572–78.

Valiyev, A. (2011). Social capital in Azerbaijan: Does it help to build democracy? *Caucasus Analytical Digest, 31*(21), 11–18.

Vaughan-Williams, N. and Stevens, D. (2016). Vernacular theories of everyday (in)security: The disruptive potential of non-elite knowledge. *Security Dialogue*, *47*(1), 40–58.

Vivoda, V. (2010). Evaluating energy security in the Asia-Pacific region: A novel methodological approach. *Energy Policy*, *38*(9), 5258–63.

Vuori, J.A. (2008). Illocutionary logic and strands of securitization: Applying the theory of securitization to the study of non-democratic political orders. *European Journal of International Relations*, *14*(1), 65–99.

Wæver, O. (1993). *Securitization and desecuritization*. Centre for Peace and Conflict Research.

Wæver, O. (1996). European security identities. *Journal of Common Market Studies*, *34*(1), 103–32.

Wakeman-Linn, J., Mathieu, P. and Van Selm, B. (2003). Oil funds in transition economies: Azerbaijan and Kazakhstan. *Fiscal Policy Formulation and Implementation in Oil-producing Countries* (pp 339–58). International Monetary Fund.

Wallander, C.A. (2000). Institutional assets and adaptability: NATO after the Cold War. *International Organization*, 705–35.

Walt, S.M. (1998). The ties that fray: Why Europe and America are drifting apart. *The National Interest*, *54*, 3–11.

Weber, M. (1994). *Weber: political writings*. Cambridge University Press.

World Bank (2017). *Azerbaijan*. World Bank DataBank.

Index